D0852816

THE TRIUMPH OF THE HOLY SEE

Pope Pius VII

The Triumph of the Holy See

A Short History of the Papacy in the Nineteenth Century

J. Derek Holmes

Burns & Oates · London
Patmos Press · Shepherdstown

First published in Great Britain and associated territories
in 1978 by Burns & Oates Limited, 2-10 Jerdan Place,
London SW6 5PT, and in the United States of America
by Patmos Press Inc., Box 833, Shepherdstown, West Virginia 25443.

ISBN (UK) 0 86012 067 8
ISBN (USA) 0 915762 06 4

Library of Congress Catalog Card Number 78-18616

Printed and bound in Great Britain by Billing & Son Ltd.,
Guildford, London and Worcester

Contents

List of illustrations

Acknowledgments
The author and publishers wish to thank the following for permission to reproduce illustrations: Radio Times Hulton Picture Library (pages ii, 8, 100, 162, 192, 204, 218, 260 and 273).
Mansell Collection (pages 34, 58, 78, 99, 118, 128 and 178).

Acknowledgments

Much of the material incorporated in this book was originally collected for a course of lectures on the history of the Church in the nineteenth century and so my first debt is to the authors whose works are listed in the bibliography. I am also indebted to those students past and present whose attitutudes inspired me to greater efforts and especially to those who expressed some interest in the subject. Finally, I must thank Miss Teresa Mulhall who once again so willingly and generously typed the manuscript with such conscientious care.

J. Derek Holmes,
Ushaw, 1978

Pope Pius IX

Introduction: An age of revolution

In 1799 Bartolomeo Alberto Cappellari, a Camaldolese friar and the future Pope Gregory XVI, published his work, *Il Trionfo della Santa Sede* which would later have a profound effect on the ideology and the organization of the Catholic Church throughout the world. However, Cappellari's anticipation of the definition of papal infallibility and the victory of the Holy See over national and Gallican churches seemed totally unrealistic at a time when Pope Pius VI was dying as a prisoner of the invading, if retreating, French forces and when the Church as a whole seemed to be in a state of inevitable decline as well as general confusion. Of course other Catholics were also able to share Cappellari's theological faith in the Church. Pius VI himself wrote:

> God willed that the Church should own her birth to suffering and the cross, her glory to ignominy, her light to the darkness of error, her progress to the assaults of her enemies, her strength to privation and adversity. Thus her brilliance has never been more clear than when all men strove to quench her flame. For as gold is tried in the fire so are the friends of God tried in tribulation.

But if Pius VI shared Cappellari's faith in the Church, he did not necessarily share his prophetic vision of its future.

The relationship between the Christian Church and secular society or the civil authority is almost as old as Christianity itself, as is the further question of the primacy and the position of the See of Rome. Monasticism continued to flourish even within an ostensibly Christian society as some Christians continued to feel obliged to reject 'the world'. The early Christian Church experienced the power as well as the decline and fall of the Roman Empire, while during the pontificate of Gregory I the first moves were made towards the creation of the Papal States and the organization of an ordered hierarchy of the Western Church under the direct control of the Pope. But the development of ecclesiology is never an isolated phenomenon either historically or ideologically and must be seen in the light of the other political or social movements of the time.

The nineteenth century was a period of political, economic, social, intellectual and religious revolution. The American Declaration of Independence in 1776 coincided with the publication of Adam Smith's *Wealth of Nations* advocating the system of *laissez faire* and 'free enterprise'. Economic developments were creating a very new and different society, while the position of the Church, often hitherto an established Church, was immediately linked with constitutional issues involving Church and State, and with the political consequences of first the American and then the French Revolutions. Of all the major Christian churches, the Roman Catholic Church suffered most immediately and directly because France proved to be one of the major centres of revolution, while some of its most violent repercussions were felt in the Catholic parts of Germany, in Spain and Portugal which had been mainly responsible for the geographical expansion of the Church since the fifteenth century, in Italy and in Rome itself. Furthermore a great deal of the violence of the revolution was deliberately directed against the Catholic Church, which was inevitably transformed in the process. Social and economic as well as political changes brought about fundamental changes in the Church itself – in the position of the Pope within the Church and his relations with other bishops, in relations between Church and Society at large, and in relations between Church and State.

The American Revolution originally made little impact on the attitudes and opinions of European ecclesiastics. Although the career of John Carroll, the first Catholic bishop in the United States, showed that Roman Catholicism and democratic republicanism were not incompatible and that it was possible to establish a Roman Catholic Church without being dominated by Rome, it would be many years before Catholics in Europe were able to learn the value of those lessons. Conditions in America strongly contributed towards the growth of dissenting Christianity and the notion of separating Church and State. Many of the immigrants had originally arrived in search of freedom of conscience, while freedom from the social restraints of the Old World inevitably emphasised the voluntary principle of ecclesiastical membership. Primitive conditions on the frontier obviously affected the religious and the secular attitudes of the colonial pioneers as well as the practice of religion, and most of the pioneers were in fact only remotely in touch with organized religion. The pietistic and individualistic religious revivals which swept through the colonies also put greater emphasis on personal contact with God than on ecclesiastical or clerical authority and greatly increased the numbers of dissenters as well as their hostility to established churches.

Meanwhile, the intellectual leaders of American opinion were increasingly influenced by the arguments of writers like John Locke in favour of the separation of Church and State, and freedom of conscience on the basis of natural rights; religion was part of that untouchable realm beyond the reach of legal or political authority. Furthermore, as a result of various crude attempts to establish Anglicanism in New York, some Americans became convinced of the necessity of separating Church and State; religious liberty could be guaranteed only when religious practice was secure from intervention by the State. And as dissenters in New York began to take the offensive against an Anglican establishment supported by English law and English authority, their campaign began to merge with the wider political attack on English colonial policies. Thus on the eve of the Revolution the strength of dissent, the existence of so many conflicting religious opinions within the thirteen colonies and the absence of any predominant Protestant Church eventually resulted in the proclamation of religious liberty and the separation of Church and State, though the adoption of these policies was not necessarily associated with a genuine sense of religious toleration. Not all the thirteen states immediately followed the example of Virginia, Pennsylvania or Maryland where the civil rights of all Christians were respected. There was an established church in one form or another in seven of the states, while Catholics enjoyed equal rights of citizenship in only five states.

Nevertheless, the Constitution adopted in 1787 included only one remark on the subject of religion: 'no religious test shall ever be required as a qualification to any office or public trust under the United States'. The fear that the Federal Government might later seek to impose an established national religion led to the first amendment. This was a specifically religious provision to prevent Congress from allowing one religion to be preferred over others or from establishing a national church in the traditional sense of a union between the State and any particular religion or denomination: 'Congress shall make no law respecting an establishment of religion, or prohibiting the free exercise thereof'. Thus although the notion of separation at the time was much less sweeping than it became in later years, the American Revolution had effectively resulted in the first disestablishment in Christian history.

Relations between Church and State were to be transformed more directly and immediately by the impact of the French Revolution, and developments in Austria illustrate how the rationalism of the Enlightenment gave way to reaction and how Erastianism and Gallicanism gave way to a self-interested union of Church and State. Gallicanism was probably the most famous movement which attempted to restrict the ecclesiastical authority of Rome, to defend the independence of local Catholic churches and the rights of local rulers. The formula known as the Four Gallican Articles, a document drawn up by Bossuet, neatly expresses Gallican opinions. The first article denied that the Pope had dominion over temporal things; kings were not subject to ecclesiastical authority in civil matters; they could not be deposed by the church authorities and their subjects could not be dispensed from their allegiance by the Pope. The second article supported the decrees of the Council of Constance and reaffirmed the authority of General Councils over the Pope. The third article insisted that the ancient rights and liberties of the Gallican Church were inviolable. The final article maintained that, pending the consent of the Church or until a General Council had been convened, the judgment of the Pope was not irreformable; even in matters of faith and morals, the Pope was not infallible without the consent of the Church.

Bossuet himself believed that the beauty of the Gallican Church was that of the Catholic Church and depended on its inviolable link with the head of the Catholic Church, the successor of St Peter. But other writers were prepared to go much further in popularizing theories of ecclesiastical government which effectively reduced papal authority over national churches – 'royal Gallicanism', or over individual bishops – 'episcopal Gallicanism'. Although the Gallican Articles were annulled by Alexander VIII in 1690 and solemnly withdrawn by Louis XIV and the French clergy in 1693, Gallican principles were defended throughout the eighteenth century and once again officially proclaimed at the Synod of Pistoia in 1786, which supported Leopold II's attempts to reform the Church along the lines pursued by his brother, Joseph II.

During the eighteenth century, therefore, the claims of the Church of Rome were not only questioned by heretics, deists or supporters of the voluntary principle such as freemasons, but by many orthodox Catholics who felt that secular, royal or episcopal authority had a greater part to play in the reform and the government of the Church than the popes in Rome. At the same time, the Roman authorities themselves who were frequently preoccupied with secular politics lacked a united or defined view on the nature and extent of ecclesiastical authority and relations between Church and State. There was a steady decline in papal authority which was too vaguely defined to impose effective demands on Catholic loyalty. Most Catholics granted the Pope a primacy of honour, but many of them shared the opinion that ultimate authority lay with a General Council in matters of faith and morals. Only Italian theologians tended to be Ultramontane, whereas French theologians argued that the Pope alone might err in matters of faith and morals. In 1718, the theological faculty of Caen, for example, was able to dismiss papal infallibility as a 'frivolous claim'.

As Catholic bishops adopted an independent attitude on ecclesiastical issues, Catholic princes tended to ignore the political claims of the Church. The Pope was frequently regarded as a minor Italian prince rather than a spiritual leader with universal and world-wide responsibilities. But his temporal sovereignty which in theory guaranteed his international independence was often more apparent than real. The Pope had practically no control over the rulers who theoretically recognized his authority; his temporal interests were ignored and he was denied a voice at international meetings. Secular rulers had no intention of allowing the Pope to interfere in their affairs and that included church affairs, whereas most secular governments felt free to intervene in ecclesiastical matters. The influence of secular governments prevailed in small as well as in more serious ways. Benedict XIV had to connive at the suppression of the feast of St Gregory VII in France because the language of the office was considered 'disagreeably Hildebrandine'. The growing demand that kings should be masters within their own dominions lay behind the attacks on the Jesuits, who had so staunchly supported the papacy since the Reformation, and the order was suppressed in 1773.

Even in Catholic countries ties with the Vatican were reduced to a minimum and there was a tendency to support national churches which would be to a greater or lesser extent independent of Rome. Attempts were made to reduce the number of appeals to Rome and to control the publication or the enforcement of papal decrees. Governments freely reorganized monasteries, suppressed orders, reformed ecclesiastical procedures and expropriated church funds. In several European states, decayed or superfluous religious houses were closed and the economic privileges of the Church such as freedom from taxation were reduced. Maria Theresa was one of the most sincerely Catholic rulers of the century, but even she halved the number of monasteries, reduced the income and judicial privileges of the Church and restricted the activities of the Inquisition.

Leopold of Tuscany also attempted to become the effective ruler of the Church within his own Grand Duchy. He abolished the court of the papal nuncio as well as appeals to Rome, he controlled the power of the curia and restricted the transmission of funds to Rome. He then limited the powers and jurisdiction of ecclesiastical courts including that of the Inquisition and set about reforming religious life and taxing clerical incomes. Bishop Scipione Ricci was allowed to put into practice his reforming and Jansenist theories; relics were burned, side-altars abolished and Mass was said in the veracular. Rome was referred to as 'Babylon' and devotions to the Sacred Heart denounced as 'cardiolatry'. Leopold also prevented the Florentines from singing hymns at the street shrines of Our Lady and limited the number of candles to be used in churches. But since he was more interested in constitutional issues than ecclesiastical reforms, he encouraged Ricci to hold the Synod of Pistoia which endorsed the Gallican Articles as well as Jansenist opinions. However, in the following year, a rumour that the girdle of the Virgin's statue was about to be removed caused a riot in Prato and Leopold was effectively prevented from going any further by the force of popular opinion.

Erastian rulers were frequently served by writers of great ability who argued for the most part in traditional ecclesiastical terms. Zeger Bernhard Van Espen argued in favour of the clergy's right to appeal to secular rulers against the tyrannical acts of their ecclesiastical superiors. He maintained that royal permission should be necessary for the execution of ecclesiastical laws and he defended the rights of bishops against the papacy. Van Espen influenced Johann Nikolaus Von Hontheim, the founder of Febronianism, while the latter was studying at Louvain. Hontheim was a native of Trier where he eventually became suffragan bishop. In 1742 he began an investigation on behalf of the German Archbishop-Electors into the historical position of the papacy and in 1763, under the pseudonym 'Justinus Febronius', he published his conclusions in his principle work, *De statu ecclesiae et legitima potestate Romani Pontificis* which was written as a contribution towards the reunion of Christians.

Hontheim argued that although Roman primacy was of divine institution and Rome the centre of unity, the abuses of the papacy had driven Protestants out of the Church. Consequently it was necessary to restrict papal primacy within the limits of the practice of the early Church, remove medieval accretions, and restore the rights of bishops and princes which had been usurped by the Pope. The Pope was Head of the Church, supervisor of ecclesiastical administration as well as of faith and morals. But the Pope was subject to the universal church or a General Council and he was not infallible. As far as possible all ecclesiastical affairs should be kept in episcopal or civil hands, while papal claims based on the False Decretals should be annulled. Hontheim's book was put on the Index in 1764, but five years later it received the approval of the Archbishop Electors who also prepared a list of some thirty objections against the papal claims.

The Archbishop Electors were also the temporal rulers of their small states and these ecclesiastical electorates or prince bishoprics provided an obvious and nautral support for the notions of Febronianism. When Hontheim argued for state control over the Church, he was arguing in favour of what was already an established fact in the electorates. This curious identification of Church and State would shortly disappear for ever under the impact of the French Revolution. Meanwhile, in 1785, the Archbishop of Salzburg and the Electors of Mainz, Cologne and Trier issued a joint protests against the appointment of a papal nuncio to Bavaria. Ecclesiastical as well as secular rulers tended to disapprove of the appointment of papal nuncios, who tried to safeguard and extend the rights and authority of the Pope. In the following year, the Electors' suffragans met at Bad Ems in an effort to put into practice the theories of Hontheim and published the famous 'Punctuation of Ems'. The bishops proposed that papal bulls and other official Roman decisions should only be binding when they had been accepted by the German episcopate. They also denounced the judicial powers of nuncios and other traditional papal rights and jurisdiction; papal nuncios should no longer be appointed to German states and the German Diet should reconsider the entire system of Roman taxation.

However, when the bishops met at Ems to co-ordinate their anti-Roman policies, events were already moving out of their control. The interests of the prince bishops were not necessarily the same as those of other bishops and secular rulers. They failed to win the support of the bishops in Germany who simply regarded the scheme as an attempt by the prince bishops to strengthen their own position. The Austrian Emperor was also hostile because the bishops were claiming rights and authority to which he himself laid claims, while the rulers of Prussia and Bavaria were also opposed to the bishop's claims.

The First Vatican Council 1869-1870

It is sometimes said that Joseph II was Febronius' best pupil and that the ecclesiology of Febronianism was simply a manifestation of Gallicanism beyond the Rhine. But the prince bishops were frequently opposed to the Emperor as well as to the papal nuncio; their attitudes were not particularly theological, but formed in the interests of their own administrative control. The Emperor himself was also subject to secular rather than ecclesiastical influences. He cared less for episcopal rights than the auxiliary bishop of Trier, who after personal experience of the Emperor's rule was prepared in 1778 and again, after some vacillation, ten years later, to recant his Febronianism. It is revealing that the prince bishops themselves also preferred to entrust spiritual authority in the hands of the Pope rather than the Emperor because they too eventually made their peace with Rome.

Many of the policies which have been seen as the result of contemporary Enlightenment can be understood more correctly as the eighteenth century form of centralizing and strengthening the State which the rulers of western Europe had been attempting since the Middle Ages. The policies of "enlightened despotism" adopted in Austria were as elsewhere a response to certain practical and urgent necessities rather than the result of philosophical opinions. In 1740 Austria lost Silesia to Prussia. Maria Theresa's determination to regain this territory began the great series of reforms associated with her and her son, Joseph II. The reform of the armed forces demanded increased taxation which could only be raised by further political, economic and administrative reforms and by restricting the privileges of the clergy and the nobility. A new civil service had to be created and this in turn demanded a new educational system free from censorship and clerical control. In 1754 a Chair of Natural Law was established at the University of Vienna; arguments from natural law were used to reject the claims of the papacy, to circumvent defences of ecclesiastical independence or property and to demonstrate the weaknesses of the old feudal constitutions. Graduates then entered the civil service which imposed the new laws and regulations.

Joseph's ecclesiastical policy was inspired by motives which were typical of a national ruler and self-conscious rationalist in the later years of the eighteenth century as well as by his policy of economic development. He himself made it clear that he accepted the principles of religious toleration because he wanted the services of anyone regardless of their religion and he would therefore grant citizenship to all who were qualified and prepared to work in agriculture or industry. A limited degree of toleration was gradually extended to different religious groups throughout the Empire and the Inquisition, which had long ceased to have any practical importance, was formally abolished. Monasticism deprived the economy of capital and man-power, Joseph therefore secured the economic resources of monasteries, dissolved contemplative orders and converted monastic buildings into warehouses and factories. Religious orders were also suppressed and their property secularized, except for those engaged in scholarly or charitable works.

The funds provided by the dissolution of religious institutions were used to finance parochial and diocesan reorganization, extend education and to replace the older diocesan seminaries with new ones. The new seminaries would produce priests to carry out the Emperor's policies. The secular clergy could be used as highly trained and specialized civil servants who encouraged the people to obey the laws and who would teach the value of practical Christianity. In a further effort to subject the Church to the State, the clergy were forbidden to correspond directly with Rome and papal decrees could only be published with the Emperor's permission. Members of religious orders could no longer be subject to foreign superiors and bishops were required to take an oath of allegiance. The Emperor also reorganized episcopal sees and parishes, reduced episcopal incomes and prohibited pluralism. He objected to such 'superstitious practices' as pilgrimages and the observance of saints days; he opposed baroque extravagances in churches and services on the grounds that simplicity had been the mark of primitive worship. Nothing was too small for Joseph's attention and Frederick the Great is said to have referred to him as 'my brother the sacristan of Europe'.

The relaxation of censorship in 1781 was followed by a flood of publications arguing the case against the papacy and clerical or aristocratic privileges. Many of the new civil servants supported more radical ecclesiastical policies than the Emperor himself and when episcopal protests were made, the civil servants through whom they passed did everything possible to prevent any modification of government policies. On the other hand, the widest interpretations were given to instructions restraining clerical influence or easing the expression of anti-clerical opinion. As a result, the clergy began to appeal to public opinion in their sermons which were not subject to government censorship, but a weekly publication of the 'Institute of Sermon Critics' subjected these sermons to searching criticisms.

Joseph himself was always a believing and practicing Catholic who simply wanted to strengthen or enrich the State by reducing the independent power and wealth of the Church. He had no intention of weakening the authority of the Catholic faith over his subjects. Nevertheless scepticism and irreligion became fashionable among the educated middle classes who began by rejecting the superstitious trimmings of a baroque Catholicism suppressed by government decree, but then discarded the idea of a revealed religion as well. There is also evidence that the joint impact of Joseph's reforms and the popularization of rationalist ideas even had an effect on some of the lower classes in Vienna.

At the same time, not only the peasants, who had benefited more than any other class from Joseph's reforms, resented various aspects of his reforms and the hardships resulting from a Turkish war as well as some of the religious innovations of his reign. This restment eventually gave rise to disorders and demonstrations. Events began to get out of hand, discontent was giving way to revolt, especially following the revolution in France during 1789, so that the retreat from 'enlightened despotism' and the start of a policy of repression had begun even before the death of Joseph. He himself decided to modify or abandon those policies which had resulted in the spread of ideas which were calculated, in his own words, to 'undermine all religion, morality, and social order'. His brother, Leopold II, issued new regulations designed to ensure that the education of university students did not in future result in a loss of faith. The Board of Censorship was reminded not to allow publications which ridiculed the clergy, the teachings of religion or the constitution of the Church.

Leopold's successor, Francis II, leaned heavily on his ministers who had been convinced by the crises within the Hapsburg dominions as well as by the revolution in France that lasting stability could only be secured by the complete abandonment of fundamental reform and the restoration of the weakened influence of the clergy and nobility. Furthermore, following the declaration of war on France, the government needed the support of the clergy, and the restrictions on various forms of public devotion were gradually relaxed. The Commission for Ecclesiastical Affairs were dissolved and its president compulsorily retired so that even those regulations which were still officially in force could not be imposed as strictly as before.

The opponents of 'enlightened despotism' associated reform with revolution. They argued that violent upheavals were the inevitable and natural result of undermining the power and the privileges of the clergy and nobility, and the situation in France became a classic illustration of their argument. The arrest and trial of some Austrian 'Jacobins' during 1794 provided evidence even closer to home. The various activities which have gone down in history as the 'Jacobin Conspiracy' were probably little more than an attempt to organize active opposition to the policies of Francis II. But it was claimed at the time that anger and disappointment at the abandonment of 'enlightened despotism' had led some of its supporters into 'subversive' paths and that it was now necessary to reverse the dangerous policies of 'enlightened despotism'.

Opponents of Joseph's reforms were particularly critical of his educational reforms and they now maintained that education should once again be influenced by the traditions of Catholicism. Many of the graduates involved in the 'conspirary' had picked up their radical opinions at the university, and the President of the Supreme Judiciary called for a new alliance between Church and State, which would restore Catholicism to its former splendour and magnificence and enable it to repair the serious damage done to the minds of the Austrian people by the Enlightenment. The Governor of the Tyrol where 'Jacobin' activities had been discovered among the students also recommended that the influence of Catholicism should be restored in the choice of teachers and textbooks, in the character of the curriculum and the whole tenor of education in general.

Over two years work by the Hungarian Diet's committee on education was simply scrapped and a new commission was constituted with the significant title, *Studien-Revisionskommission*. The Emperor expressed the hope that this commission would develop an educational system which would produce well-behaved, religious and patriotic citizens which, in his view, the existing system had obviously failed to do. Although the composition of this commission did not completely satisfy the Cardinal Archbishop of Vienna, by 1806 even the Deputy Minister of Police was complaining of the extent to which the clergy had recaptured control of the educational system.

In view of these and later developments both in Austria and elsewhere, it is interesting to read the judicious remarks made in 1794 by the Chancellor of State, Prince Wenzel Kaunitz, who has been described as 'the real author of Josephism'.

The Clergy must be honoured by the State and respected by the people. But it would in my opinon be very dangerous to concede them excessive influence and arbitrary powers, or to adopt our civil and police laws to ultramontane principles .... Such a course would bring the government into collision with the spirit of the times which cannot easily be changed ...... I very much hope that small, shortsighted minds which have been thrown into utter confusion by the unexpected events of our time .... will not succeed in leading the government astray by their numerical majority .... It is my conviction that justice is the securest foundation of States.

Pope Gregory XVI

I: The Revolution and the Church in France

The American Revolution had a profound effect on European opinion and made a powerful contribution towards preliminary moves in favour of political reform. The Americans had appealed to natural law and the rights of man in their declarations of universal principles and had succeeded in establishing a republic in the name of a sovereign people. Their example captivated European 'liberals', stirred romantic enthusiasm and disturbed the principle of submission to an established order. Those who shared the political ideas of the Enlightenment were aroused; Condorcet and other revolutionaries adopted some of their proposals from the new Republic, while French officers like Lafayette who had fought on the side of the Americans received a political education which enabled them to form the nucleus of a liberal nobility.

Furthermore, by 1787, partly at least as a result of the support which the French had given to the Americans during the war of independence, the royal treasury was practically bankrupt. This financial crisis was an immediate and direct cause of the French Revolution, which was originally started and led by the nobility. At first the financial problems were alleviated by a policy of borrowing, but eventually the deficit became so great that it was necessary to undertake fundamental reforms. In 1787 Calonne introduced a comprehensive plan of reform and in order to secure its acceptance he called into existance an Assembly of Notables of the privileged orders. This was in itself an initial surrender in the sense that the monarch was forced to consult the aristocracy rather than simply inform his subjects of his demands.

It has been argued that these moves brought about the first revolt, the revolt of the aristocracy – clergy and nobility, because this Assembly refused to accept the reforms which included an attack on clerical manorial rights and the nobles censured the idea of a universal land tax which would have infringed their privileges. An attempt to secure financial reform in spite of the judicial aristocracies of the Parlements also failed. The aristocracy resisted, sometimes violently, and demanded a meeting of the Estates General as the only representative body able to agree to new taxation. In short, the French crown was forced to abandon absolute monarchy in the face of the resistance of the privileged classes to financial reform by calling the Estates General.

Some historians, on the other hand, would argue that the crown attempted its own revolution by calling in the Third Estate and doubling its representation in the Estates General. In either case, however, until the end of 1788 the struggle was against the King, whereas from 1789 the main issue was the conflict between the Third Estate and the other two orders over the middle class attack on despotism and privilege, the bourgeois demand for a just and rational society based on equality of opportunity. The *ancien régime* was a political and social system founded on privilege justified by service, whereas the supporters of the Revolution wanted to establish a system founded on equality. And the Gallican Church was not only a stronghold of privilege as an essential part of the *ancien régime,* but it also suffered from internal divisions between its privileged and its less privileged members.

Eighteenth-century society was based on a religious foundation. Ecclesiastical establishments were taken for granted and even non-believers could hardly conceive of any possible alternative. The *philosophes* were agreed that the State could not function without religion and that in France, religion could only mean Roman Catholicism, though some of them might have preferred a civic religion and a few revoluntionary idealists were later inclined to establish new cults. Rousseau regarded a state religion as absolutely necessary and Voltaire who publicly proclaimed the necessity of crushing the beast – the Roman Catholic Church – had a chapel built on his manor where he made his Easter duties. However, as the *Abbé* Raynal, another of the *philosophes*, pointed out, the State was not made for religion but religion for the State which therefore had the right to judge and control its precepts and its doctrines.

On the eve of the Revolution, the French Church enjoyed the moral leadership of the nation, the protection of the Government and played a crucial part in the lives of all Frenchmen from the cradle to the grave. The Church monopolized education, marriage and care of the sick. The Church had its own courts, its clergy were a privileged class and only Catholics enjoyed the rights of citizenship. By the second half of the eighteenth century, Protestants were no longer actively persecuted and in 1776 one of them was a minister in all but name, yet it was only in 1787 that Frenchmen were allowed to register as Protestants and to practice their religion in private.

The French Church was also exempt from taxation and had become extremely wealthy. By 1789, as a result of bequests and legacies, the industry of its monks and the financial skill of its clerics, the Church was the greatest landed proprietor in France. Tithes seem to have averaged out at about an eighteenth, but varied according to the district from about a fiftieth to a fifth. The annual income of the Church has been estimated to amount to some 180 million francs and its expenditure to about 150 million. However, rumour and gossip exaggerated the wealth of the Church and at the same time seriously underestimated its financial contributions to the community by the money spent on charity and education, chiefly by the religious societies which had been established during the religious revival of the seventeenth century. In 1789 the Church provided over two thousand hospitals and there were fewer secondary school pupils in 1842 than there had been in 1789. Furthermore, several of the bishops in the second half of the eighteenth century were active in improving the economic life of their dioceses by digging canals, draining marshes, organizing associations of peasants, as well as giving grain to the poor.

The crown had nominated French bishops and abbots since the sixteenth century and by the middle of the eighteenth century the aristocracy almost monopolized the positions of wealth, honour and authority in the French Church. Bishops were recruited almost entirely from the ranks of the aristocracy and younger sons frequently moved into their episcopal palaces before the age of thirty. Although most of the appointments were made conscientiously, the very way in which particular bishops had been appointed or promoted could never be ignored or forgotten whatever subsequent zeal or abilities they might display. And, of course, since birth was considered more important than faith or merit, there were the inevitable, if occasional, scandals.

Bishop Grimaldi of Mans enjoyed the company of rather dubious women and on Sundays preferred to hunt on his estates rather than officiate in his cathedral; on one occasion he forced his horse through a religious procession in pursuit of his prey. When Louis XVI was asked to nominate Loménie de Brienne to the capital see, the King was said to have remarked that the Archbishop of Paris should at least believe in God! On another occasion Louis complained that a particular archbishop was alleged to owe many debts; 'Sire', replied the cleric, 'I will find out from my administrator whether that is the case and will then do myself the honour of reporting to your Majesty'. Such prelates inevitably preferred the pleasures of the court to the labours of a diocese and willingly left the work of ecclesiastical administration to others; when one bishop asked 'Have you read my Pastoral?', he received the reply, 'Yes, my Lord, and have you?'.

Cardinal de Rohan, His most Serene and Most Eminent Highness, Louis René Édouard, Prince of Rohan-Guéméné, Cardinal of the Holy Roman Church, Prince-Bishop of Strasbourg, Grand Almoner of the Court, Landgrave of Alsace, Prince of the Holy Roman Empire and in 1771 Ambassador Extraordinary at the Court of their Imperial and Royal Majesties in Vienna, member of the French Academy and Rector of the Sorbonne – wished to seduce Marie Antoinette. He therefore bought a superb necklace which he intended to present to her one evening in a shrubbery in the park at Versailles. Unfortunately the Cardinal was a little short of money. He did not actually pay for the necklace which the jewellers became anxious to repossess. The Cardinal was then fooled by an adventuress playing the part of the Queen and the subsequent scandal did nothing to improve the reputations of either the Throne or the Altar. It is, however, only just to recall that de Rohan led an exemplary life when he was forced to leave his ostentatious mansion at Strasbourg and flee from the Revolution. He sheltered many priests and seminarians with whom he lived simply and, in his own words, as 'a priest of Jesus Christ' and 'a poor man'.

Most of the French bishops, however, were neither particularly scandalous nor particularly edifying. They tended to be more concerned with political issues than with spiritual matters and were more attracted by the pleasures of this world than the prospect of eternal happiness in the next. Altogether there were only about half a dozen scandalous bishops, but the public was much more interested in their careers than those of their more virtuous colleagues like the Bishop of Castres who lunched on bread dipped in watered wine or the Bishop of Perpignan who frequently spent whole nights before the Blessed Sacrament. In any case, the ordinary people were either almost ignorant of or largely uninfluenced by episcopal scandals. They were much more likely to be alienated by the condition of a local abbey or religious house.

French abbeys were notoriously wealthy. Citeaux enjoyed an annual income of some 122,000 francs, while Cluny had almost 100,000 francs for the monks and twice as much again for the abbot. Furthermore, the evil effects of the system of privilege were shown in the possibility of holding a number of benefices and the consequent evils of non residence. More than half the revenues of the great French abbeys went to titular 'abbots' who might be aristocratic ecclesiastics supplementing their incomes or tonsured courtiers free from any ecclesiastical obligations. It has been estimated that some four fifths of the abbeys in France were held as mere sinecures.

Some monasteries and religious houses, orders like the Caupuchins and Carthusians, and especially the teaching and charitable orders of nuns kept strictly to their religious rules. Older foundations, however, particularly monasteries, tended to be lukewarm. Serious scandals and actual decadence were rare, but poverty and obedience were not much in evidence and the wealth of the monks was not redeemed by social utility – a fact that did not go unnoticed in such a critical age. Voltaire was not alone in his opinion that monks did nothing for a living except to bind themselves by inviolable oaths to be slaves and fools and to live at the expense of other people. Furthermore the number of vocations had declined and there were on average only about ten monks in each house. Seventeen Cistercian houses had only one monk each, twenty-two houses had two and seventy-nine houses had three. In short, the devotion of Trappists or Carmelites and the work of Trinitaires ransoming captives from pirates were forgotten or ignored as attention concentrated on the aristocratic Benedictine abbesses who threw hunting parties, noble canonesses with temporary vows as they waited for handsome suitors and even the otherwise industrious Benedictine scholars of Saint Maur who relaxed by indulging in hearty eating and heavy drinking.

But if the higher clergy were often extremely wealthy, the inferior clergy were generally desperately poor because the wealth of the Church was very unevenly distributed. Canons, parish priests and even curates in the larger towns often enjoyed an enviable standard of living. On the other hand, parish priests in the country were often very poor indeed, while their curates suffered the added humiliation of having to seek the renewal of their faculties every year. The tithe owners of almost half the parishes in France were chapters or monasteries who paid the *curés* barely enough on which to live. But although the country clergy might be poor, on the whole they lived good and moral lives and enjoyed a special position within their communities as spiritual and temporal local leaders, as ministers of the sacraments and minor civil servants.

Edme Rétif was the father of fourteen children. He began each day by praying with his family and servants, and each evening he read and commented on the scriptures, recited a short prayer and catechized his children. His son, Nicolas, a parish priest in the diocess of Auxerre, gave a thousand francs of his income of 1,500 francs to the poor. Nicolas rose at three in the morning and meditated on the Scriptures until six in order that he might better instruct his flock. After celebrating Mass, he visited his parishioners until midday. He provided schools at his own expense to which he compelled his parishioners to send their children. When the bishop proposed to move him to a larger parish, Nicolas replied that he had already married the church of Courgis and would be faithful to her until death. It is very clear from the *cahiers* or the lists of grievances submitted to the Estates General that many Frenchmen respected their parochial clergy, despised the idle monks and canons, and hoped to secure for their priests a fairer share in the wealth of the Church.

The parochial clergy, for their part, mostly welcomed the meeting of the Estates General and largely supported the aims of the revolutionary middle classes in their attack on privilege. The regulations governing the elections of the Estates General enabled the parish priests to dominate the electoral assemblies of the clergy who were able to vote individually, whereas canons and monks could only vote through their representatives. The divisions among the clergy as well as the strength of the lower clergy were reflected in numbers of clerical representatives, four fifths of whom belonged to the Third Estate; of the 296 clerics elected, there were 208 parish priests, but only 47 were bishops.

The wider divisions within the French nation were demonstrated on May 1789 when the deputies of the Estates General marched in a religious procession to the Church of St Louis for a Mass of the Holy Spirit. The nobility were distinguished from the Third Estate by their position in the procession as well as the splendour of their clothes. Musicians marched between the ordinary priests and their glittering bishops so that, as one cynical and angry parish priest remarked, distant spectators would not be in danger of confusing them. Nevertheless, with the inauguration of the Estates General which had not met since 1614, the representatives of the nation now had an opportunity to air their grievances and to demand reforms.

After the opening of the Estates General on the 5th of May, the Third Estate attempted to alter the traditional system of voting by separate estates and to establish a united chamber where their greater numbers would be more effective. On the 13th of June three parish priests joined the Third Estate. 'We have come', declared one of them, 'preceded by the torches of reason, spurred on by ardour for the public good and by the demands of our own conscience to join our fellow citizens and brothers'. The priests were welcomed with embraces and tears of joy and their example was followed by others. On 17 June the deputies of the Third Estate declared themselves to be the National Assembly, a revolutionary break with the old French Constitution, and two days later the clergy voted to join them.

Although not all the clergy favoured this move nor all the bishops opposed it, the clergy's decision was a direct result of their suspicions of aristocratic bishops and, at least according to some contemporaries, effectively 'made' the Revolution. The clergy played a decisive part in destroying the power of the monarchy and nobility by joining the National Assembly where the bourgeoisie were the predominant power. Between 20 and 23 June, the National Assembly defied a royal command to disperse and on 27 June the King gave way and ordered the first two estates to join the third, but not before the first elements of mob rule had appeared, directed in part against the clergy.

Maximilien Robespierre later commented that in most European countries there were three powers:

> the monarchy, the aristocracy and the people, and the people is powerless. Under such circumstances a revolution can break out only as the result of a gradual process. It begins with the nobles, the clergy, the wealthy, whom the people supports when its interest coincide with theirs in resistance to the dominant power, that of the monarchy. Thus it was that in France the judiciary, the nobles, the clergy, the rich, gave the original impulse to the revolution. The people appeared on the scene only later. Those who gave the first impulse have long since repented, or at least wished to stop the revolution when they saw that the people might recover its sovereignty. But it was they who started it. Without their resistance, and their mistaken calculations, the nation would still be under the yoke of despotism.

On 11 July 1789 the King dismissed a popular minister, appointed a reactionary one and summoned royal mercenaries to Versailles. These decisions coupled with high food prices and widespread unemployment whipped up the popular fury which resulted in the attack on the Bastille. The Parisian mob, hungry for bread and terrified of a military coup, forced the royal family to return to Parish. Members of the

Assembly followed and both the King and the Assembly became the prisoners of Paris which was increasingly independent of the King's government and the controlling factor of the Revolution. The prisoners who poured out of the dungeons of the Bastille consisted of four forgers, two lunatics and a dissipated young nobleman, but the destruction of the Bastille was more important as a symbol of the destruction of privilege.

Peasants throughout the country followed the example of the mob in Paris by burning down their local manor houses and the records of their feudal dues. Militias were formed to defend citizens against aristocrats and to meet the danger of anarchy, while several towns refused to obey the officials of the King and would only take orders from the National Assembly. It was in an effort to pacify the people that the Assembly in a state of delirious enthusiasm abolished feudalism on the emotional night of 4 August. Bishops joined with nobles in renouncing their feudal dues, tithes and such privileges as immunity from taxation. The feudal system and the domination of the aristocracy over rural areas was destroyed. The work of financial and ecclesiastical reform was begun and the way was open for that declaration of rights proclaiming liberty, equality and national sovereignty which effectively marked the end of the *ancien régime.*

Irreligion played hardly any part in the collapse of the Gallican Church which was a direct result of the destruction of the *ancien régime.* France at the time was a genuinely Catholic country and some historians have even claimed that with the usual exceptions of prostitutes, publicans and old soldiers, religious practice was more general between 1650 and 1789 than it had been before. There were, of course, regional variations as well as differences of commitment. Less than half of the population made their Easter duties in the cities of Paris and Bordeaux, while the fact that some ninety per cent in the dioceses of Auxerre and Châlons made their Easter duties does not necessarily imply that they were all deeply pious Catholics. The irregular distribution of religious practice in France, as elsewhere, is to be explained by a combination of historical and political, intellectual and moral, ethnic and geographical factors. But the events of the Revolution would finally divide those who practised their religion out of a sense of Christian conviction from those who were simply responding to political, social or economic pressures.

There is, however, some evidence that members of the upper classes were already neglecting the practice of their religion and although many middle class families, particularly in the provinces, remained faithful to their traditional beliefs, the intellectual development of the rising generation was undoubtedly influenced by the *philosophes* who dominated the circles of the middle classes as well as the *salons* of the ruling class. Furthermore, there were few great theologians in this age of reason and rational religion; an age increasingly dominated by the literature of the Encyclopedists, Voltaire's mockery of superstition and Rousseau's sentimental deism. The masonic lodges in particular provided a liberal, mystical and occult philosophy to rival the austere and authoritarian religion of Catholicism, though Catholicism and Freemasonry did not come into conflict until the nineteenth century and many contemporary Catholics were themselves Freemasons.

Originally, the French Church was neither inevitably nor necessarily opposed to reform, while the Estates General was neither anti-Catholic nor even anti-clerical in spite of a few manifestations of anti-clericalism in the *cahiers*. There was not a great deal of support for the idea of religious equality or for depriving the Catholic Church of its social and educational role, and there was no demand at all for its disestablishment. Many members of the Constitutent Assembly were sincere believers who regularly practised their religion. Many others were Catholics if only out of a sense of conformity rather than conviction. But only a few members were irreligious or anti-Catholic and even they thought that religion was necessary. The idea of a secular, lay state was unknown and even alien to the men of the time. In any case the Assembly was in need of local agents such as parish priests who could explain its decrees and instruct the ignorant in their political duties.

However, there already existed the attitudes as well as the issues which might lead to conflict. Two contradictory notions dominated the Assembly: the theory of individual liberty and a belief in the omnipotence of the State. Thus, the Assembly quickly accepted the principle of religious freedom and less quickly recognized the civil rights of Protestants and Jews. But at the same time, the Assembly claimed the right to reorganize the Church without consulting either the clergy or the papacy. If the ecclesiastical authorities refused to accept this new situation, the State might them seek to impose its authority by force, and liberal tolerance would give way to persecution. Similarly, the clergy were also in a somewhat ambiguous position and the lists of clerical grievances included two distinct sets of demands.

On the one hand, the clergy emphasized the need to reform the system of benefices, to secure the redistribution of property and to establish the principle of promotion on merit. On the other hand, they also stressed the need to reinforce the privileged position of the Church by enforcing Sunday observance, condemning anti-Christian publications and even revoking the grant of toleration to Protestants. The clergy united with the middle classes in some aspects of their attack on privilege, but opposed moves towards universal religious toleration and other ecclesiastical reforms associated with the *philosophes*. The clergy supported initial phases of the Revolution, but were then unable to prevent the development of another phase which they regarded as hostile to their interests.

On 2 November 1789 and in an effort to solve the financial crisis, a decree drawn up by Mirabeau placed all ecclesiastical property 'at the disposal of the nation, which would make itself responsible for defraying the reasonable expenses of worship, the sustenance of ministers and the relief of the poor'. In a wry comment on the phrase 'at the disposal of the nation', one cleric congratulated the deupties on their 'wonderful progress in the science of embezzlement'. The nationalization of Church property, which was of only fleeting value to the State, inevitably led to the reorganization of ecclesiastical administration since tax-payers were now responsible for supporting the Church financially and paying the salaries of the clergy as well as providing for the education of children and the care of the sick and the poor. Although the confiscation enabled the Revolution to survive by meeting its internal and external expenses, what is perhaps more significant in the long term is that it created a body of new property owners who had a vested interest in the success of the Revolution and a genuine fear of any clerical restoration.

The decision to nationalize ecclesiastical property was also associated with an attack on monasticism. In February 1790 those religious orders not engaged in educational or charitable work were dissolved and religious vows which had already been declared to be without legal validity were now prohibited altogether. Of course, the cost of supporting monks was not one which the State would readily accept, but there were ideological as well as financial considerations. The financial measures adopted by the Assembly had destroyed the economic basis of religious orders, but monastic life was also declared to be incompatible with the rights of man. Utilitarianism combined with anticlericalism and Voltairian prejudice. The wealth and the abuses of monks, the hostility of the laity and parochial clergy, the tendency of religious to appeal to Rome, titillating rumours of forced vocations, all provided the background for an attack on what was generally and increasingly considered to be part of the *ancien régime* which was about to be swept away by the new revoluntionary sovereignty.

Large numbers of monks seized their chance of freedom and some monasteries were almost emptied; only two out of forty monks remained in the Abbey of Cluny. The reason for this exodus may be partly due to the fact that, whereas the *milieu* of the *ancien régime* had allowed men to drift into monasteries, the life of monasticism after 1789 seemed doomed to extinction; these were, after all, the days of liberal idealism before the great disillusion. There were some noble exceptions. The Trappists, Carthusians and Capuchins tended to remain faithful to their vows, while communities of women were generally united in their desire to remain in the religious life.

However, the attack on the monasteries was interpreted by some ecclesiastics as a further infringement on the rights of the Church. The clergy had already lost a great deal during the progress of the Revolution and were becoming increasingly suspicious of the secular authorities. The bishops themselves first protested against the religious policies of the Assembly on the issue of abandoning the State religion without the consent of either the papacy or a national synod. Conscious of the necessity and implications of religious toleration, and in spite of the opposition of some of its own numbers as well as in the country at large, the Assembly consistently refused to declare that Catholicism was the religion of the State with exclusive rights of public worship. When the bishops were overruled, they refused to take any part in the discussions on the Civil Constitution of the Clergy.

On a latter occasion, Talleyrand was prepared to state:

> Regardless of my own part in this affair, I readily admit that the Civil Constitution of the Clergy, decreed by the Constituent Assembly, was perhaps the greatest political mistake of that Assembly, quite apart from the dreadful crimes which flowed therefrom.

The actual responsibility for reorganizing the French Church fell to the Constituent Assembly whose members, both cleric and lay, often shared Gallican or Jansenist attitudes and sympathized with the ideas of Edmond Richer. Gallicanism was still strong, areas of 'mixed' ecclesiastical or secular jurisdiction had not been satisfactorily defined, while French lawyers and civil servants had already maintained that, apart from doctrinal matters, the secular power had the authority to reform ecclesiastical organization and discipline. There were, of course, several types of Gallicanism – royal, episcopal and parliamentary. Members of the French Parlements were traditionally hostile to the papacy and the Jesuits and sympathetic to the Jansenists. Other members of the Parlements were also influenced by anti-clerical or even sceptical ideas. The parliamentary Gallicanism of royal servants, who were often more concerned to defend the interests of the crown than the King himself, was partly responsible for the anti-religious development of the Revolution, since, somewhat ironically, the reigning monarch Louis XVI did not in fact share the common Gallican outlook of the time.

In some ways the Civil Constitution of the Clergy seemed to put into practice some of the more extreme principles of Gallicanism and it was certainly imposed by the civil authorities on the grounds that it was solely concerned with the discipline or organization and not with the doctrines or the dogmas of the Church. Thus the Pope was no longer allowed to collect money in France nor to invest French bishops with their spiritual powers. The Constitution recognized the Pope's primacy of honour, not of authority or jurisdiction, though 'without prejudice to the unity of faith and the communion which will be maintained with the visible head of the universal Church'. But the Constitution was also influenced by the arguments of Edmond Richer, who had maintained that the contemporary Church should return to the practices of the early Church. The power of the keys rested with the whole body of Christians and all episcopal authority, including that of the papacy, should be reduced. Parish priests and their flocks should be given greater authority in the Church. Parishioners should have a voice in the election of their pastors, who should then exercise ecclesiastical authority on their behalf.

The Civil Constitution of the Clergy undoubtedly provided some of the reforms which the French Church so desperately needed. Ecclesiastical organization was adapted to the secular administrative framework. Dioceses now coincided with civil departments and some 57 dioceses were suppressed. Parishes were reorganized on a more logical basis, while chapters and beneficies without the cure of souls were abolished. Bishops and priests were to be elected like other civil servants, though curates were still appointed by their parish priests. Episcopal incomes were estimated more realistically and priests were given reasonable incomes graded according to their responsibilities.

Salaries, duties and the extent of pastoral responsibilities were clearly laid down. Bishops were required to reside in their dioceses and priests could be dispossessed by the civil authorities if they were absent for more than a fortnight or took on employment which interfered with their professional duties. Provincial synods were allowed and the bishops who could not act without their episcopal vicars were to be advised by a council whose decisions were binding. Any appeals from an episcopal decision were to be heard by the metropolitan or his council, there was no question of an appeal to Rome. A newly-elected bishop was to write and enter into communion with the Pope, but without requesting papal confirmation; he would be consecrated by the senior or metropolitan bishop and ordain his own priests.

The clergy in general did not dislike the Constitution to the point of rejecting it and most of the bishops were in favour of finding ways to make it acceptable, but there were several obvious difficulties. In the first place, even some of the reforms were not universally acceptable. Some clerical incomes were actually reduced and many of the parishes in towns, no less than 33 out of 52 in Paris, were even abolished. The system of election might mean that ecclesiastical appointments were in the hands of a group of men which did not include a single cleric or representative of the bishop, which had little immediate knowledge of the parish in question, and which included anti-clericals and public sinners, heretics and atheists. Although the French clergy might have been indifferent to the fate of the religious orders or the authority of Rome, they were not necessarily in favour of sacrificing their religious liberty to the State, while their bishops could hardly welcome the new restrictions on their prerogatives.

Gallican bishops who had formerly been suspicious of the Roman authorities began to appreciate that Rome might offer the only possible support against the increasing dangers of state control. The Assembly was imposing changes without consulting the Church and on 29 May 1790 Archbishop Boisgelin of Aix-en-Provence warned of the necessity of referring the question either to an episcopal synod or a national council, or alternatively to the Pope. However, the Assembly would not permit a synod or a national council to meet since this might provide a platform for counter-revolutionary propaganda because all the bishops were aristocrats, and the Assembly was no more concerned about the opinions of the Pope than had been some of the Gallican monarchs of the past.

Pius VI himself had already been disturbed by the reforms adopted in France and he was also offended by the abolition of his privilege of collecting annates, the first year's revenue from benefices. On 29 March 1790 he had condemned the principles of the Revolution, especially the principle of religious freedom, in a consistorial allocution, though this had remained secret through the influence of Cardinal de Bernis, the French representative to the Holy See. The Pope also formally disapproved of the Civil Constitution of the Clergy in a letter to Louis XVI which arrived too late to prevent the royal assent but which reinforced the King's personal doubts about it. When the King finally promulgated the Civil Constitution, the Pope again disapproved, but failed to make an official decision and continued to evade the issue. It would seem that Pius VI refused to accept the Civil Constitution of the Clergy, but feared to provoke a schism. He mistakenly imagined that the new Constitution would be so difficult to apply that the Assembly would be forced to make concessions, whereas when it was faced with difficulties, the Assembly resorted to force rather than conciliation.

On 30 October, Archbishop Boisgelin issued the *Exposition des Principes sur la Constitution Civile*. This was a moderate summary of the arguments against the Civil Constitution and a request that the Assembly should suspend the execution of its decrees until the Pope had spoken. Boisgelin himself was fairly confident that Rome would eventually agree. He did not condemn the Constitution, but simply claimed that it was neither permissible nor constitutional to reform the Church without consultation and merely requested that the Pope should give his approval and remove any canonical difficulties before the decree was enforced. Nevertheless, some historians would argue that in substance the first Ultramontane act in modern Church history occurred when the *Exposition* was sent to Pius VI with a request that he would dispense from canonical objections to the Constitution.

The Assembly, however, was unwilling to seem dependent on a papal decision. Furthermore, the inhabitants of Avignon had rebelled against the rule of the papacy and requested to be incorporated into France; their supporters in the Assembly began to combine with anticlericals. Time was running out. There would be few purchasers of ecclesiastical property unless they were confident that the new ecclesiastical policies would not be reversed and tension increased throughout the country as the sales of Church property drew near. Local authorities had begun to elect parish priests and bishops according.

to the new legislation, but the first bishop elected could not find another to consecrate him. Some bishops ignored their new and reduced diocesan boundaries. Other dioceses and parishes were left vacant on the deaths of their incumbents which created administrative difficulties in keeping secular as well as ecclesiastical records. And perhaps worst and most ominous of all, violent clashes broke out between Catholics and Protestants.

Exasperated by the internal situation developing in France and angry at the Pope's delay in issuing a statement, though confidently assuming that he would eventually yield, the Assembly passed a decree which imposed an oath accepting the Civil Constitution on all priests holding office; those who refused to take the oath were to be deprived of their parishes. The imposition of the oath on 27 November 1790 marked the end of national unity and the beginning of civil war. The Constituent Assembly had not intended to fall into schism, but by the imposition of the oath it had created an official religion of the Revolution which would be rejected by the majority of the Catholic faithful. Once Catholics found themselves persecuted, they inevitably looked for support to others who were being persecuted by the forces of the Revolution and Roman Catholicism became the religion of the counter-revolution.

Only two bishops in the Assembly, Talleyrand an opportunist and Gobel a weakling, were prepared to take the oath. Hardly a third of the clergy in the Assembly were willing to follow their example, though their names were called out individually as the crowd outside demanded that the 'rebels' should be hanged. 'We have taken their property', whispered Mirabeau, 'but they have kept their honour'. The motives of the bishops who refused to take the oath were inevitably mixed. Some of them resented their recent fall from their former high position, others were influenced by their loyalty to their colleagues and many of them feared the danger of a schism. The five bishops outside the Assembly who took the oath included one who was depraved, one who was hopelessly in debt and one who was highly eccentric if not actually mad.

On the other hand, about half the clergy in the country including many devout parish priests proved willing to take the oath. These were less influenced by the example of the bishops in view of their previous conduct than by the improvement in their own status and finances as well as the other genuine reforms in the Constitution, by the facts that the King had sanctioned the document and the Pope had remained silent. The Pope only condemned the Constitution and the oath when the schism in the French Church had already taken place. Furthermore, the circumstances under which the oath was taken were such that terms like 'loyal' and 'disloyal' had very limited validity. The oath itself was neither obviously anti-Christian nor anti-Catholic and those who refused to take the oath as well as those who took it were subjected to religious and pastoral as well as to political, social or personal pressures. The total number of jurors varied at different times and in different places. Many of the priests who took the oath did so with reservations and many of them retracted following the papal condemnation.

The new Constitutional Church was threatened from the outset by the difficulty of consecrating the newly-elected bishops. Of the seven bishops who had taken the oath, three were insignificant bishops who did not have their own dioceses, two would have been unpopular if not decidedly odd choices, and a sixth refused to consecrate other bishops. However, the accomodating Talleyrand eventually agreed to consecrate bishops for the Constitutional Church and incidentally in so doing performed his last episcopal function. Had Talleyrand refused to co-operate, it is likely that more and more of the constitutional clergy would have returned more quickly to the Church of Rome.

The attitudes which people adopted to the constitutional clergy largely depended on local conditions and local sympathies in favour of the Church or the Revolution. Many of the non-juring clergy could not be replaced, while some of the priests who took the oath remained on good terms with their congregations. Many of the constitutional clergy proved to be excellent parish priests and many of the constitutional bishops, some of whom attempted to protect the non-jurors, were undoubtedly worthy men. On the whole, difficulties arose with the arrival of a new cleric, especially if the non-juror simply left his presbytery to take up residence at the other end of the village. Then there might well be mutual and bitter denunciations, boycotts or simultaneous services, stone throwing by children or cock crowing by women as the constitutional priest passed through the village.

At the time, only a few vocal fanatics wanted to exploit these religious differences or to support the constitutional clergy and to persecute the non-jurors as a result of their hatred for superstition and the Church of Rome or their enthusiasm for primitive Christianity or a civic religion. A decree of 7 May 1791 had confirmed the religious freedom and the rights of the non-juring clergy to celebrate Mass in constitutional churches. However many of the constitutional clergy began to complain against the non-jurors, while constitutional bishops occasionally made bitter attacks on the orthodox. Verbal battles sometimes coincided with local riots and there was serious trouble particularly in the west of the country. For its part, the Assembly used a new oath in favour of the Civil Constitution as a test of patriotism and priests who refused to take it were suspected of rebelling against the law and the fatherland. Thus the non-juring clergy became generally regarded, especially by the mob, as traitors to the Revolution. Furthermore, the King compromised himself as well as the Roman clergy by refusing to confess to, or to attend the Masses of, the constitutional clergy. The mob retaliated by preventing him from attending services conducted by non-juring priests and forcing him to attend Mass celebrated by one of the constitutional clergy.

A new and more anti-clerical Legislative Assembly came into power during 1791 and adopted measures which effectively ended the liberty of the non-juring clergy and suppressed the freedom of Catholic worship. Like the Constituent Assembly which it succeeded, the Legislative Assembly was dominated by its minority, in this case, left-wing jurists and members of the Jacobin club. Meanwhile, as a result of the threat of foreign invasion and fears of internal insurrection, non-juring clergy were interned as part of local security measures and the Catholic laity fell under suspicion where they were not actively persecuted. As the future of the Revolution seemed threatened both at home and abroad, the Roman clergy were increasingly regarded as supporters of a counter-revolution. In fact, however, the French bishops and clergy were already divided between those who believed that their future liberty depended on a return of the old order and the moderates who were already beginning to look for some form of compromise.

On 29 November 1791 the Assembly declared that non-jurors were under suspicion and liable to expulsion if any trouble occurred in the communes where they lived. By an unfortunate coincidence the King vetoed this measure at the same time that he vetoed other measures which were directed against the *émigré* nobility. The interests of the French Church, the nobility and the monarchy were becoming identified. Although the actions of the National Assembly would discredit Gallicanism and Febronianism, and help to forge a new alliance between Throne and Altar, the non-juring bishops at this time were still more royalist than papal since they believed that their temporal authority had come from the King and their spiritual authority was directly from God, only mediately through the Pope. The alliance was also reinforced by the fact that in September 1791, the French had justified their annexation of Avignon by appealing to the sovereign will of the people; the interests of the papacy as a secular as well as a religious power seemed to be identified with the interests of other secular and 'legitimate' rulers.

On 20 April 1792 the French declared war on Austria. The Austrian invasion and the disorganized rout of the French troops inevitably gave rise to cries of 'treason!' It was rumoured that the bodies of non-juring priests had been found on the battle field in Austrian uniforms, in spite of the fact that there had never been any real fighting at all. Non-jurors were regarded as traitors, a fifth column in league with the *émigrés* and the invading forces, and this association was actively encouraged by some of the *émigrés* as well as by a few of the Roman authorities. After all, the Pope had already condemned the 'Declaration of the Rights of Man' in a secret consistory during 1790 and in the following year had greatly stimulated counter-revolutionary activity by formally condemning the principles of the Revolution and the Civil Constitution of the Clergy. Furthermore, the Pope gave moral support to the plans of the Austro-Prussian alliance to rescue the French King and Queen from the Revolution. The attitude of the Pope was in fact one of the reasons which eventually prompted the French monarch to break with the Revolution and make his attempt to join the allies at Varennes in June, 1791. The King's flight marked the beginning of the persecution of the non-juring clergy and subsequently led to his own execution in January, 1793.

The flight of the monarch also brought to an end his limited protection of the orthodox clergy, while the continued successes of the enemy and an insurrection in the Vendée, aggravated by an economic and financial crisis intensified the persecution of the clergy. Priests who were not prepared to identify themselves with the ideology of the Revolution and its religious policies either went 'underground' or faced the prospect of exile, deportation or imprisonment; and in due course the success of the invading forces caused a panic in Paris which resulted in the Prison massacres of 1792. Marat called on his supporters not to 'leave behind in Paris a single enemy to be gladdened by our defeats and, in our absence, to slaughter our wives and children'. On Sunday, 2 September a platoon of the National Guard dragged three clerics from a cab taking them to jail and hacked them to pieces. For the next two days massacres occurred in most of the prisons where suspects were held and on a less extensive scale in various provincial centres.

There were almost 1,400 victims who were judicially murdered after travesties of trials. They included political prisoners and aristocrats, prostitutes and ordinary criminals, three bishops, some 220 priests and even children. The scenes were often hideous. The body of the Princess de Lamballe was dismembered and her head carried on a pike to the Queen Marie Antionette. The wife of the minister of the interior who previously sympathized with the Revolution wrote of 'Women brutually violated before being torn to pieces by those tigers, intestines cut out and worn as turbans; bleeding human flesh devoured'.

When Toulon surrended to the British fleet on 2 September 1793, the Convention ordered the policy of terror which continued until the fall of Robespierre in the following year. By 1793 the only priests who were able to escape the persecution were those who exercised no ministry, who had taken the so-called oath of liberty and equality, and had not been denounced by six citizens. More than 30,000 French priests fled abroad to a life of menial employment, poverty and charity, though many others continued to act as priests in hiding and ministered to their people in secret. Other priests hid their identity or adopted a different profession. Some obtained certificates of loyalty, passed themselves off as patriots or even joined the militia.

The actual horrors of the persecution varied according to local circumstances. If the persecution was intense in some areas, it was almost non-existent in others. It would seem that between two and five thousand priests were executed and many were imprisoned throughout the country. Ninety priests interned at Nantes were transferred to an old barge under the impression that they were about to sail to the opposite side of the river and to freedom. The plugs were then removed and they were drowned. Five hundred priests awaiting deportation to Guiana were crammed into a prison ship built for half that number; the ship was blockaded by the British and threequarters of them died in less than a year. From February 1784 some 850 priests were put on three old ships formerly used in the slave trade. Their conditions were so appalling that their detention became known as the 'dry guillotine' and only 274 of them had survived when they were released a year later. The Recollects and Carmelites of Arras marched to execution singing the vespers of the dead. When a secular priest was taken to execution in his vestments as a mark of contempt, he recited the *Introbio ad altare Dei* at the foot of the Scaffold. On 17 July 1794

Pope Pius VI

sixteen Carmelite nuns went to the guillotine; they renewed their vows at the foot of the scaffold and then sang the *Veni Creator* until the last of them had perished. The Sacramentines of Bollène thanked their judges and executioners, and one of them kissed the scaffold before mounting it. The Ursulines of Valenciennes sang the *Te Deum* and prayed for their executioners when they were condemned.

French Catholics on the whole seemed either unable or unwilling to resist the persecution of their priests and religious, and the attack on their Church. However, it is almost impossible to judge how far this was simply the result of fear or apathy and how far it should be seen as a manifestation of a decline in Catholicism since the Counter-Revolution. Personal attitudes were incredibly confused. Modeste Babin of Poitiers was betrayed by two priests whom she had helped. Her executioner was Pierre Verdier who had usually sat beside her in their parish church duing the old days. When Verdier himself died some sixty years later, he was holding the cross which Modeste had given to him on the guillotine. The only real resistance to the persecution of the Church was the insurrection in the Vendée with its population of traditional if not superstitious peasants who had been evangelized at the beginning of the eighteenth century by St Grignion de Montfort.

The people of the Vendée, which in this context refers to the entire country from the north of Poitou to Brittany and even Normandy, had originally welcomed the Revolution and the abolition of feudalism as well as the opportunity of purchasing ecclesiastical property. However, three-quarters of the local clergy and almost all of the local laity had refused to accept the Civil Constitution of the Clergy. Their spontaneous and sporadic resistance, including the boycott of constitutional priests, sometimes gave way to serious clashes. The peasants of the Vendée were also poor and found themselves subjected to high taxation at a time of raging inflation when food was scarce. Finally the threat of foreign invasion which had led to conscription occasioned the outbreak of a revolution under the slogan 'Long live religion'.

Civil wars are almost always notoriously bitter and ferocious, and in this case both sides were guilty of atrocities. With rosaries on their wrists and pictures of the Sacred Heart on their chests, the rebels of the Vendée cut the throats of their prisoners, shot local republicans and killed any constitutional priests who had the misfortune to fall into their hands. The revolt later became associated with the defence of the monarchy as local nobility and gentry came to provide the more experienced leadership that was required. But, not unnaturally, the revolt in the Vendée simply confirmed the fears of republicans that the non-juring clergy were in league with royalist *émigrés* and were enemies of the State.

The suspicions and hostility of the anti-clericals inevitably began to extend to the constitutional clergy. The unfortunate Constitutional Church was unable to defend itself against Government interference nor could it avoid the complete subordination of the spiritual to the temporal. In any case, the State Church did not enjoy even the nominal allegiance of most Frenchmen because sceptics and free-thinkers joined with the orthodox in refusing to recognize the civil role of the local constitutional clergy. The gradual decline in the status of the Constitutional Church was first seen in the adoption of festivals and public ceremonies in which it played no part, and in various measures which deprived clerics of their influence over education; former monks and nuns were eventually banned from teaching altogether.

The Legislative Assembly manifested its comtempt for the Constitutional Church by confiscating Church property and abolishing clerical fees, secularizing the registration of births, marriages and deaths, and by legalizing divorce, which effectively marked the introduction of the secular State. The Assembly also prohibited the wearing of ecclesiastical dress except for religious services, encouraged the rejection of celibacy and defended married priests. Finally, the Assembly allowed any French town or village to close the churches within its boundaries. The whole movement divorcing the State from the Constitutional Church was associated with an attempt to replace the public role of Catholicism with a new revolutionary religion, a national philanthropic deism, an optimistic and humanitarian religion, and occasionally with something worse.

The first attempts to establish a revolutionary religion were mingled with Catholic observances. Civil 'sacraments' provided the necessary solemnities on the occasion of births, marriages and deaths. Christian names were replaced by republican names such as Brutus or Cato, Marat or Peletier, 'Liberty' or 'Federation' and later with 'Love of the Devil'. On the Feast of Federation on 14 July 1790 Bishop Talleyrand celebrated Mass on the altar of the Fatherland, surrounded by four hundred priests wearing tricolour sashes over their albs. At the first session of the Legislative Assembly in 1791 the sacred book of the constitution was carried in procession as the deputies rose to their feet and removed their hats.

On 18 July 1793 was celebrated the feast of the translation of the heart of Marat to the Cordelier's club room where it was suspended in an urn from the roof amid applause. The end of the monarchy and the acceptance of the constitution was celebrated on 10 August 1793. A colossal statue of the Goddess Nature was built on the site of the Bastille; water spurted from her breasts into an ornamental pool; a member of the Committee of Public Safety gave a speech of invocation and drank from the fountain to a salute of eighty-three guns. During the following month the Feast of Brutus was celebrated in the Church of Saint-Cyr.

The policy of terror, however, was accompanied with the phenomenon of 'de-Christianization', which added sacrilege and vandalism to the attempt to introduce a revolutionary religion as a replacement for Christianity. De-Christianization took place by fits and starts, without rhyme or reason, going to ridiculous extremes which were followed by bursts of embarrassment and even repentance. Nevertheless nine months of confusion and crisis, of terror, panic and madness provided opportunities for adventurers and exhibitionists, intriguers and criminals, drunks and prostitutes, street urchins, ne'er-do-wells and village idiots. Former priests and monks demonstrated their hatred for the vocations which they had abandoned or only reluctantly accepted in the first place. Fouché, who had once been a minor seminarian, celebrated the republican baptism of his daughter, dedicated a bust of Brutus in one of the churches in Nevers, ordered priests to marry within a month and placed inscriptions over the gates of local cemeteries describing death as 'an eternal sleep'. On a later occasion he presided at a ceremony in which donkeys with crucifixes tied to their tails were formed into a procession and made to drink toasts from chalices.

A further impetus was given to the process of de-Christianization with the abjuration of the constitutional Archbishop Gobel of Paris who, having recanted his schism in prison, would later die on the scaffold crying out 'Long live Jesus Christ!' Gobel refused to abandon his priesthood and his faith is not really in question, but he had always obeyed the secular authorities, probably out of fear, even to the point of inducting a married priest. He now agreed, under pressure, to surrender his episcopal functions. Accompanied by his vicars general and young men wearing surplices and chasubles, he went before the Assembly to surrender the certificate of his priesthood, his pectoral cross and ring, and replaced his mitre with a red bonnet. According to the President of the Assembly, Gobel was surrendering 'the gothic baubles of superstition' for the social and moral virtues of the Supreme Being.

The honour of the Constitutional Church, however, was to some extent redeemed by Bishop Grégoire of Blois whose revolutionary fervour was accompanied with a deep devotion to the Church. Grégoire refused to follow the example of Gobel in spite of the pleas of his colleagues or threats of the guillotine. He declared that he was 'A Catholic by conviction and sentiment, a priest by choice, I have been elected bishop by the people; but it is neither from them nor from you that I hold my appointment'. Grégoire demanded his rights of freedom of worship and continued to act as a bishop. Although many followed the example of Gobel, Grégoire himself presided at religious ceremonies wearing the symbols of his office throughout the reign of terror.

Clerical apostasies were the highlights of de-Christianization ceremonies. During the terror many priests returned to the secular state and surrendered their legal functions, if not their priesthood. Others made the most abject surrenders, adding blasphemy or buffoonery to their apostasies, divorcing themselves from their breviaries or even 'debaptizing' themselves. Marriage offered the safest refuge. Some priests argued that a civil marriage had no religious significance and married their old housekeepers or friendly nuns who were under the impression that they were performing a pious act by saving a priest. Some of these marriages were simply fictitious unions which might or might not be maintained in later life. Other priests took their marriages seriously and adopted another profession, while a few priests indulged in the scandal of enjoying a spectacular marriage ceremony.

Of the eighty-two constitutional bishops consecrated in 1791, ten had already died including eight on the scaffold, five of whom retracted their errors before dying. Of the rest, a third apostatized including nine who married, another third surrendered their ecclesiastical functions, but the last twenty four preserved their lives and their honour. However, over 20,000 of the 28,000 constitutional clergy abandoned their ministries. Those who remained faithful suffered the same fate as their orthodox brethren, and of the 484 clerics from all over France who appeared before the revolutionary tribunal in Paris at least 319 belonged to the Constitutional Church. Of course, the apostates were not acting voluntarily and most of the apostasies were insincere, conditional or qualified. Nevertheless the de-Christianization campaign effectively succeeded in destroying by discrediting the Constitutional Church.

During the de-Christianization campaign, the Cathedral of Notre Dame was turned into a Temple of Reason and Liberty. The festival of Reason was celebrated in the cathedral where an artifical mountain was built with a flame of Truth and crowned with a Temple of Philosophy from which emerged the Goddess of Reason and Liberty, suitably played by an actress from the Paris Opera. Later, the cult of reason gave way to the cult of the Supreme Being and Robespierre's attempt to establish an official deist religion. Statues of Atheism, Selfishness and Nothingness were burnt to be replaced by a somewhat blackened statue of Wisdom. Children carried tricolours, crowds sang, girls threw flowers, mothers held out their children, men drew their swords, fathers gave their benedicitions and all united in proclaiming 'Long lives the Republic'.

Although the cult of the Supreme Being declined after the fall of Robespierre, the idealistic spirit of the Revolution still needed a ritual and the people needed a religion. This demand gave rise to Theophilanthropy which was not in itself hostile to Christianity and which some of its supporters regarded as more 'Christian' than some of the notions of God put forward by the orthodox.

> Merciful God, thy suppliant people seek
> Protection for the mother and the child,
> Thou couldst not strike an infant for the sake
> Of imagined crimes imputed to the weak.

The liturgy of Theophilanthropy was clearly inspired by the Mass. There were hymns, an examination of conscience, readings from the sacred texts of the principal religions and, as a replacement of the dismissal at the end, the reader urged his congregation not to quarrel over opinions, but to love one another. Other ceremonies replaced baptisms and first communions, marriages and funerals. However, Theophilanthropy enjoyed a limited intellectual appeal rather than popular enthusiasm and it too eventually failed.

It is difficult now to appreciate the contemporary enthusiasm for and symbolic importance of the new revoluntionary rites. It is easier to smile at their anachronisms and peculiarities. However, with all their limitations, they reminded men of the old argument that religion was the best guarantee of popular morality, while attempts to replace Catholicism provided the strongest social and political argument in favour of its restoration. Over the next few years, it became increasingly clear that Catholicism had survived both the destruction of the French

Church and the creation of rival forms of worship, though the actual process of restoring the Church would prove to be spasmodic and was marked by violent reversals.

The persecution of religion declined following the fall of Robespierre and the collapse of the first coalition against France which the Pope had supported. The French Government guaranteed religious freedom and this was followed by a revival of the constitutional and orthodox Churches, though the strength and persistence of this revival varied considerably. In fact whenever persecution slackened, priests came out of hiding, exiled clerics returned and with a few newly-ordained priests as well as those constitutional priests who had been reconciled they began the work of building up missions and restoring Catholic discipline and the Christian apostolate. However, the freedom which the Church enjoyed at this time was only grudgingly conceded and was not universal. Priests were still subject to local intolerance and persecution was resumed with the threat of political reaction.

The future divisions which would plague the French Church were already emerging. Many priests jeopardized the religious revival by associating it with political or monarchical reaction and some of them actually indulged in counter-revolutionary activity on the local level. In the absence of the bishops, priests had turned to other priests for advice and in particular to the *Abbé* Emery, Vicar General of Paris and Rector of Saint Sulpice. Emery was in favour of doing everything possible to save the French Church without betraying either its teaching or its discipline. He therefore took a more moderate line on the interpretation and lawfulness of oaths of loyalty than did the exiled bishops, though by 1797 both the Archbishop of Aix and the Bishop of Boulogne were beginning to appreciate that Catholicism could exist with all forms of legitimate government and that the survival of the Church should not be dependent on the stability of a particular government.

There were a few other signs, though isolated and somewhat premature, of an increasing awareness of the need for compromise. In 1796, the Pope urged the French clergy to obey their new Government. This had not been published in France because the head of the Constitutional Church had prompted the Directory to demand a withdrawal of all papal statements opposing the Revolution, especially the condemnation of the Civil Constitution of the Clergy, which Pius VI refused to do. In 1797, Camille Jordan secured the restoration of civil rights to all those priests who were prepared to make a harmless declaration of loyalty to the Republic. However, the law was never in fact applied.

The Directory reverted to its original attitude of hostility, the non-jurors were presented with an 'Oath of Hatred' against the monarchy and the exiles and deportations began all over again.

In 1797, Cardinal Chiaramonti, the Bishop of Imola and future Pius VII, preached on the theme that the new ideas of the Revolution were not irreconcilable with those of the Church, but that they would only be effective if they were interpreted in a Christian way; liberty, equality, fraternity and democracy must be based on Christianity. This sermon foreshadowed Dupanloup's acceptance of the principles and liberties of 1789 as well as Montalembert's speech to the Malines Congress in 1863. Chiaramonti's homily merely accepted the facts of the situation and outlined a pragmatic *modus vivendi*. Nevertheless, he was later bitterly criticized by Ultramontane conservatives, especially when he signed the Concordat with Napoleon and then went to Paris for his coronation as Emperor. The opinion of Barruel and de Maistre that the Revolution was simply satanic seemed confirmed beyond all doubt when the same Pope was subsequently kidnapped and imprisoned. As a result, in 1837, the Pope's biographer would explain that the passages on revolution and democracy in his homily had been inserted by those who had been anxious to please the French.

Meanwhile, by 1796, the internal and external enemies of the Revolution had been defeated, the French had taken the offensive and were about to descend into Italy under the youngest of their new generals, Napoleon Bonaparte. Pathetic attempts to raise a papal army were practically useless and the security of the Papal States was totally dependent on the success of the Austrians in the north of Italy. On two separate occasions the Pope had to make territorial concessions to the French, pay a considerable ransom and surrender many works of art. In due course, the French authorities ordered General Berthier to occupy Rome, remove the Pope and establish a Roman Republic. The General concealed his real intentions and received the military surrender of the city by promising to respect religion and the property and the person of the Pope. After waiting in vain for the expected revolution, he entered the city, deposed the Pope and by an 'Act of the Sovereign People' established a consular regime. The cardinals were arrested and the octogenarian Pope was ordered to leave Rome within three days.

There were apparently few republicans in Italy at the time and the French were forced to defend their satellite republics from internal and external enemies. During 1799, a popular rising of the *Sanfedisti* or the *Congregation of the Holy Faith* threatened the republican regimes in Naples, Florence and Rome. Although the motives of the peasants were undoubtedly mixed, they proclaimed their intention of saving and restoring the Church, the Pope and the city of Rome. Their defence of relics and images should not disguise their conviction that essential matters of faith were also at stake. Bonaparte himself seems to have appreciated this because, following his victory at Marengo, he based French power in the north of Italy on a restored Church, rather than on the new political ideology. In the meantime, however, Pius VI was not to be saved. The French took care to keep moving him away from the Austro-Russian army which was invading Lombardy and he died at Valence in 1799.

The death of the Pope illustrated the mixed attitudes adopted by supporters of the Revolution towards the Church. The local municipal officer recorded the Pope's death in the words 'Jean Ange Braschi, exercising the profession of pontiff'. On the other hand, one of the earliest decrees of the First Consul Napoleon on 30 December 1799 was to order funeral honours for 'a man who had occupied one of the highest ranks on earth'. The authorities at Valence who had so confidently declared that the late Pope would also be the last, were obliged on 31 January 1800, wearing full uniform and *crêpe* armbands, to follow the hearse drawn by caparisoned horses which took the Pope's body to its temporary resting-place, while the cannon of the garrison fired salvoes in its honour.

Napoleon was not only a great general, but a great administrator and a great statesman. He centralized and reformed the government of France, improved its finances and promoted its economic prosperity, codified the laws and established a system of public education. As a statesman, Napoleon was determined to end the schism in the French Church. He believed that religion was an agent of law like money, honours or punishments; religious peace and the social utility of religion were both maxims of his policies. 'Society cannot exist without inequality of wealth, and inequality of wealth cannot exist without religion'.

> What is it that makes the poor man take it for granted
> that ten chimneys smoke in my palace while he dies of cold --
> that I have ten changes of raiment in my wardrobe
> while he is naked – that on my table at each meal
> there is enough to sustain a family for a week? It

is religion which says to him that in another life
I shall be his equal, indeed that he has a better
chance of being happy there than I have.

When Napoleon seized power, the French Church had been almost devasted. Although the people in some areas had remained unshakeably loyal to the Catholic Church, most of the bishops were in exile, the number of priests, who were no longer paid by the State, had been drastically reduced by death, schism or apostacy and seminaries had ceased to exist. Some forty three 'Roman' dioceses were without bishops. Parishes and the faithful had been abandoned or neglected and churches were in ruin. The Revolution had permitted and encouraged the development of an active hostility to the Church and revealed the extent of the de-Christianization of the French people which now mainfested itself in an indifference or apathy towards the Catholic faith. Intellectuals were publicly atheistic, civil servants and ordinary citizens were openly hostile. Nevertheless, in spite of everything, many French people remained wedded to the Christian morality which had governed the life of the nation from time immemorial and to the Catholic liturgy which marked the significant stages of human life from the cradle to the grave.

Napoleon recognized that the attempts to establish a French Church independent of Rome had failed; both Catholicism and the Revolution were facts of life and their supporters must learn to live together in a spirit of coexistence if not of tolerance:

> My political method is to govern men as the majority of them want to be governed. That, I think, is the way to recognize the sovereignty of the people. It was by making myself a Catholic that I won the war in the Vendée, by making myself a Moslem that I established myself in Egypt, by making myself an Ultramontane that I gained men's souls in Italy. If I were governing a people of the Jewish race I would rebuild the Temple of Solomon.

But if Napoleon wanted religious peace, he also wanted a Church which would serve the State. 'The people must have a religion and that religion must be in the hands of the government'.

In spite of Napoleon's attitudes and diplomatic tactics, his material promises and physical threats, including one to break off the long and difficult negotiations, in spite of a calculated and premature publication of agreement and a draft altered at the last minute, the papacy secured a good deal in its Concordat with Napoleon and did not yield on any essential point. The papacy did not wish to see a restoration of the old Gallican Church, while the quasi-official character of Roman Catholicism was recognized as 'the religion of the great majority of the French people'. The Catholic liturgy was restored and replaced the constitutional forms of worship, the revolutionary cults were abandoned and the Pope's rights over the canonical institution of bishops were recognized.

The Pope signed the Concordat on 15 August along with three papal briefs intended to ease its application. The first called on all legitimate bishops to resign, the second called on the constitutional bishops to return to the unity of the Church and the third authorized the absolution of repentant married priests, but not bishops, and the convalidation of their marriages. Over three thousand priests and three hundred religious were in this way reconciled with the Church of Rome. In an effort to unite constitutional and 'Roman' Catholics, all the bishops were to resign and if any refused, the Pope would declare their sees to be vacant. Napoleon, as First Consul, would then nominate a new hierarchy including a fair proportion of the constitutional bishops. Cathedrals and churches were to be handed back to the clergy who would also be paid a suitable salary, but the Church completely renounced any claims to confiscated ecclesiastical property. The public practice of the Catholic religion was freely allowed so long as it conformed to Government regulations necessary for public order.

This last provision became significant immediately because when Napoleon published the Concordat he coupled with it a series of regulations, the notorious 'Organic Articles', in order to safeguard the position of the Government. The spirit of these articles was not simply Gallican but distinctly Erastian. It was an attempt to increase episcopal authority over the clergy, the secular authority over the episcopate and to reduce or control the authority of the papacy over the French Church. Roman documents and decrees could only be received in France with the permission of the Government and no Roman representative was allowed to exercise jurisdiction in France without the Government's consent. Seminaries could not be established without the approval of the First Consul who also had to approve of their regulations, one of which included the demand that professors must subscribe to the Gallican decrees. The articles also gave the civil contract precedence over the religious in marriage, put Protestantism on the same level as Catholicism, demanded Government approval for all religious feasts except Sundays and required public prayers to be said for the Consuls and the Republic.

The point was that having satisfied French Catholics by coming to an agreement with the Church, Bonaparte had to reassure republicans that the Church would be subject to the State and not the other way round. Napoleon clearly felt unable and unwilling to accept a weaker position in ecclesiastical affairs than the former rulers of France. He could not at one and the same time offend constitutional and royalist bishops, Jansenist or Gallican lawyers, senators and university teachers, sceptical Jacobins and republicans, many of whom were anti-clerical and all of whom were anti-Ultramontane.

Napoleon himself treated bishops simply as agents of his policies. He reappointed some of the most accommodating bishops who he regarded as ecclesiastical prefects. On one occasion, he instructed a counsellor of state to,

> Write to the Bishop of Orleans to ask him for information about one Lecoq and what manner of man he is. Tell him that I have an idea that Prejean is in the West; he should see whether he can have him arrested.

For their part many of the bishops accepted Napoleon's understanding of their role as prefects in clerical dress and willing co-operated with the secular authorities. The civil prefects helped bishops to deal with disobedient priests, while the bishops preached on the duties of respect and obedience which were owed to the civil authorities.

Napoleon himself was described as the modern Cyrus or Alexander, Constantine or Charlemagne. One of the former constitutional bishops described him as 'the most perfect of heroes that have yet come from the hands of God' and the Prince de Rohan simply declared, 'The Great Napoleon is my tutelary god'. Monsignor de Boisgelin, though with some reservations, referred to the legitimate Government, both national and Catholic, without which there would have been neither religion nor fatherland. The clergy as a whole were too few and too old, and sometimes too compromised during the Revolution, to dissociate themselves from these Erastian tendencies or to engage in a religious apostolate which in any case they would not have been allowed to exercise. The new order included former Jacobins and republicans who would have been only too willing to control any unduly apostolic or evangelizing cleric. In the meantime the Napoleonic regime was prepared to honour those priests who kept in their place – in church preaching the civil and military virtues.

Napoleon later introduced a catechism which answered a question on the duties of Christians towards their rulers and particularly to the Emperor Napoleon in the following way:

> Christians owe to the princes who govern them, and we, in particular, owe to Napoleon I, our Emperor, love, respect, obedience, loyalty, military service and the taxes ordered for the preservation of his Empire and his throne.

The reasons given for these duties and obligations to Napoleon were,

> because God, who creates Empires and apportions them according to His will, by heaping upon him His gifts, has set him up as our sovereign and made him the agent of His power, and His image on earth. So to honour and serve our Emperor is to honour and serve God Himself.

Those who failed in their duties to the Emperor were reminded that, according to the words of St Paul, they were opposing the order established by God and so rendered worthy of eternal damnation. An attempt was even made to celebrate the feast of Napoleon's name saint and the obliging Cardinal Caprara discovered an Egyptian martyr of the fourth century called Neopolis or Neopolus, later corrupted to Napoleon. Unfortunately for the Cardinal and the Emperor, Neopolis was the name of a place, not a person, and the courage and sufferings of the 'Saint' commemorated at Lauds and Mass on the Feast of the Assumption were simply figments of Caprara's imagination.

Nevertheless, in spite of Napoleon's blatant Erastianism, it is impossible to overestimate the significance of the concordat in the history of the papacy and it soon became a model for other treaties defining relations between Church and State. Originally neither side really liked the concordat. The Pope disliked it because Catholicism was not restored as the established religion of France and because important issues and traditional ecclesiastical rights over the family, marriage or education were simply ignored. Furthermore, the publication of the Organic Articles seemed to show that Bonaparte was acting in bad faith. It was not immediately obvious that, as one historian has put it, 'the genius of Napoleon accidentally confirmed the popes in a power which seventeen centuries of Vatican politics had been unable to achieve'. In due course, however, Pope Pius VII himself was to appreciate that,

> to Napoleon more than to anyone, save God alone, is due the restoration of our holy religion in the great Kingdom of France . . . . Savona and Fontainebleau were only mistakes due to temper, or the errors of an ambitious man: the Concordat was the saving act of a Christian and a hero.

In the first place, the Concordat allowed the French Church to exist and contributed to the religious revival which was beginning to take place in the country. Previously, the Church had lacked any public influence, vocations and money; the hierarchy was in exile and the clergy were dispersed. The Church was now allowed to rent property, but not to buy it, though the Church could hardly afford to do so at the time. Church buildings handed back to the ecclesiastical authorities were often in a deplorable condition and there were fewer and fewer priests to take charge of them. The shortage of vocations was particularly frightening. Between 1802 and 1814 about six thousand priests were ordained which was less than would have been ordained in a single year during the *ancien régime*. Nevertheless, the Church had survived. Furthermore, persecution had not only failed to destroy Catholicism, but even sometimes helped to strengthen religious feeling and this partly stimulated a religious revival. In some circles, missing Mass came to be regarded as a lack of good taste and it became fashionable to wear a rosary as a necklace. Some zealous prefects even made regulations governing the sale of drink and the conduct of dances. A transformation was beginning to take place which would have seemed quite impossible only a few years before.

Although Napoleon regarded monks as 'unprofitable creatures', he welcomed the services of teaching and nursing sisters. In December, 1800, 'citizeness Duleau, formerly Superior of the Sisters of Charity' was authorized 'to train pupils for service in the hospitals'. Other nursing and teaching orders were allowed to resume their work and at La Rochelle the Sisters of Wisdom were escorted back to the hospital by the mayor and the commanding officer of the garrison with military honours. Napoleon regarded contemplatives as 'lazy' but many of them were able to overcome this difficulty by opening small schools within their enclosures. By 1814, there were some 1,800 houses of women religious throughout the country. Napoleon would not allow the restoration of the Benedictines, the Franciscans or the Dominicans, but in 1804 the Brothers of the Christian Schools were officially re-established, while missionaries like the Lazarists and the Holy Ghost

Fathers were not only authorized but even subsidized. Missionary congregations could provide Napoleon with information on conditions in Asia, Africa or America and their missionary role could disguise their political or commercial importance.

The immediate administrative effect of the Concordat was to centralize authority in the hands of the episcopate and the secular Government, but ultimately this authority would come into the hands of the Pope who was not only to enjoy his traditional power of investing bishops, but was given a new one, that of deposing them. The agreement with Napoleon allowed the Pope to demand the resignation of French bishops, something that would never have been tolerated before the Revolution. Not unnaturally the removal of former bishops was to prove one of the most difficult points in the negotiations. Cardinal Consalvi commented; 'You can read as much as you like in the history of the Church and you will find no comparable example. To get rid of a hundred bishops is something that just cannot happen'. This subordination of the episcopacy was neither planned nor foreseen, but it was quickly appreciated by the papacy and incidentally was unaffected by Napoleon's Organic articles.

The Pope issued a rather categorical letter to the exiled bishops demanding their resignations. Forty eight of the bishops did so, but another thirty seven refused, whereupon the Pope declared that their sees were vacant. Some of the royalist and Gallican bishops refused to recognize the Concordat and set up the schismatic *petite église* which even continued after it had been denounced by the King following the restoration of the Bourbons in 1815. These schismatic bishops were influenced by theological claims as well as political loyalties. They reminded the Pope that their episcopal jurisdiction came directly from God and that the Pope had no right to ignore or to dispose those who were lower than himself in the ecclesiastical hierarchy. These claims would later be contradicted by the first Vatican Council which maintained that bishops received their spiritual jurisdiction through the Pope who enjoyed the fulness of spiritual jurisdiction and who could remove them if he so wished. However, it would be quite impossible to imagine any Pope before the French Revolution attempting to remove the Gallican episcopate at a stroke. The schismatic bishops also felt a sense of personal injury. They were the same bishops who by maintaining their links with Rome over ten years before had given the Pope the power to attack them now. And when the Pope conferred canonical powers on a former constitutional bishops and disobedient priests, it must have seemed that the loyal and the orthodox were being punished while heretics and schismatics were being rewarded.

The fact that the Concordat was an extreme example of Gallican principles drawn up in the interests of a thoroughly Erastian sovereign who had no claim at all to the divine right of kings inevitably discredited Gallicanism and strengthened Ultramontanism within the French Church. Even the Gallican Church could not trust a Government which reduced it to the level of a public servant or a department of state. In due course the French Church turned to the Holy See for support against a secular ruler who showed such little understanding of its spiritual values. Consequently, even before the separation of Church and State in 1905 left Pius X as the sole authority in ecclesiastical matters, the stage was being set for the Ultramontane autocracy of Pius IX. In any case Gallicianism was becoming increasingly irrelevant as Ultramontanism developed and both spiritual and secular rulers united against the forces of revolution. Furthermore, as European states became more secularized the chief supporters of Gallicanism such as theologians and lawyers lost their influence or their interest in ecclesiastical affairs. Gallicanism had always proclaimed the supremacy of a General Council over the papacy. But during the nineteenth century the success of Ultramontanism would be illustrated by the fact that the Pope alone was able to define the doctrine of the Immaculate Conception, while the only General Council held would define papal infallibility.

Napoleon's policies not only helped to destroy the credibility of Gallicanism, but he also effectively destroyed the centres of Josephism and Febronianism by his reorganization or destruction of the great Catholic states of the Rhine and the prince bishoprics. Even before the French occupation of the Austrian Netherlands, resistance to the authority of the Emperor had reduced support for Josephism and increased the strength of Ultramontanism. The support of the Pope seemed a necessary counter-balance to the claims of the Emperor. After Napoleon's reorganization of Germany the ecclesiastical princes, who had previously sought administrative independence of Rome, were forced by the loss of their territories and the reduction of their authority to seek the support of the Pope rather than independence from him. The German territories annexed by France became subject to the ecclesiastical policies of the Republic where the Catholic reaction inevitably reinforced Ultramontanism. German territories which included large proportions of Catholics became subject to Protestant princes and

Catholic bishops, priests and laity under Protestant rulers began to look to the papacy for support. Even in some of the remaining Catholic states in Germany where the Church lost its independent episcopacy and the clergy were reduced to the level of a civil bureaucracy the support of the papacy assumed a new significance.

The careers of Karl Theodor Anton Maria von Dalberg, who became Prince Primate of the Confederation of the Rhine in 1806, and his vicar general, Ignaz Heinrich von Wessenberg, show that the notion of establishing a German national church largely independent of Rome was not immediately destroyed by Napoleon's measures. But such a development was circumvented by the papacy's policy of signing concordats, not with the German Confederation, but with the individual states, who tended to regard the plans of Dalberg as a threat to their own Erastian control. The German states often preferred to deal directly with the Holy See than with a strong united Catholic Church in Germany which might directly or indirectly challenge their authority. After the destruction of the old French and German ecclesiastical structures by the forces of the Revolution, the Roman authorities were apparently determined not to allow the restoration of national episcopal structures which might again challenge the power of the Holy See. As a result of the political turmoil in Germany, many episcopal sees had been left vacant, sometimes for years. It had been necessary to seek dispensations from the Pope himself as the 'Universal bishop' and, when the time came to reorganize the German Church, famous old traditional sees were either eliminated or reduced in importance. Trier and Mainz became suffragan bishoprics, while Constance and Worms disappeared altogether. In future, German bishops as well as their French colleagues would be reduced to the level of papal officials, rather than papal rivals.

The provisions of the concordat also ended lay patronage and reinforced the clerical and hierarchical organization of the French Church which inevitably in time increased the power of the Pope. Furthermore the French Government appointed bishops, paid their salaries and could veto their appointments of the clergy. Bishops were unable to leave their dioceses, ordain priests, establish cathedral chapters, call synods or take part in metropolitan councils without permission from the State. This financial and administrative dependence on the secular authorities led the bishops to turn increasingly to the papacy. French bishops who had never questioned the principle of doctrinal unity now came to regard papal authority as the only defence against the

Erastian power of the State. Meanwhile, as the bishops became increasingly dissatisfied with Erastianism, the ordinary clergy were becoming more and more disillusioned with the exercise of episcopal Gallicanism.

According to the concordat, parish priests were appointed and curates moved by the bishops. Priests were not allowed to leave their dioceses and special prayers could not be said nor sermons preached without episcopal permission. The country clergy in particular were completely under the control of their bishops, some of whom seem to have enjoyed exercising their new authority. One of them remarked that he only had to lift a finger to have his clergy doing exactly what he wanted. In 1837, 3,500 priests were moved, one bishop moved 150 of his priests in a month, and between 1836 and 1842 all the priests in some dioceses had been moved. 'It was both sad and amusing', wrote Ollivier, 'to meet, on different roads, a pile of shabby bags followed by an old woman in tears and a priest reciting his breviary'.

What was even worse was the fact that a piece of gossip repeated by a mayor, teacher or squire was enough to have a priest punished or sent to another parish without being given an opportunity of defending himself. Priests, dismissed without proof and without even knowing the names of their accusers, were sometimes forced to find employment as coach-drivers or road-sweepers. Feeling abandoned by the bishops, parish priests and their curates began to turn to the Pope who seemed to offer such a striking contrast to a bishop like the Gallican Archbishop of Besançon. The Archbishop usually prayed in a private oratory decked with satin hangings and attended only by his chosen personal servants. On his rare episcopal visitations he insisted on the presnece of the local *maires*, swords at their sides, standing behind his chair as he dined. The most famous clerical protest came in 1839 when a couple of priests attacked the effects of the Concordat on the ordinary clergy. The French bishops angrily deposed them, but not before they had laid their case before Gregory XVI who received them favourably and commented that he had not realized before that the French bishops were such 'popelets'.

When Napoleon was proclaimed Emperor of the French in 1804 he made enquiries whether the Pope would be prepared to come to Paris to annoint him. Both Pope and Emperor were anxious about the significance and the implications of the ceremony, while the Pope was conscious of the further danger of alienating other European rulers as well as his Catholic supporters. In the event, the Austrian Emperor was outraged and the Tsar broke off diplomatic relations with the Pope. Joseph de Maistre claimed that the crimes of Alexander Borgia were less revolting than this hideous apostacy by his feeble successor. Before leaving for Paris the Pope attempted to secure some modifications of the Organic Articles and the removal of former constitutional bishops who still refused to be reconciled with the Holy See. But he eventually had to begin his journey with nothing more than promises that the French Government would not encourage the continuing opposition of the constitutional bishops.

The studied discourtesy of Napoleon's treatment of Pius VII was part of his calculated policy. It began with an 'accidental' meeting in the forest of Fontainebleau which saved Napoleon from having to provide a more public and deferential welcome for his distinguished guest. At the actual ceremony Napoleon kept the Pope waiting for almost two hours before putting the crown on his own head. He later explained his refusal to go to Confession or receive Communion on the grounds that he still had too much faith to wish to commit a sacrilege. Napoleon's discourtesies only ended with the arrangements made for the Pope's journey home. The new Emperor wished to show that he was the master and the Pope his chaplain. The Pope was simply there to sanction and to strengthen the claims of Napoleon's succession. But if Napoleon's Erastian attitude was similar to that of Joseph II, his actual invitation to the Pope was hardly typical of the Hapsburgs and was a most un-Gallican act.

The direct and immediate fruits of the Pope's visit to Paris were almost marginal. Pius VII had successfully insisted on a religious ceremony of marriage between Napoleon and Josephine, though even this was a quasi-clandestine ceremony conducted by Napoleon's uncle, Cardinal Fesch; it was later annulled in a French ecclesiastical court when Napoleon married Marie Louise of Austria in 1810. The Emperor had refused to modify the Organic Articles or to abolish the divorce laws in the Civil Code, to enforce Sunday observance or allow the restoration of religious orders, to return papal territory or to re-establish Catholicism in France. But if Catholicism was not recognized as the religion of the State, Napoleon had behaved as if it was and constitutional bishops, deserted by the Government, tended one after the other to submit to the Pope.

Napoleon proved more accommodating on such minor issues as improving clerical pay and pensions, allowing closer episcopal control over clerical discipline, returning some secularized churches and restoring seminaries. However, the real success of the papal visit was almost accidental and was to be found in the popular demonstrations which took place, illustrating the popularity of the Pope among the French people. These demonstrations were one of the first signs of a new attitude towards the papacy, the development of a new Ultramontane sentiment and a rejection of de-Christianization, constitutional churches and the political persecution of Pope Pius VI.

Relations between Napoleon and the Pope were again disturbed when the latter refused to annul the marriage of Napoleon's youngest brother Jerome and when another brother, Lucien, sought refuge in Rome after marrying his mistress. The final break, however, came as a result of Napoleon's Italian policies. When the Emperor announced the introduction of the French Civil Code, which allowed the possibility of divorce, the Church was faced with another threat to its moral authority. A moral issue could not be dealt with in the same way as a matter of political sovereignty or ecclesiastical property, of administration or organization. Finally, Napoleon's military policy brought matters to a head. He marched his troups through papal territory and occupied Ancona. The Pope regarded this as a direct threat to his political sovereignty and threatened to break off diplomatic relations. In 1806 Napoleon used Ancona as a base for his successful invasion of Naples. He then demanded that the Pope should regard all the enemies of France as the enemies of the Holy See, banish them from his territories and exclude their ships from his harbours. The Pope formally rejected these demands on the ground that he could not possibly depart from his policy of peaceful neutrality or lose his political independence.

The Pope also refused to contemplate Napoleon's idea of incorporating Rome within a new confederation in his Empire. Such a move would prejudice the Pope's position as a Common Father of the Faithful throughout the world and by involving him in the political struggles of Europe compromise his role as a minister of peace. In 1808, Napoleon ordered one of his generals to occupy Rome and proposed that the Pope should join the Italian Confederation. The Pope refused and the Emperor decreed that the Papal States should become part of the Empire, whereupon he was excommunicated. The excommunication of Napoleon reinforced the resistance, national, liberal and Catholic, which was developing throughout Europe, but especially in Italy, Germany and Spain. On the other hand, it is significant that when a group of devout Catholic nobles formed the Knights of the Faith to defend the Church they associated this cause with support for the legitimate Bourbon King. Napoleon himself was at least indirectly responsible for the subsequent abduction of the Pope. The journey was hurried and unpleasant. Local rulers were embarrassed by the presence of the Pope who was taken by circuitous and hilly roads in order to avoid the crowds. Pius VII suffered fatigue and developed dysentery. Yet his journey from Grenoble through Provence to Savona provided further opportunities for those demonstrations of devotion which the Emperor was so anxious to avoid.

For almost five years the Pope was practically isolated from all but a couple of personal servants. He was not even allowed to choose his own secretary, confessor or advisers and was eventually deprived of pen and ink in an effort to break him. The Cardinals were in Paris and the Church was almost totally disorganized as the Roman Congregations were without superiors and staff as well as their archives. The Pope himself retaliated by refusing to institute the bishops nominated by Napoleon and the number of vacant sees increased throughout Europe. After several unsuccessful attempts had been made to get round this difficulty, three devout bishops were sent to the Pope in 1811 to plead in favour of the radical proposal that failing investiture by the Pope, bishops nominated by Napoleon should be instituted by the Metropolitan of the Province. Ten cardinals, two archbishops and seven bishops also pleaded with the Pope to make all possible sacrifices for the sake of the Church. The Pope verbally and provisionally agreed, but he soon realized that deprived of his counsellors, abducted and imprisoned, spied on and reduced to impotence, he had surrendered a crucial aspect of traditional papal power, the investiture of bishops, and he therefore repudiated what he had done.

The Emperor, however, blandly announced that the Pope had agreed and then went on to try to persuade a National Council to adopt a resolution admitting the possibility of a canonical episcopal investiture without the Pope. Had this move been successful, the future development of Ultramontanism might well have become impossible. However, the bishops took the usual oath of obedience to the Pope and refused to register any decree on investiture without the consent of the Pope, which was to be obtained by a deputation from the Council and bear the Pope's own signature. Napoleon denounced the bishops as traitors, dissolved the Council and arrested three of the leading episcopal opponents. The Emperor then attempted to secure from the bishops individually what they had refused collectively. After securing eighty five signatures in favour of the new procedure of investiture, he simply announced that the Council had not in fact been dissolved.

The Council of Bishops affirmed collectively what had already been agreed privately, but included the condition that their agreement must also receive papal approval. This approval was granted, though the Pope wrote the decree as one coming from himself as Supreme Pontiff, insisted that the Council itself had been invalid and excluded the bishops in the Papal States from those bishops who could be invested by their metropolitans. Almost incredibly, Napoleon refused to concede this exception. Pius for his part refused to make any further concessions and was thereby saved from the consequences of his own surrender of papal control over the investiture of bishops with spiritual authority.

The Pope was then removed to Fontainebleau where Neapoleon hoped to force his submission on returning from Russia. Care was taken to avoid those demonstrations which had taken place in Provence or at Nice by traveling in disguise and through Turin and Lyons at night. The Pope was again taken too quickly, fell sick and caught fever. At one stage he was unable to stand and in such pain that he could not resume the journey and he received the last sacraments. Napoleon returned from Russia in January 1813 determined to reach a settlement with the Pope. Pius himself had been isolated from all but the Emperor's supporters and did not know of the changed situation following the defeat of the *Grande Armée*. Nor was the Pope aware of the increasing opposition to Bonaparte and support for himself which was growing, especially among French and Italian priests. Many of the younger clergy in particular were becoming passionately anti-Gallican, while cathedral chapters were refusing to elect Napoleon's nominees. The Emperor for his part had revoked favours granted earlier and discontinued giving subsidies to seminaries and foreign missions. The Pope also knew nothing of Bonaparte's violent treatment of the more obstinate bishops, his conscription of seminarians or purging their professors and the closing of Saint-Sulpice.

It was in this isolated situation that Pius VII implicitly surrendered the temporal power and papal authority over episcopal investiture. The Ultramontanes, now organized in bodies like the Knights of the Faith, whose hopes had been raised by Napoleon's defeat in Russia, were shocked and horrified. Fortunately, the Pope had only signed confidential and provisional proposals to serve as the basis for an understanding, and he considered that Napolean had once again betrayed him when these were published as a concordat. When the Pope's advisors were allowed to return to him, they set about cancelling the so-called Concordat of Fontainebleau by publishing a letter in the Pope's own hand in which he declared that his conscience revolted against proposals which he had only signed out of human weakness. Once again Napoleon isolated the Pope and kept the letter secret, but the Battle of the Nations at Leipzig was the beginning of the end. Bonaparte sent envoys to the Pope offering to restore his temporal sovereignty, but Pius refused to negotiage until he had returned to Rome and enjoyed his complete freedom. The Pope's return to Rome became a triumphant procession. Everywhere he received those tremendous demonstrations which marked the rise of Ultramontanism, while Napoleon himself was on the way to Elba.

François René, Vicomte de Chateaubriand

Jean-Baptiste Henri Lacordaire

II: Papal authority and political reaction

The reaction against the French Revolution had of course begun long before the fall of Napoleon in 1815, while the development of Ultramontanism was already an established feature of Roman Catholicism. However, before outlining the progess of Ultramontanism after the French Revolution, some consideration must be given to one or two of the leading writers who provided the basis of its intellectual content and were instrumental in its success during the nineteenth century. Much of the philosophical and theological reaction to the Revolution came from Traditionalists of whom there were basically two types. Most of the Traditionalists supported the old political and religious traditions of France against the new revolutionary spirit. They regarded the revolution as a disastrous attack on the valuable religious, social and political traditions of the French nation which should now be restored. However, there were also Traditionalists in the technical sense. These maintained that certain basic beliefs which were necessary for man's spiritual and cultural development and for his well-being were not simply the result of human reasoning, but were handed on from one generation to the next through the medium of language and had been derived from a primitive revelation. These two types of Traditionalism were often associated, but they were not inseparable. Not all monarchists accepted the notion of a primitive revelation and not all the philosophical Traditionalists supported the restoration of the *ancien régime*.

Furthermore, although the Traditionalists attacked the philosophy of the Enlightenment and were in a sense 'anti-rationalist', they were not simply irrational, but offered a reasoned defence of their position and even appealed to reason in support of their criticisms of the thought of the eighteenth century. During the eighteenth century, Christians apologists had tended to adopt a rational approach and used philosophical arguments in favour of the existence of God, while countering attacks on Christian revelation with arguments supporting the authenticity of the biblical accounts of miracles, prophecy and the life of Christ. However, after the French Revolution and under the influence of the Romantic Movement, Christian apologists began to reject rationalistic philosophy in favour of arguments based on the claim that Christianity best fulfilled the needs of man and society.

The *Genius of Christianity* by Francois René, Vicomte de Chateaubriand, appeared four days after the proclamation of the Concordat with Napoleon. A few years later Chateaubriand would break with Napoleon, but in 1802 he was full of praise for 'the mighty man who has snatched us from the abyss'. while Napoleon himself was said to have wept as he read Chateaubriand's emotional and imaginative work. Chateaubriand had previously scandalized his fellow *émigrés* in London by publishing a paper which was considered politically unacceptable and even anti-Christian. However, the bloodshed of the Revolution prompted him to reflect on the frivolity of his earlier life and to alter his opinions dramatically. As a poverty-stricken *émigré* in England Chateaubriand learned of the execution of his brother and sister-in-law through the newspapers; he knew that his wife and sisters were in prison at Rennes, and he also lost his mother who died as a result of the hardships which she suffered during the Revolution. On her deathbed, his mother implored one of her daughters to remind Chateaubriand of the religion in which he had been raised. His sister wrote to him, but by the time her letter arrived she had also died as a consequence of her imprisonment. As a result of these two voices from the tomb rather than from any great spiritual illumination, and as a result of an emotional rather than an intellectual conviction, Chateaubriand became a Christian.

Chateaubriand then attempted 'to summon all the powers of imagination and all the interests of the heart in support of that religion against which they had been armed'. He consciously reacted against the rationalism of the eighteenth century in adopting an apologetic approach which tried to transfer the religious debate from reason to feeling and he argued that the study of history proved that Christianity was the main source of European art and civilization by the continuing stimulus which it gave to the intellectual and spiritual aspirations of mankind. Chateaubriand appealed to the aesthetic qualities of Christianity as the most human, the most poetic, the most favourable to arts and letters, and to liberty, of all the religions which ever existed. In fact, Chateaubriand has been described as 'the fountain head of Catholic liberalism'. 'Christianity', he wrote, 'is opposed in spirit and determination to arbitary power'. 'I shall never again become an unbeliever', he declared, 'until someone proves to me that Christianity is incompatible with liberty'.

In effect, Chateaubriand's argument was that the intrinsic excellence of Christianity showed that it came from God, rather than the more usual argument that Christianity must be judged excellent because it had been proved to have come from God. However, the aesthetic and consoling qualities to be found in the Christian religion do not prove that it is true and consequently Chateaubriand has been accused of substituting aesthetic considerations and emotional reasons for rational argument. Chateaubriand, however, was replying to those opponents of Christianity who condemned its doctrines as repellent and who argued that it was hostile to human freedom and human culture, that it impeded the development of moral consciousness and had a stifling effect on the freedom of the human spirit. He was writing against those who argued that Christianity was a barbarous and cruel religion, the enemy of art and literature, and detrimental to human happiness. Certainly, the *Genius of Christianity* was published at the right time and in a form well suited to the men of the period. Even many agnostics and athesists had become convinced of the utility of religion, while some of them experienced a real need for it. Consequently, even if Chateaubriand did not bring about a revival of Catholicism, he definitely helped to re-awaken the sympathy and interest of the intellectual *élite* in Christianity.

From the philosophical point of view, Louis Gabriel Ambroise, Vicomte de Bonald, was a much more significant thinker. He had been a member of the Constituent Assembly in 1790, but had gone into exile during the following year where he suffered considerable poverty. In due course he supported Napoleon and then, following the restoration, the Bourbon monarchy. De Bonald began his literary career with an attack on the *philosophes*, and especially on Montesquieu's *Spirit of the Laws* and Rousseau's *Social Contract*. He emphasized the need for a religious basis of society and contrasted this necessity with the in-sufficiency of philosophy as as adequate social foundation. He denied the so-called state of nature, the social contract, the democratic origins of power, the rights of man and especially the right of freedom.

De Bonald's social philosophy was based on the notion that there were three units in every society. 'In cosmology God is the cause, movement the means, body the effect. In a State the government is the cause, the minister the means, the subject the effect. In a family the father is the cause, the mother the means, the child the effect'. In the family, authority belonged naturally to the father, but ultimately came from God; it was not the result of any contract or compact.

Similarly, political sovereignty belonged to the monarch as a result of the nature and the conditions of human society. Democracy tainted the relationship of cause and effect between the ruler and the ruled as divorce broke the trinity of cause, means and effect in the family.

In the name of tradition de Bonald laid down a rigid social and political system to preserve the past and to reject democracy. This rigid order, he argued, came from God. God was the cause, Christ was the means and human society was the effect; and the centralized and authoritarian organization of the Catholic Church was the archetype of all regimes. Let a strong government apply the laws properly, prohibit everything that tended to destroy the legitimate order, entrust the Jesuits with a monopoly of education and all would go well with the world. Like de Maistre, de Bonald insisted on the unity of power or sovereignty. Sovereignty must be one, independent and absolute, though this did not mean that it should be tyrannical or arbitrary; he also supported hereditary monarchy on the grounds that sovereignty must also be lasting. On the other hand, de Bonald was a Gallican who did not give to the Pope the pre-eminence given by de Maistre.

It is not easy to deal objectively with the writings of Count Joseph de Maistre, many of which were occasional, sarcastic and paradoxical, provocative and deliberately exaggerated. His initial reaction to the French Revolution had been enthusiastically favourable, but he later went into exile and became active in counter-revolutionary movements. His life of deep moral earnestness was based on severe and austere religious beliefs; he was a member of a religious organization which made periodic nine day retreats and a group of men who spent the night before execution with condemned criminals as an act of charity.

De Maistre was violently opposed to the rationalism of the eighteenth century. He accused the *philosophes* of concentrating on abstractions and ignoring the traditions which manifested the operation of divine providence. He invoked tradition as a defence against reason and respect for society against individualism. The only true basis of society lay in authority – a spiritual authority vested in the papacy and a temporal authority committed to human kings. Authority itself came from God. History, not intelligence, revealed the truth, and history was also under the control of divine providence. De Maistre condemned as fictional the notion of an abstract human being without a history or a nation, and the idea of the State as the product of a contract or a convention. Man was unable to construct either a constitution or a religion on *a priori* principles and the notion of a natural religion or a purely philosophical religion, a deliberate construction of the human reason, was equally absurd. Belief in God was handed down from a primitive revelation to mankind, while Christianity itself was a further revelation of God.

Eighteenth-century philosophical thinkers had argued in favour of democratic theories of the sovereignty of the people but, according to de Maistre, such theories were fundamentally unsound, while the practice of democracy had resulted in disorder and anarchy. Human nature was such that Government was necessary and absolute power was the only alternative to anarchy; it was necessary to return to the historically grounded and providentially constituted authority – Christian monarchy and the unique sovereignty of the infallible papacy. De Maistre himself was very conscious of what he called the 'great inconveniences' involved in accepting claims of absolute power, but absolute power should not necessarily be equated with arbitrary or tyrannical power, and the only alternative was anarchy. Furthermore, the exercise of absolute power was in practice inevitably restricted by a variety of factors and secular sovereigns were also subject to the jurisdiction of the Pope, who had the right to judge their actions from the religious and the moral points of view.

Nations could only be defended from the abuses of authority by a sovereignty which was superior to all others, namely the papacy which had saved European civilization from the barbarians and had proved to be the only stable institution in Europe during the last eighteen hundred years. De Maistre's most faous book, *The Pope*, was published in 1819 and its wide circulation coupled with its immediate influence would seem to show that many Catholics were beginning to share the views which de Maistre was supporting and advocating. De Maistre argued that the Pope must be the unquestioned leader, the supreme arbiter and guide of all peoples and all sovereigns. The Pope was the supreme instrument of civilization, the creator of every monarchy, the guardian of arts and science, and the natural protector of liberty. The Pope was sovereign in the Church; as sovereign, his decisions were not subject to appeal and since he exercised sovereignty in his teaching, that teaching must be infallible. Since the Pope was infallible, he laid down the principles of morality and spiritual life, and was the manifestation of God's purpose. Those schismatic Christians who failed to acknowledge the authority of the Pope would fall into Protestantism and the inevitable consequence of Protestantism was a state of philosophical indifference.

Like so many reactionaries, de Maistre's 'protest against the present tended to raise up an image of the past no less radical in its implications than the revolutionary dream of the future'. De Maistre became completely committed to a new and revolutionary Ultramontane position as he tried to persuade French Gallicans who understood his concept of secular sovereignty and shared his belief in the truth of Catholicism of his conviction that Gallicanism had weakened French Catholicism and prepared the way for the French Revolution. In de Maistre's mind, the spiritual authority of the papacy was closely linked with his absolutist understanding of government, though infallibility was divinely promised in one case and humanly supposed in the other. Inevitably however de Maistre's name became a symbol of the alliance of the Throne and the Altar because of the use made of his theories by later extremists whose ideas were often more excessive and doctrinaire than his own. Furthermore, it was only too easy for simple and unflexible minds to misunderstand him, like the bishop who called on his people,

> to continue to obey in the civil order whoever derives his sovereign power from above, however evil his morals, whatever his religious beliefs, whatever the abuses, apparent or real, of his government, and however impious and tyrannical the laws he enacts in order to pervert you.

During the nineteenth century many French Catholics came to regard support for the monarchy as a religious obligation. They behaved as if the survival of the Church depended on the survival of the monarchy. De Maistre himself, on the other hand, had tried to persuade secular rulers that it was in their best interests to give to the Church the freedom and assistance which it desired. He treated the issue of supporting and maintaining the Church as a political question, and even though this was doubtful from a theological point of view, it was less compromising for the Church than the attitudes adopted by later Catholics.

De Maistre's bold and imaginative apologetic encouraged Catholics at a time when the Church seemed in danger of collapse, but he failed to appreciate, as did many of the new apologists, that the Revolution had resulted from social and economic factors as well as from subversive ideas or religious decline. Too many French Catholics followed him in rejecting the Revolution as satanic and supporting the alliance of Throne and Altar. His writings helped to perpetuate their intransigent and unrealistic opposition to everything associated with the Revolution.

De Maistre had effectively warned against the dangers of republican anarchy, but his alternative, an absolutist political system, was potentially just as dangerous. In the event, although de Maistre had worked sincerely for the welfare of both Church and State, his ultimate influence in France was probably detrimental to the cause of the Catholic religion as well as political stability.

It is sometimes argued, understandably but not entirely convincingly, that Traditionalists like de Bonald became the founders of Ultramontanism and that the political theorists of the Bourbon Restoration such as de Maistre first brought to light the particular motive which led to the declaration of papal infallibility – the nineteenth century hunger for authority. It is true that at the time of the Vatican Council Cardinal Rauscher found it necessary to warn the Fathers against the arguments of laymen like de Maistre whose talent, he claimed, was more seductive than reliable. But it is too crude to claim that de Maistre merely postulated the doctrine of papal infallibility on the basis of his political ideology, or that he considered secular sovereignty and papal infallibility simply as parallels; nor is it fair to argue that he secularized the ecclesiastical and theological notion of Tradition and interpreted it politically. Nevertheless, although the Roman theologians eventually condemned philosophical Traditionalism and even originally questioned some of its political implications, they undoubtedly welcomed the rejection of Gallicanism and the spread of Ultramontanism as well as the criticisms of the Enlightenment, the attacks on the French Revolution and support for the Bourbon Restoration. For the Church to have avoided the temptation of being identified with the supporters of reaction, it would have needed the leadership of far sighted men of genius, but unfortunately, apart from some significant exceptions such as Cardinal Consalvi, the ecclesiastical authorities almost unanimously sided with the forces of counter-revolution.

There are a few constitutional monarchists and liberal Catholics in France who were willing to accept many of the implications of the Revolution, but on the whole the history of the Bourbon Restoration was dominated by political and religious extremists. Following the defeat of Napoleon, the most influential French politicians and theologians argued that only by returning to the past, as completely as possible, would it be possible to save French society and civilization; the Revolution ought to be undone and could in fact be undone. Some aristocratic and clerical extremists anticipated the restoration of the *ancien régime* with its three orders as it existed before the

Revolution, though the philosophical prejudices of the eighteenth century had given way to a new and different appreciation of the role of religion. Throne and Altar were now united, not least in their need of mutual support. Religion was not merely an agent of the law as it had been under Napoleon, but a political necessity. Even unbelieving public officials felt obliged to adopt a hypocritical attitude towards the profession and practice of the Catholic faith, rather than the cynical and irreligious approach of their predecessers.

The political attitudes of King Louis XVIII and his advisers were similar to those who had led the aristocratic revolt in 1789, while the predominant outlook of the new French hierarchy was monarchist, aristocratic and Gallican. Morally irreproachable, the bishops believed that neither the Throne nor the Altar could survive without the other and most of their clergy adopted the same views, exhorting their flocks to act as good royalists and good Christians, and sometimes in that order. Unfortunately, the men of the Restoration showed a complete lack of understanding of the social and political situation in both affirming and applying their principles. They were demonstrative and even theatrical in their political and religious claims, which inevitably provoked a suspicious and then a hostile reaction. There were still many Jacobins and Bonapartists in France who were bitterly opposed to the family of the Bourbons as well as to the Catholic religion; and between 1817 and 1824, no less than twelve editions of Voltaire and thirteen editions of Rousseau were reprinted.

Roman Catholicism was again recognized as the official religion of France and no longer simply as the religion of the great majority of the French people, and this in spite of the fact that some Frenchmen were decidely hostile to Catholicism and many more quite indifferent. At the same time religious toleration was granted and legal safeguards protected the owners of confiscated ecclesiastical property. The Napoleonic Concordat had to be re-affirmed since attempts to return to the old concordat or to negotiate a new one had to be abandoned in view of Rome's hostility to Gallicanism and the papacy's determination to base all future concordats on the pattern of that with Napoleon. Incidentally, the Organic Articles were not withdrawn and the Gallican Articles were still taught in seminaries.

The first administration of the Duc de Richelieu, which proved too royalist even for the King, removed the divorce laws from the Civil Code, deprived married priests of their pensions and even tried to return civil registers to the clergy. The Pantheon was purged of the infidel remains of Voltaire and Rousseau, and handed over to the Church for religious functions. The control of secondary education and the appointment of teachers in primary schools was surrendered to the bishops, while a leading ecclesiastic was appointed Grand Master of the University. New legal sanctions were introduced against attacks on religion and sacrilege. Thefts from churches were punishable with solitary confinement or hard labour for life, while profanation of sacred vessels or of the consecrated host was to be punished by death: the condemned man was to be led to execution with his feet bare and his head covered with a black cowl; his right hand was to be amputated before the death sentence was carried out. It is only right to point out that no one was actually put to death for sacrilege and few people suffered as a result of the laws governing the censorship of the press. The only real victim was the Government which was stupid enough to enact such legislation.

The clergy themselves were not afraid of resorting to strongarm tactics or moral blackmail in an effort to revive the practice of religion. Lists of non-communicants were displayed in church porches and ecclesiastical authorities refused Christian burial to former revolutionaries, actors, duellists, divorcees or Jansenists, though occasionally mobs of sceptics and anti-clericals might force their way into churches with bodies to be buried. Missions seemed to be one of the most effective means of converting the indifferent to the practice of religion. The missionaries usually preached a violent and menacing form of Catholicism and their sermons largely consisted of threats of hell-fire, denunciations of sin and sentimental appeals to the emotions. Spectacular services were organized with mass confessions and group communions, sermons in cemeteries and processions led by military bands. The clergy sometimes conducted ceremonies of reparation for the sacrileges committed during the Revolution and erected enormous calvaries to the memories of Louis XVI, Louis XVII and 'the august Marie Antoinette'.

In spite of, or perhaps because of, their excesses, the missionaries were sometimes extraordinarily successful. On one occasion, a group of missionaries had to be protected from women armed with scissors who wanted to cut relics from their clothes. 10,000 people out of a population of some 145,000 went to a general communion at Marseilles and 7,500 out of a population of 36,000 at Montpellier. Only 20 men usually made their Easter duties at Tulle, but 1,300 attended a general communion. Usurers made restitution, thieves restored property and women gave up their lovers. Unfortunately these effects seldom proved to be permanent, while the missionaries further alienated the traders who lost business, the non-practising Catholics who found themselves boycotted and the liberals or the sceptics who were amused if not disgusted by religious theatricals. In due course, this hostility gave rise to opposition. Anti-clericals began to organize pamphlet campagins; preachers were hooted as crowds sang songs outside and hooligans threw stink-bombs into churches.

Religious extremism and the consequent political threat to the Church hid the real revival which was taking place within the French Church and disguised the extent to which its character was already changing. During the Revolutionary and Napoleonic regimes, the French Church had been deprived of training facilities as well as economic support. Confiscated seminary buildings were not returned to the Church and there was no endowment to build new ones under the settlement with Napoleon. Furthermore, those who did ofter themselves for the priesthood were dependent on charity since the 500 francs given by Napoleon in 1804 was hardly a living wage, and finally seminarians did not escape military service. Consequently, by the turn of the century, the supply of new secular priests was drying up.

In 1806 at least one sixth of French parishes were without a priest and a quarter of the incumbents were over sixty. In 1816 one-third of the country's parishes were vacant and by 1820 this would mean about 20,000 parishes. Yet by 1830 most of the vacancies had been filled. The figures of ordinations throughout the nineteenth century are most revealing and reflect the changing fortunes of the French Church. There were 715 ordinations in 1814, 1,400 in 1821, and 2,350 in 1829 when the number of secular priests had grown from 36,000 to over 40,000. There were 1,100 ordinations in 1841, 1,300 in 1847, 1,753 in 1869, 1,582 in 1877, but only 825 in 1913. During the middle years of the century, the numbers of monks and nuns increased even more dramatically: in 1789, there had been some 70,000 regular clergy in France; there were only 3,000 in 1847, but 17,700 by 1861. When the Jesuits were re-established in 1814, only about 800 survivors remained, but by 1820 there were almost 2,000 Jesuits and over 6,000 in 1850.

The increasing number of vocations was undoubtedly partly due to the fact that the bishops were free to organize recruitment and training, to establish both minor and major seminaries, while the governments of the Restoration raised the stipends of parish priests from 1,000 to 1,200 francs and of curates from 500 to 800. The Church was also

also helped in its exapansion by the fact that the religious budget was increased threefold under the Restoration, though the sums contributed by the faithful increased in even greater proportion, reaching more than 42 million francs, whereas they had never been more than 2.5 million under Napoleon. But there was also a dramatic change in the qualities as well as the numbers of parochial clergy.

Before the Revolution priests had tended to come from a particular class, but they now came from the ranks of the ordinary people and they were men with a genuine sense of vocation since there was little prospect of desirable promotions or financial gain. Before the Revolution, and as a result of the wealth of the Church, ecclesiastical promotion came to be regarded as the prerogative of gentle birth. In 1789 only 5 members of an episcopate of 134 could be regarded as men of humble origins. Betweeen 1814 and 1829 seventy of the ninety episcopal appointments were made from the ranks of the aristocracy, whereas between 1830 and 1847 only eighteen of the seventy two bishops nominated were also members of the nobility. By the end of the century there were only four nobles out of an episcopate of ninety, but the radical change in the character of the hierarchy was evident long before then. As bishoprics ceased to be sinecures attracting men with a taste for high living, the principal members of the French hierarchy would soon be the sons of a cobbler and a tailor, and the illegitimate son of a seduced peasant girl.

But although there were more priests by the end of the Restoration, there were probably fewer practising Catholics particularly in the towns. The attempt to use the Government and its public servants in an effort to promote a religious revival was to prove self-defeating, while the alliance of the Throne and the Altar seemed to threaten religious toleration, if not religious freedom. Clearly the increasing and dominant influence of the Church was one of the most important factors in the ultimate failure of the Bourbon Restoration and the subsequent revolution, and the Church was to pay the price for its imprudence when anti-clericals were given the opportunity of showing as little understanding of the concepts of freedom and tolerance as had the extremists of the Restoration.

In 1824 Charles X, an extreme reactionary and fanatical Catholic had ascended the throne and to the amusement of many Frenchmen had been anointed with the oil of St Louis on the forehead, shoulders, breast and arms, before prostrating himself like an ordinand in the sanctuary of Rheims Cathedral. Uninstructed peasants as well as middle class readers of Voltaire no longer appreciated but were even astonished at the performance of such anachronistic medieval rites and ridiculed their significance. Charles' reign reinforced the alliance between the Church and the aristocracy of the *ancien régime*, which obviously alienated the educated liberal middle classes who inevitably also became anti-clerical. In 1830 a political movement which began as an attempt to force the King to dismiss an unpopular minister turned into the July Revolution which was directed as much at the Church as at the monarchy. The crisis precipitated by the King's attempt to secure control of the Chamber would not have turned into a Revolution without such factors as the accumulated resentment which had built up against the Church.

However, the revolutionary riots of the middle and working classes during the July Revolution could not possibly be compared with the bloodletting of 1789, though the destruction of the Bourbon regime inevitably involved an attack on its loyal ally, the Catholic Church. Episcopal residences, seminaries and novitiates were raided and looted. Two or three bishops fled from the country and priests went about in lay dress. Churches were closed during the week and some priests were afraid to open them even on Sundays. But on the whole priests were despised rather than hated and they were no longer feared following the collapse of the Bourbon regime. Christianity was regarded as largely irrelevant, while Catholicism was politically discredited and once again became the religion professed by the majority of French people, rather than the religion of the State. There was no religious ceremony at the coronation of Louis Philippe and although the new King used to attend Mass with his family, the monarchy was no longer officially Catholic. The legal restrictions imposed on the Church by the new administration – a reduction in the ecclesiastical budget, the expulsion of religious orders, the abolition of military chaplains – were simply meant to irritate and further weaken an already moribund organization. It was said that religion was dead and already decomposing. Most Frenchmen spoke of the Church as if it were a corpse and when referring to the Church politely held their handkerchiefs to their noses.

The Revolution of 1789 had devastated the Church, Napoleon had contemptuously used it as an agent of law and order, while attempts to restore religion under the Bourbons had further alienated many Frenchmen and had finally resulted in a violent reaction. When Louis Veuillot was still a sceptic and beginning his career in journalism, he did not know of any parents who spoke to their children about religion and none of his acquaintances ever carried out their religious duties. According to a report drawn up by Jean-Baptiste Henri Lacordaire, less than ten per cent of the senior pupils in the royal colleges of Paris made their Easter duties and only one per cent of them kept the faith after leaving. Pupils at Saint-Cyr who received communion in uniform were likely to be challenged to a duel by their comrades on the grounds that they had dishonoured the school, while Hughes-Félicité Robert de Lamennais recorded that thirty pupils in another school used the sacred host to seal their letters to their parents.

But in spite of the Church's association with the cause of the Bourbon monarchy, Pope Pius VIII refused to adopt the advice of his nuncio in Paris, Gallican bishops and aristocratic *émigrés*, all of whom were opposed to any recognition of the new French regime. The Pope told the French clergy to support the established rather than the legitimate ruler, and in general the French clerby adopted an attitude of prudent reserve rather than political opposition to the regime of Louis Philippe. This was partly a result of the instructions of the Holy See which was very conscious that the strength of French anti-clericalism could not easily be opposed, but there was also another reason. The priests who tended to support the Bourbons were now growing old and were not inclined to seek a fight whereas the younger priests were increasingly being influenced by new leaders who were seeking reforms both within the Church and in its policies. Meanwhile, in spite of the opposition of both extremists and more liberal Catholics, the papacy and the new monarchy decided to continue with the working arrangement which existed between them, and the Napoleonic Concordat remained the basis of relations between Church and State: the King still nominated French bishops and his Government continued to pay clerical stipends. Unknown to their contemporaries, the Pope and the King decided to maintain the existing relations between Church and State, just at the time when some French Catholics were about to propose a radical change and even the complete separation of Church and State.

In appearance de Lamennais was rather like a short and thin sacristan, and he was in fact once described as a timid, priestling, weakly, stunted and glum. Pope Leo XII, however, was more perceptive. In 1824 Lamennais was welcomed in Rome as the herald of Ultramontanism. He stayed at the Vatican and had several private audiences with the Pope who remarked, 'That man needs gentle handling . . . He is a fanatic; he has talent and good faith, but he is one of those perfectionists who, if allowed, would convulse the world'. Lamennais' conversion to

Catholicism had inevitably been followed by a vocation to the priesthood, and his determination to make a total sacrifice of himself eventually overcame his deep sense of fear and respect for the majesty and the grandeur of the priesthood. As he celebrated his first Mass in 1816 he distinctly heard Christ's voice telling him, 'I am calling you to carry my cross – nothing but my cross, do not forget'. Lamennais himself producly declared, 'I will teach them what it means to be a priest'. For Lamennais there were no obstacles, only inexorable and logical conclusions; the ideal was always within reach and must be achieved. Hence his contempt for the French bishops whom he described as tonsured lackeys; 'They are men who have no desire to act, but give them a kick in the appropriate place and you will find they have moved a hundred paces'.

Lamennais was remarkably prophetic and much of what the Church later achieved could be found in his writings, the definition of papal infallibility, the abandonment of the temporal power, the acceptance of democracy and liberalism, the separation of Church and State, the development of biblical studies, liturgical and pastoral reform, and the growth of Catholic Action. With his brother Jean Marie, who was also a priest and who helped to found the Brothers of Christian Instruction and other religious congregations, Féclicité worked for the reform and the revival of Catholicism. In 1809, he produced *Réflexions* which condemned the philosophers of the eighteenth century and outlined a programme for the reform of the French Church. He was horrified by the subservience of the French bishops to Napoleon and greatly admired the resistance of the Pope. However, an apostle of liberty who was also a champion of Ultramontanism had little chance of being heard at the time. His book passed almost unnoticed except by the police who confiscated it. In 1814, Lamennais and his brother published a work in three volumes on the tradition of the Church and on the institution of bishops which again criticised Gallicanism and advocated Ultramontanism, and in 1817 he published the first volume of his *Essay on Indifference in Matters of Religion*.

Lamennais insisted on the social necessity of religion and rejected the eighteenth century notion that an autonomous ethics was possible apart from religion or that a satisfactory human society could exist without religion. Man himself could not develop as man without religion which, as the basis of morals, was necessary for society; a society without religion would degenerate into a group of individuals fighting for their own interests. At the same time Lamennais consciously and explicitly rejected the theory that religion was merely socially or politically useful for keeping the people in order. Christianity was true as well as socially useful and was socially useful precisely because it was true. He then went on to argue that heresy prepared the way for deism which prepared the way for atheism and resulted in a complete indifference opposed to the nature of man and destructive of his being.

At the time the Catholic Church in France seemed to be assuming the character of a State Church and declining to the status of a Government department by its gradual submission to the demands of the State. Although the Bourbon régime had not been hostile to the Church, measures had sometimes been adopted to appease the increasingly powerful anti-clerical and 'liberal' parties. Lamennais, therefore, argued that the State should be consistently liberal and should give to Catholics the same constitutional liberties granted to Protestants and Jews. The Catholic Church could only win the attention and respect of those who had been influenced by philosophical scepticism if it was free to reform itself, to educate and to exercise its own influence; and if the Vicar of Christ on earth would give to the Church and the world the leadership which he alone was providentially able to give.

According to Lamennais, the Pope was not only the Lord's Anointed and God's representative on earth, he was also the expression of the universal will of man and the trustee of the whole human race. The authority of the papacy, therefore, was both absolute and infallible, 'the infallible organ of the testimony of the human race to the one true religion'. The Pope must regain his right to intervene in the affairs of this world so that he might give effect to the principles of the Gospel. He alone could safeguard the freedom of the children of God against Erastian interference, just as he alone could establish that fraternal order between the nations of which a secular agreement like the Holy Alliance was a mere mockery.

Contemporary conditions and political realities obviously prevented the restoration of the traditional relations between Church and State. Modern governments were forced to tolerate all religions or to recognize more than one; they were atheist, professing no particular faith, and the will of the people rather than the will of God was presumed to be the supreme arbiter of what was lawful and just. Originally Lamennais had distrusted the people and supported monarchism on the grounds that the latter was stable and orderly, whereas democracy was unstable and might even destroy Christianity. However, he eventually began to try to secure the rising forces of democracy in favour of the Church and he argued that the people had the right to overthrow a ruler who ceased to be the representative of God's power. In due course Lamennais became more and more democratic and uncompromisingly Ultramontane. Monarchs were equated with tyranny and oppression, and revolutionaries with democracy and freedom. Ecclesiastical establishments implied submission to civil governments, while a liberalism or sovereignty of the individual reason which excluded all superior authority would inevitably lead to anarchy and to atheism.

Lamennais hoped to replace Gallican notions about relations between Church and State with Ultramontane opinions. National churches might easily be controlled or dominated by the State, whereas the universal Church of the union of all Catholics under the Pope could not. This reasoning reinforced Lamennais' conviction that only religion could provide the necessary order for society:

> No pope, no church;
> No church, no christianity;
> No christianity, no religion;
> No religion, no society.

Lamennais argued in favour of an alliance between the Church and democratic freedom to replace the alliance between Throne and Altar. He concluded that the fall of the Bourbons was inevitable and that the French Church itself might also fall unless it broke with the monarchy. By now Lamennais was defending freedom of conscience as well as freedom for the Catholic Church, a free society with free speech, press and education, the separation of Church and State, and an assembly elected by universal suffrage. His reputation was enormously enhanced when, as he had predicted, the Bourbon monarchy fell in 1830 and with the success of the Revolution, Lamennais urged his fellow Catholics to break with the past and the Bourbons, and with all forms of legitimist, royalist and absolutist regimes.

Thus, Lamennais became one of the promoters of both Ultramontanism and Liberal Catholicism which would eventually oppose each other, but which for the moment and for some time to come were united. It is important to distinguish between Lamennais' Traditionalist apologetic, Ultramontane ecclesiology and Liberal Catholic politics which were not necessarily linked together. Liberal Catholicism was condemned in *Mirari vos* during 1832 and Traditionalism some two years later in *Singulari nos*, but Ultramontanism was eventually canonized. De Bonald was a Traditionalist and a Gallican, not an Ultramontane nor a

Liberal. Lacordaire was a Liberal and an Ultramontane without being a Traditionalist. Until 1829 Lamennais himself was a Traditionalist and an Ultramontane, but not a Liberal. As a result of these distinctions, it was sometimes claimed that those followers of Lamennais who remained in the Church were Ultramontanes rather than Traditionalists or Liberals and this was sometimes, though not always, true. Lamennais' 'disciples' included several future bishops such as Gerbet, Gousset and Doney, Emmanuel d'Alzon, the founder of the Assumptionists, the historian Rohrbacher and the liturgist Guéranger. The biographer of Guéranger who later completely identified himself with the Ultramontanes, unscrupulously concealed or even denied the facts of his early association with Lamennais.

Lamennais' most famous supporters were, of course, Lacordaire and Count Charles Montalembert. Lacordaire had been converted to Catholicism partly as a result of his desire to improve the social order for which Christianity was a necessary means, and partly as a result of a sentimental or romantic anguish somewhat reminiscent of Chateaubriand. 'I remember crying one day', he wrote, 'when I heard the Gospel of Saint Matthew read. When one cries, belief is not far away'. Lacordaire argued that in the nineteenth century the Church could be considered as superior to the State, or absolutely independent of the State, or Church and State might support each other by making reciprocal concessions. The first, he believed, was the true position which could no longer be restored, while the third position inevitably involved Erastianism or Gallicanism. Consequently Lacordaire maintained that the two institutions must be absolutely independent and this was probably one of the reasons why he accepted an invitation from the Bishop of New York to go to the United States where the principle of separation was already being adopted. However, when the July Revolution broke out Lacordaire met Lamennais and was later invited to collaborate in establishing a newspaper which would fight to secure those liberties for the Church which had been won for the country. Meanwhile, having read the first issue, Montalembert hurried back from Ireland where he had been meeting the Great Liberator himself, Daniel O'Connell, to join in the new venture.

Dieu et la liberté was the motto of *L'Avenir*, which might well be contrasted with the title of the unofficial journal of the French clergy during the Restoration, *L'ami de la Religion et du Roi. L'Avenir* argued that Catholicism was an essential condition of social stability, but that a revolutionary period was not a time of normal stability or of a common faith and that during such a period different beliefs should freely contend in order that the truth might prevail. Secular governments should respect and secure the freedom of all rather than favour any particular ecclesiastical establishment. However, the idea of a liberal regime was soon supported for its own sake and defended as both proper and permanent; it ceased to be a weapon in the fight for ecclesiastical liberty and became a fundamental part of the Catholic faith. *L'Avenir* rejected the divine right of kings in favour of the sovereignty of the people and advocated the separation of Church and State as well as freedom of conscience. In fact, the newspaper supported complete religious and educational liberty, freedom of press and association, universal suffrage and the decentralization of government. Lacordaire himself was particularly critical of examples of Erastianism. He criticised the method of appointing bishops by ministers of State who might be Protestants, atheists or Jews and the humiliating way in which priests collected their stipends from the tax collector's office: 'It was not with a cheque drawn on Caesar's bank that Jesus sent His Apostles out into the world'.

The newspaper, recently described as 'the most important Catholic journal of the nineteenth century', quickly won international fame and its contributors included Lamartine, Victor Hugo, Honoré Balzac and Alexandre Dumas. Lamennais had been influenced in his own conversion to democracy by the struggles of Catholics in Ireland, Belgium and Poland against their non-Catholic governments and his newspaper now supported their cause. The co-operation of Catholic and Liberals as advocated by Lamennais was actually realized in the Belgian Revolution, while the passing of the Catholic Emancipation Act in England during 1829 was also interpreted as a sign of the times because it freed the Church from political control and was a practical application of the principle of separating Church and State.

For several months, the newspaper had a daily circulation of about 2,000 subscribers, both cleric and lay. Two numbers were seized by the police within the first five weeks and the editors were prosecuted for attacking the government, but acquitted. They were, however, defeated in bringing an action for libel and fined for opening a school in defiance of the law. The Gallican periodical *Ami du clergé* joined various legitimist publications in attacking Lamennais, while some of his other opponents even forged a letter in which he apparently called for help in 'smashing' the hierarchy. Many of the French bishops, who still tended to be Gallican and monarchist, issued pastorals in 1831 denouncing the newspaper, and seminarians who were suspected of being influenced by it had their ordinations postponed.

Consequently, after only a year, *L'Avenir* ceased publication as a result of a decline in the number of subscribers. Liberals as well as Catholics were prejudiced against the 'unnatural' union which Lamennais proposed, while the editors did not try to win support slowly and tactfully, but by their over-enthusiastic haste simply shocked their readers into hostility. It was obviously easier for a newspaper to advocate the separation of Church and State, and an end to Government stipends, than for the bishops and clergy to accept the implications of such measures. The newspaper was discontinued and Lamennais, Lacordaire and Montalembert went to Rome to seek papal support on the questions at issue. The Pope was so distant that Lamennais and his friends had been able to fashion him into a myth, to 'lend him the colours of his own hope', and to ignore the developments which had taken place in the Papal States since 1815. Lacordaire's fateful promise was about to be realized.

> We will, if need be, carry that protest to the city of the apostles, to the steps of the confession of St Peter, and we shall see who will dare to stand in the way of the pilgrims of God and of liberty.

In 1815, the papacy had emerged from recent struggles with a new prestige and not only among Catholics. The French Revolution which had originally been welcomed with such enthusiasm throughout Europe soon became an object of horror and a justification for all those who opposed contemporary developments. This reaction provided the opportunity for the triumph of the Holy See and at this time the hostility of the papacy to the revolutionary spirit of the age would become one of its strongest weapons. The prestige of the papacy was also greatly increased by the character of the reigning Pope and the abilities of his Secretary of State. By his patience and courage during his trials, his sincere piety and lack of vindictiveness following the downfall of Napoleon, Pius VII had won the respect and veneration of millions. The Pope provided shelter for several members of Napoleon's family fleeing from the 'White Terror' in France and he later wrote to the Prince Regent in an effort to improve the conditions under which Napoleon was being held in exile on St Helena. Of all the continental powers the papacy had been Napoleon's most consistent opponent and on his defeat the triumph of the Holy See was inevitable, though the popes themselves had only indirectly contributed to his downfall. Furthermore,

Hughes-Félicité de Lamennais

only Pius VII had resisted Bonaparte's attempt to dominate the Church, a fact which more than anything else converted Lamennais to Ultramontanism. As a result, Europeans felt a new sense of respect for the Holy See and this was to be a crucial factor in the restoration of the temporal power.

Cardinal Ercole Conslavi represented the Holy See at the Congress of Vienna and by his astuteness he won back a great deal that had been lost during the preceding years. However, this papal success at the Congress of Vienna which restored almost all of the Papal States, including the legations and enclaves in northern Italy, was ultimately to prove the most disastrous event in the history of the papacy during the nineteenth century. It is arguable that the election of Pius VII was the occasion on which the temporal power of the Pope might have been surrendered; this would have been in the best interests of the papacy and future popes would have been free to devote their full attention to spiritual matters. However, it was considered inconceivable at the time to attempt to preserve papal independence without temporal sovereignty, in spite of the fact that this independence was more apparent that real. On one very revealing occasion the Austrains were only willing to return *some* of the former papal territories to the Pope and they only did this when they were retreating from Italy which was about to fall again under French control as a result of Bonaparte's victory at Marengo in 1800. On another occasion it was suggested to Pius VII at Savona that he should return as Bishop of Rome and Head of the Church, but without his temporal sovereignty. The Pope himself was prepared to accept this on condition he was guaranteed his spiritual freedom and allowed to choose his own advisers; unfortunately, Napoleon refused to agree.

But in spite of the restoration of the Papal States and the growing identification of the interests of Throne and Altar, the Pope had refused to excommunicate Napoleon during the hundred days or to give his spiritual blessing to the new order of security established by the Russian and Austrian Emperors at the Congress of Vienna. The Pope who had maintained his neutrality under Napoleon was determined to avoid becoming involved in the Congress System which was intended to destory revolutionary forces wherever these might appear, while the famous Holy Alliance which defended the Divine Right of Kings was considered too Erastian to receive papal support. In 1820 the Papal Government again refused to join the Congress of Troppau which also accepted the obligation of suppressing revolutionary movements.

Although the Papal Government was willing to prevent the spread of revolution by imposing a strict censorship, for example, it did not want to see Austrian troops across the river Po where they might be able to dominate Italy. The Holy See actually protested to the Congress of Troppau when Austrian troops proposed to cross papal territory in order to suppress a rebellion in Naples and refused to send any papal troops, though the Papal States were also immediately threatened by this particular revolution.

In short, the Papal Government adopted two incompatible policies, that of defeating revolutionary movements, while maintaining the absolute neutrality of the Papal States. The principle of isolation, however, was ultimately impossible because papal independence could only in fact be maintained if the French and Austrian powers were finely balanced, otherwise the Holy See became subject to the predominant power. Furthermore, the popes proved unable to resist the revolutionary movements within the Papal States without external support and in time the temporal power became completely dependent on what was happening outside the papal territories. Between 1831 and 1870, the popes were only able to survive in their own lands for a few years without the protection of foreign troops and the rule of the Pope came to an end as soon as these were removed. Of course, political alliances would have involved the popes in foreign wars which were clearly incompatible with their religious position. But this dilemma was an inevitable consequence of the existence of the temporal power. Territorial integrity and political neutrality were inconsistent aims. The popes refused to join foreign alliances or to impose military conscription and hoped to defend their territories by condemning violations as sacrilegious which was hardly an effective defence in an increasingly secular and nationalistic age.

The situation within the Papal States was made worse by the policies of reaction adopted after the restoration when a clerical and absolutist regime was once again and sometimes ruthlessly reimposed. The provisional government under Agostino Rivarola behaved without much prudence or skill, while later governments seemed almost incredibly provocative. Those who had collaborated too openly with the French or who had accepted French honours were dismissed from their positions, secular as well as religious. Distinguished professors were dismissed from universities and clergy who had taken oaths of loyalty were evicted from their benefices. Those individuals who had been closely involved with the arrest of the Pope were sent to the galleys. Various

Napoleonic legal codes which had reformed civil and criminal procedure were cancelled and an ecclesiastical commission was established to supervize the return of secularized religious property.

Of course, such moves hardly amounted to a 'White Terror' and some of them, such as the abolition of conscription and divorce, were understandable and even justified. The situation throughout Europe was tense at the time, the records of other secular rulers were not particularly impressive, while the most violent acts of revenge in Rome took place during the military and secularist regime of Murat. Nevertheless the Pope was a religious leader, not simply a secular ruler, and the restoration of feudal justice and the Inquisition (even though it was advised not to use torture), the return of Jews to the ghetto, filling in the excavations at the Colosseum, the abolition of uniformity in weights and measures, street lighting or vaccination, seemed obscurantist and vindictive in the extreme.

Cardinal Conslavi who was an outstanding administrator and statesman adopted different policies because he appreciated that young people 'who had never lived under papal government, took a very poor view of it'. In 1816 he introduced a constitution clearly influenced by the French principles of unity and uniformity, and he appointed laymen to subordinate, but still important offices of administration. He reformed the administration of justice; the use of torture and the old system of justice were abolished in favour of a modified Napoleonic code. He also reorganized the taxes and the finances of the Papal States, and the system of education. He attempted to improve agriculture and transportation within the papal territories and to establish a textile industry. He also began a programme of public building and restoration that was eventually destined to transform the Eternal City. However, these more liberal policies were not always supported by more conservative cardinals and clerics, while Consalvi himself did not long survive Pius VII and died within six months of the Pope's death in 1823. Metternich believed that Consalvi had been responsible responsible for the refusal of the Holy See to support more fully the measures which had been taken to suppress the liberal revolutions in Spain and Italy during 1820 and 1821. The Chancellor, therefore, made it clear that Austria would oppose the choice of Consalvi as successor to Pius VII, while the *Zelanti* among the Cardinals already distrusted him as too liberal in his reforms and too willing to compromise in the agreements which he made with secular governments.

The Roman authorities made some incidental or isolated attempts at reform. There were improvements in the planning, servicing and maintenance of the city of Rome which were financed by a fairer re-assessment of the rates and which also eased the burden of taxation on the poor. But, the popes in the first half of the nineteenth century were usually more interested in matters spiritual than secular concerns and although this was to their credit it did not benefit their secular subjects to whom the Papal Government must have seemed irrelevant or inefficient when it was not positively harmful. Pope Leo XII, for example, was actively involved in the revival of Catholicism by encouraging missions both in Europe and abroad, and in 1825 he held the first Holy Year since 1775. However, as a secular ruler, he believed that all would be well if the standard of morality was higher in the Papal States. He, therefore, closed the Roman wine shops in 1824 and two years later, banned the waltz at the carnival. In 1829 the same Pope declared that whoever decided to be vaccinated was no longer a child of God; smallpox was a judgment from God, vaccination was a challenge to heaven. On a later occasion, during a cholera epidemic in Rome and as a protection against the disease, Gregory XVI led a procession through the streets, carrying the picture of our Lady said to have been painted by St Luke.

It is surely significant that the popes who played such a vital role in the revival of Catholicism throughout the world should have been, perhaps inevitably, political 'failures' at home. At the beginning of the nineteenth century the missionary expansion of Catholicism seemed permanently threatened by the suppression of the Jesuits which had deprived the Church of well over three thousand missionaries, by the intellectual atmosphere of the Enlightenment as well as theological dissensions within European Catholicism, by the Erastianism in the Iberian peninsula and the turmoil of the French Revolution, the colonial expansion of Britain and Holland, and the Church's own unwillingness to adapt to local cultures seen in the famous controversies over the use of Chinese and Malabar rites. As a result of the revolutionary crises in France, the Franciscans and Dominicans, the Lazarists, the Fathers of the Foreign Missions and the Congregation of the Holy Spirit had all been effectively suppressed, while the finances and resources of the Congregation of Propaganda were siezed when the French occupied Rome. Napoleon himself was not unwilling to use the missionary societies to further his own interests but his quarrels with the Pope effectively ended most of his schemes. The missionary crisis still continued after the restoration of the Congregation of Propaganda and the French missionary societies; vocations were few and money was short so that by 1820 the Church seemed faced with total disaster. Yet only fifty years later Catholic missionaries would be found in all parts of the world and the flood of Catholic immigrants from Ireland, Italy and Germany would transform the situation in the United States of America.

Pius VII, Leo XII and Pius VIII all gave active and financial support to the work of Propaganda and missionary societies such as the Picpus Fathers, the Marists and the Oblates of Mary Immaculate, but the real breakthrough came in 1831 when Cappellari became Pope Gregory XVI. As a religious leader Gregory XVI proved to be brilliant. He encouraged the revival and reform of monastic orders and the creation of new religious congregations. He welcomed and promoted new devotions, especially devotions to our Lady and those devotions which best reflected the traditions of Rome. As a former Prefect of Propaganda, Gregory had a particular interest in the spread of the Church throughout the world and in an allocution to the Cardinals, declared that the establishment and enlargement of the missions was his chief care.

The Pope reorganized Propaganda and endowed it with additional funds and with a new library which he himself had collected. He supported new missionary congregations and enterprises, directly restored and controlled missionary colleges and seminaries, and by reviving the policy of creating vicars-apostolic attempted to circumvent the ancient rights of Portugal and Spain over the appointment of missionary bishops. Gregory's support for Catholic missionary activity was accompanied with a determination to establish papal control in the new mission fields. He strengthened the episcopate in the United States and Canada, in England and Australasia. He appointed bishops or vicars apostolic in north Africa, Egypt and western Asia, in India, Burma, Siam, Malaya, Indo-china, China and Korea, and in the East Indies as well as several of the Pacific islands. He also encouraged the ordination of native clergy and the consecration of native bishops. Finally, in 1839, Gregory issued his famous instruction, *In Supremo*, where he condemned the opposition of many Christians to the emancipation of negroes: 'All Catholics', he declared, 'whether priests or laymen are forbidden to pretend that slavery and the slave trade are lawful'.

However, the papacy showed itself to be less concerned with the political emancipation of Italian Catholics. The Papal States had been badly governed during the eighteenth century, but after 1815 they were considered to be the worst governed territories in Europe apart from those of the Turkish Empire, though this dubious distinction should probably have been given to the Kingdom of Naples and Sicily. After the restoration, there was too much clerical control, while too many opponents were punished or exiled. The re-establishment of clerical control over justice and administration was associated with restrictions, censorship and the return of older methods of judicial procedure. Clerical extremists could not bring themselves to allow laymen in the Papal States to hold political or administrative office, while the inability or the refusal of the papal authorities to adopt measures of political or economic reform inevitably forced Italian nationalists to adopt a thoroughly anti-clerical ideology.

It would, of course, be unfair to condemn the papal government without also appreciating the obvious limitations of political practices and economic theories such as '*laissez faire*' which were widespread at the time. Neither the English Reform Bill of 1832 nor the Poor Law of 1834 were as democratic or an enlightened as was sometimes suggested. The Italian peasant was probably no worse off than his Irish counterpart, or the men, women and children then working in the mines and the new factories of industrial Britain, while capital punishment was rare compared with England. According to contemporaries, the Papal States were hopelessly corrupt, but if it was important to know a cardinal in Rome, it was still a help to know a duke in England.

Nevertheless, such factors as the lack of public control over finances and the clerical monopoly of political life, the failure to adopt the same constitutional and political, economic and judicial principles which were being increasingly recognized in western Europe, the absence of an established rule of criminal law with swift and open procedure as well as trial by jury, were to give the Papal States an unenviable reputation. In time the papal regime was described as one in which the police could, at their pleasure, imprison a man or place him under house arrest, deprive him of his employment and his civil rights, enter his house, close shops and impose fines. The fact that these events did not happen every day and were repeated far more frequently and viciously in other parts of the world did little to preserve the good reputation of the Papal Government.

The inhabitants of northern Italy particularly disliked being ruled by the papacy, but since these legations were the only economically prosperous parts of the Papal States, it was impossible to grant them independence without giving up the temporal power itself. It was, however, quite impossible to restore a reactionary regime in the legations where for well over a decade the inhabitants had enjoyed the benefits of French political, judicial and administrative institutions which, in their view, far outweighed the disadvantages of French taxation, conscription and even exploitation. In any case, the Austrian Chancellor, Prince Metternich, did not want these areas to become centres of disaffection since they were closely linked, economically and culturally, with Austrian Lombardy. Consequently, before returning these territories to the Pope, Metternich had insisted on the maintenance of the existing secular administration, a general amnesty, and guarantees for the owners of secularized property as well as the creditors of the previous regime. Limited reforms granted some lay participation in government, suppressed feudal rights and authorities, and clearly distinguished administrative from judicial powers, which were no longer to be exercised by priests. However, these reforms were never fully implemented, they failed to satisfy reforming liberals and were condemned by conservatives as French or Jacobin.

Discontent was widespread throughout the papal territories, but especially in the legations, and an obvious example of the evils of the Papal Government can be seen in the formation of voluntary bands of *Sanfedisti* into violent and unruly 'Centurians' to combat the political opposition which was developing in the lodges of secret societies. The *Carbonari* or 'charcoal burners' were secret revolutionaries and nationalists fighting against the Pope and the Church, while the *Sanfedisti* were a type of secret police who adopted the deplorable if common practice of using spies. At Ravenna in 1825 the Cardinal Legate, acting on information provided by the *Sanfedisti* and using the emergency powers conferred on him by the Pope, sentenced seven men to death, fifty four to forced labour, six to life imprisonment, fifty three to imprisonment, two to exile and two hundred and eighty six to police supervision. An attempt to assassinate the Legate was followed by a number of arrests, summary trials and hangings, the bodies being left on the gallows as an example to others, Later reactions were equally harsh. In 1843 a conspiracy to kidnap three important ecclesiastics, including the future Pius IX, and to hold them as hostages, was taken too seriously and resulted in seven executions, more than fifty individuals being condemned to the galleys and the imposition of martial law.

Some ecclesiastical officials and loyal supporters of the papacy were critical of the political system operating within the Papal States. The most famous of these critics, who at this time included the future

Pius IX, was Cardinal Giuseppe Sala who actually presented a comprehensive plan for the reform of the Papal States in which he criticized the confusion of the sacred and the secular, the pervading conservative attitudes and the fact that the Papal Government 'had lost or forgotten the art of understanding men'. In order to separate the spiritual from the temporal, he recommended that all secular tasks should be entrusted to laymen and that the position of the Pope should be clearly distinguished from his role as a secular ruler, the essential spiritual function of the papacy from its accidental temporal rule. Sala believed that 'We have often confused the spiritual with the temporal, sacrificing the former in the endeavour to maintain the latter, and we have thereby lost them both'.

The popes and most of their officials, on the other hand, felt committed by history, principle and prestige to the theocratic government of the Papal States. They either refused or failed to see that geography, politics and the climate of opinion would inevitably combine to destroy this independent theocracy in the middle of the Italian peninsula. Contemporaries were adopting political principles which made any appeal to 'legitimate' political or legal rights anachronistic and with which no theocracy, however enlightened, could come to terms. The idea that sovereignty belonged to the people could not be reconciled with the current Catholic theological claim that it came from God. At the same time, there was no historical reason for a Church which had so often come into conflict with secular powers to support the political principle of legitimacy and even less the principle of absolutism.

However, the existence of the Papal States influenced and even dominated the decisions of the popes who made confused judgments about the theory of political questions. Both Gregory XVI and Pius IX denounced democratic liberties precisely because the extension of such liberties to the Papal States was incompatible with theocratic government. The thoery of popular sovereignty was considered inapplicable to the theocratic Papal States because it was thought impossible to separate the Pope's spiritual autocracy from his temporal authority. Of course, many other rulers also failed to solve the political or social problems of the time, but the popes had religious as well as political subjects, and they universally condemned movements in the world at large which seemed similar to those causing problems within their own dominions. Furthermore, these practical considerations were inevitably reinforced by the ideological alliance between Throne and Altar as well as actual experience of the effects of revolution.

Pope Leo XII was not ignorant of the enormous progress which had been made by the Church in the United Stated and he explicitly recognized that 'The Catholic religion has flourished under republican as well as under monarchical regimes'. But although the Church might gain immediate benefits from a revolution and the establishment of freedom, ecclesiastics generally felt that the shock to the monarchical system, at least in Europe, would ultimately be disastrous not only for the Church and the Papal States but for society as well. The Church, therefore, supported 'legitimate' monarchs even when they were opposed to its interests. Irish Catholics were ordered to submit episcopal nominations to the veto of their Protestant King, while French Liberal Catholics were to be silenced in the interests of their agnostic ruler. Other Catholics were expected to make even greater sacrifices.

In 1827 a Concordat modelled on that with Napoleon had been negotiated with the King of the Netherlands. Bishops were to be elected by chapters, but the King was given the right of exclusion and a veto over episcopal appointments of the clergy. The concordat, however, did not settle questions of education and, under the influence of Lamennais, the Belgian clergy began to demand freedom of education and to resist royal attempts to control the training of priests. The monarch retaliated, while Pope Leo XII advised Belgian Catholics who were being persecuted 'to maintain an attitude of passivity' until such time as the Holy See saw fit to intervene. With the advent of the Belgian Revolution, the Roman authorities urged the bishops to be moderate and demanded that the clergy should remain loyal to the King.

These policies were obviously adopted in the interests of the Concordat and because of the principle of legitimacy, though the Pope would undoubtedly have also been influenced by the demands of diplomatic neutrality and the interests of Catholics in Holland. When Belgium finally broke away from Holland in 1830, the Pope refused to appoint a Vatican representative until 1842, and even then the attitude of the Holy See continued to be somewhat ambiguous. The first nuncio appointed made a clumsy attempt to control the Belgian hierarchy and had to be withdrawn. His successor, the future Leo XIII, who was much more conciliatory, was rebuked by the Secretary of State for not sufficiently defending papal rights and he was replaced by a notorious opponent of 'liberalism'.

The Pope's reaction to the Polish revolt of 1830 was even more notorious. In June 1832 Gregory issued a letter condemning 'those authors of lying and trickery who, under cover of religion, defy the legitimate power of princes, break all the ties of submission imposed by duty and plunge their country into misfortune and mourning'. He advised Polish Catholics to obey their 'mighty emperor who would show them every kindness'. This appeal was published by the Russians when they were beginning to carry out their policies of repression throughout the country. It was not revealed that the Pope had also sent a letter to the Tsar in which he condemned the persecution and deceit of the Russian Government in Poland. Meanwhile, Nicholas continued his policy of strengthening his political authority by imposing religious uniformity, regulating the affairs of the Uniate and Polish Catholics, forbidding the reception of converts into the Catholic Church, removing marriage and education from the control of the clergy, governing seminaries and closing convents. When Gregory eventually learned of the persecution of the Church in Poland he was horrified and distressed, and he sent a moving protest to the Tsar begging him to change his policies.

Gallicanism was increasingly becoming something of an anachronism, especially after 1830 when the French King no longer possessed a legitimate divine right and the Government was effectively not even Christian at all. However, Erastianism itself still survived. Although secular rulers appreciated the social utility of religion, they still preferred the help of a Church under their own control. In an effort to avoid conflicts between Church and State, the papacy adopted the policy of signing Concordats with various secular regimes. The character of these Concordats largely depended on the contemporary situation and on the particular country involved. The Concordat with Bavaria in 1817 secured ecclesiastical rights over censorship and education, whereas the Concordat with Prussia in 1821 made scanty provision for the support of clergy or seminaries and allowed the Prussian King to veto episcopal elections, and to control communications with Rome as well as the publication of episcopal instructions. It is significant that both Bavaria and Prussia should have followed the example of Napoleon in altering the content of the Concordats in their own favour. But it is also interesting that Cardinal Consalvi should have safeguarded the right of the Pope to have a decisive voice in the episcopal nominations of the German states.

The policy of signing Concordats showed that the papacy was forced to co-operate with secular regimes in restricting the activities of the Church within particular national boundaries and so undermined the position of the local Church. Governments were able to restrict ecclesiastical activities and the Catholic Church was expected to secure the loyalty of Catholic subjects. Catholicism was unable to exercise a formative influence on the age and was forced to adopt the role which had originally been envisaged for it during the eighteenth century Enlightenment. On the other hand, these Concordats eventually contributed towards the increasing dominance of the papacy within the Catholic Church and helped to secure papal primacy against the claims of local hierarchies and national churches. As far as the Roman authorities were concerned, Concordats, with all their faults, were always made with the popes and not with local or national bishops.

Unfortunately, these Concordats later became regarded as the final settlements in relations between Church and State. The Church was guaranteed some rights and liberties by the secular régimes, but tolerated and even institutionalized some situations which could not be considered as right or favourable for the Church at all times. The Roman authorities were then unable to meet particular situations flexibly or on their merits, while the papacy was in danger of losing the capacity to adapt itself to the particular situations of individual countries. This inflexibility was reinforced by the conservatism of theological studies in Rome as well as by the defence of the Papal States. It is clearly part of the Pope's teaching office to help to define the limits of doctrinal belief, but during the nineteenth century the new and dominating position of the papacy was frequently used to oppose the development of unfamiliar or untraditional theological views. In spite of the growth of Ultramontanism, the defence of the Papal States also restricted the popes from developing and intensifying an alliance between the papacy and the faithful which might have been used for the benefit of the Church as a whole. Incidentally, in some ways the policy of signing Concordats went against the spirit of the time because any increase in 'foreign' or 'alien' authority during this extremely nationalistic century usually created further problems. However, it is also arguable that if this Ultramontane development had not taken place, the continued existence of national churches in an age of nationalism might eventually have endangered the unity of the Catholic Church throughout the world.

Of course, not all these developments had actually taken place when the 'pilgrims of liberty' were on their way to Rome, but the pattern of events was already clearly emerging. During the election which followed the death of Pius VIII in December, 1830 the *Carbonari* took the opportunity provided by risings in Parma and Modena to seize Bologna and to establish a provisional government which won the support of the cities of the legations and almost all the cities of Umbria and the Marches. They declared that the temporal power of the papacy had now come to an end. This revolution was part of the Italian reaction to the events which had taken place in France and to the promise made by the French that they would not allow foreign powers to restore order outside their own terriories. Pope Gregory XVI, however, immediately requested Austrian intervention on his election as Pope in 1831. Thus, when Lamennais, Lacordaire and Montalembert went to Rome in December 1831, the Austrians had already been asked to suppress the revolt in the Romagna, while the Pope himself did not need to be reminded of the necessity of supporting law and order, and in the light of recent disturbances, of the danger of adding fuel to the flames of revolution.

Furthermore, the papal nuncio in France, the French Government and hierarchy were all warning the Pope against Lamennais, while some of the most apostolic French clergy, including Dupanloup, had already come out against him. Lamennais himself believed that the Austrian, Prussian and Russian Governments had also sent diplomatic notes asking the Pope to express his disapproval. Certainly, Prince Metternich was hostile and, interpreting the issue completely politically, played an important part in securing the subsequent condemnation. Metternich later boasted of what he had done to Charles Saint-Foi, a friend and former pupil of Lamennais, and on a later occasion, the Chancellor caused further trouble by sending to Rome a pamphlet which identified Lacordaire's position with that of Lamennais. Lamennais for his part either failed to appreciate or simply ignored the fact that the Pope's theological or spiritual position was being influenced by contemporary politicians and political attitudes.

Lamennais argued that there was no inconsistency between Ultramontanism and political Liberalism. The people inherited the tradition and the Pope was their mouthpiece interpreting this tradition as Rousseau's legislator interpreted the general will. The cause of Pope and people was identified with that of truth and freedom, as opposed to the pretensions of temporal rulers and aristocracies. The Papal States were unique precisely because the truth was given by God to the people and expressed on their behalf by the Pope. Consequently, a Pope could not be tyrannical because he was united with the people in truth, whereas tyranny came from rulers, particularly from heretical or unbelieving rulers, whose interests were merely selfish. Incidentally, this justification of the temporal power would later be continued by Montalembert.

Roman officials, on the other hand, believed that authority came directly from God and that temporal authority was bestowed by God on legitimate princes. Gregory XVI was therefore faced with the unenviable alternatives of apparently undermining his own position by condemning Lamennais' ideas or fomenting revolution if he approved of them. And he was only too well aware that the French Revolution and the rule of 'freedom' had brought about the despoliation of the Church, the secularization of education, the closing of convents and monasteries, the persecution of priests and nuns, the abduction of two of his own predecessors and the worship of the goddess of reason on the altar of Notre Dame.

The three 'pilgrims' were first asked to explain their position in a memorandum. Some time later Lamennais was told that the Pope was aware of his good intentions and of his services to the Church, but that he was also pained by the raising of dangerous questions and the expression of rash opinions. The three men were informed that the memorandum would be studied and that they could now return home. Lamennais and Montalembert requested an audience with the Pope and this was granted on condition that nothing was said on the points at issue. Furthermore, when the audience took place Cardinal de Rohan, one of the enemies of *L'Avenir*. was also present, the Pope himself was not particularly friendly and the meeting simply consisted of a cold exchange of platitudes.

Originally Lamennais himself had remained behind in Rome, but then on his own and against the advice and the pleas of Lacordaire, he decided to reissue the newspaper. In the meantime, there had been a regular consultation on the issues in question, with written reports from a number of theologians. The original examiners included Ventura, a friend of Lammennais, and Banaldi who was not particularly reactionary as well as Cardinal Lambruschini. All of them concluded that the work of Lamennais did in fact include certain errors and the *consensus* of opinion was that the papal pronouncement should be along the lines actually followed in *Mirari vos*, the publication of which was to be described by Montalembert as 'the most disastrous act in the annals of the Church of France'.

This was Pope Gregory's first encyclical and much of it was taken up with the conventional material which is suitable and usual on such an occasion. Lamennais himself as well as his newspaper were neither mentioned nor named, but both were implicitly censured in such passages as the description of freedom of publication as abominable or detestable, the disapproval of the separation of Church and State, and the condemnation of universal liberty of conscience as sheer madness and the result of indifferentism. Lamennais, Lacordaire and Montalembert immediately published a declaration of submission in the *Tribune Catholique*, but the three men were already beginning to draw apart even before Lamennais made his final break with the Church.

Mirari vos had been sent to Lamennais with a covering letter recognizing his services and qualities, but pointing out that although it might be necessary to tolerate freedom of worship or liberty of the press, it was wrong to regard these as good in themselves. Lamennais stopped publishing *L'Avenir* as he had promised, but he also told the Pope that in submitting to ecclesiastical doctrine and discipline, he felt entirely free in his opinions, words and actions in the temporal sphere. Gregory replied that he expected an unqualified acceptance of the doctrines of legitimist absolutism and a rejection of those democratic principles advocated in *L'Avenir*. Consequently, Lamennais' later publication of *Paroles d'un Croyant* was a flagrant reassertion of a qualification in his submission which the Pope had already refused to accept.

The danger of a public conflict between Lamennais and the Roman authorities was heightened by the French Gallicans in *L'Ami de la Religion* who sarcastically attacked the papalist condemned by the Pope and who insinuated that his submission had been insincere. Lamennais' brother was also harassed and threatened with dismissal from charitable institutions which he had helped to establish, while Ventura, Lamennais' close friend, was forced to resign as General of the Theatines. The French bishops did not imitate the moderation of the Pope and some of them required that candidates for ordination should reject the theories of Lamennais on oath. When the Pope sent a private letter to the Archbishop of Toulouse expressing his sorrow that Lamennais seemed to be qualifying the submission which had caused such satisfaction to the Pope, the Archbishop published the letter in *L'Ami de la Religion* to the delight of Lamennais' enemies.

In May 1833 Montalembert published his translation of a religious appeal for liberty by the Polish poet Mickiewicz, to which Lamennais added a 'Hymn to Poland'. Shortly afterwards Lamennais himself published *Paroles d'un Croyant* which was a combination of prayer, polemic and appeal in the style of Mickiewicz. Lamennais' work, however, was more subversive and anarchically hostile to all civil authority; Christ was seen to condemn the Pope and the ecclesiastical hierarchy 'because power is the child of hell and priests are only the lackeys of kings'. Lacordaire used this publication to break publicly with Lamennais and he issued his own *Considérations* on Lamennais' philosophical system. It was sometimes believed that Lacordaire's criticisms actually provoked the papal condemnation which was said to reflect his language. However, the encyclical *Singulari nos* was once again influenced by the representations of foreign diplomats from Russia, Prussia and especially from Austria whose opinions carried far more weight with the Roman authorities than the writings of Lacordaire.

Both Lacordaire and Montalembert later acknowledged that *L'Avenir* had been too aggressive and violent in advocating 'intemperate and rash theories' which had been sustained 'with that unrelenting logic which ruins the causes it does not dishonour'. On the other hand, the ultimate reason for the condemnation of the newspaper was that its principles were incompatible with theocratic government. The Pope identified ecclesiastical interests and the good of society with absolute monarchy and legitimacy in an ill-judged condemnation of political principles in terms of universal and permanent validity. Furthermore, Gregory XVI was too impersonal and legalistic in his dealings with Lamennais, whereas, however surprising it might seem, Leo XII had won Lamennais' confidence and even his affection without approving of his teaching. Finally, the ecclesiastical authorities could be patient and accommodating in dealing with hostile and secular powers, but seemed too demanding to say the least in their attitude towards Lamennais.

Although Lamennais might have gone too far and while he certainly attempted to move too quickly, his proposed reconciliation with contemporary liberalism was wiser, more practical and even more Christian that the political attitudes which the papacy did not in fact adopt during the following decades. It is significant that Cardinal Archbishop Englebert Sterckx of Malines, the Primate of Belgium from 1832 until 1867, who was influential in gaining Belgian independence, did not support the Roman authorities nor did he publish *Singulari nos*. On the contrary, he accepted religious liberty, endorsed the opinions of Montalembert and approved of the Belgian publication *Union* which began when *L'Avenir* ceased and which continued to advocate the same policies.

There were certainly grounds for rejecting Lamennais' opinions and in particular his philosophical Traditionalist opinions, but these were not the main reasons for the papal encylicals which were primarily political and social declarations, though motivated by religion. Although Gregory himself probably never really understood Lamennais' ideas, their views on the nature of the Church and the role of the papacy were utterly irreconcilable. Through his encyclicals and the growing alliance between Throne and Altar, the Pope committed the Catholic Church to the old political and social structures, but such a link with the old order was no real alternative to a more liberal policy which would have tried to influence the social and political developments of the age.

After all, at the beginning of the century, the Church did not enjoy a particularly close association with the old order, with Erastian and Gallican monarchies, and even after 1830 reactionary regimes did not prove to be very accommodating to the Church. Furthermore, the influence of the Church over the masses progressively declined as it increasingly adopted the role of acting as a shield against the forces of revolution. It was only with the election of Leo XIII that a Pope attempted to reconcile the Church with the world and the papacy was free once more to become an influential agent in the history of mankind. When the papacy was no longer fettered with the temporal power, Leo XIII could reject the thesis of the Throne and the Altar, and call for a *ralliement* with the French Republic. It is interesting that monarchist successors of those who abused Lacordaire for his association with Lamennais, would then refuse to co-operate with the Pope.

Lamennais, for his part, failed to allow for the fact that the Church had to deal with the powers of this world in defending its rights and its material interests. The Church was sometimes forced to sacrifice its own supporters and even its spiritual interests in order to avoid even greater evils. Lamennais was also too impatient and he failed to judge the contemporary situation either prudently or realistically. He foolishly forced a reluctant Pope to commit himself at a time when he could only commit himself in one way. Already, Leo XII had given his support to the old order in South America where an initial enthusiasm in favour of Catholicism turned into that open hostility which subsequently influenced the history of the Church in that area. *L'Avenir* itself also raised false fears about the sort of episcopal nominations which were to be expected from King Louis Philippe, while Lamennais had called on the French clergy to renounce their state salaries when the integrity of the Church had not then been threatened; Church and State were not yet at the breaking point.

Subsequently Lamennais' attitude to the papacy inevitably changed and the apocalyptic element in his thinking deepened. The Church and the papacy, as at present continued, must be condemned and destroyed. Lamennais later extended absolute freedom of conscience to all men and argued that society must reform itself by destroying sin in mankind, rather than by submitting to the influence of a liberated Church. In time Lamennais would be closely identified with all oppressed peoples rather that with those mainly fighting for religious liberty, and he worked for the regeneration of society through politics and religion, and not through the Church or even through Christianity. The people, not popes or kings, became the instruments of God's power. Christianity was a religion of the past which was giving way to a new one with a new social philosophy in which social and religious duties became identified. Man was perfectible, his aim was to construct the city of God and by his own efforts achieve union with God.

But in spite of the loss of Lamennais, the Ultramontane and Liberal Catholic movements continued to make progress. In 1833, Frederick Ozanam and about a hundred other intellectuals petitioned Archbishop de Qúelen of Paris, to authorize a series of sermons dealing with modern controversies and answering current objections to Christianity and Catholicism. Earlier Catholic apologists such as de Maistre were too reminiscent of the *ancien régime* and had simply opposed national ambitions and contemporary hopes. Indeed, the Archbishop himself was a Catholic royalist who had once declared that not only was Jesus Christ the Son of God, 'but he was also of a very good family on his mother's side, and there are excellent reasons for seeing in him the heir to the throne of Judea'. About two hundred people signed another petition in the following year asking for sermons which would show that Christianity was in harmony with the needs and aspirations of the individual and society.

Ozanam and his friends then offered Lacordaire a pulpit and his sermons were a great success. Conservative objections and police criticisms led to an injunction which ended the conferences, but in 1835 Lacordaire was appointed to the pulpit of Notre Dame. In his sermons Lacordaire began with the fact of the Church, its necessity, its constitution and authority, and its relations with the temporal order. He argued in favour of the infallibility of the Church and the primacy of the Pope. His audiences responded to his eloquence, his sincere honesty and the appeal of his personality. The conferences went from strength to strength in spite of, or perhaps because of, the inevitable accusations of heresy, and the sermons had a profound impact on the religious development of thousands of young men at the time.

The undoubted success of the sermons should not hide the fact that they came at the right moment. The period following 1815 proved to be one of religious, Catholic and Ultramontane revival. Bishops were more zealous and the clergy more devout. Older religious orders were revived and the Jesuits were restored, both as always dependent on papal protection. New orders such as the Oblates of Mary Immaculate or the Christian Brothers were growing and an increasing number of religious houses for women were being established. Deism, materialism and spiritualist philosophies had failed to supply the void left by the decline of dogma and the younger generation were beginning to look for some assurance that the gods were not mere figments of the imagination. In short, by 1833 all the necessary preconditions existed for a religious revival, though nothing happened while Lacordaire, on whom the revival in France was largely to centre, lived in obscurity, out of favour and suspected of heresy.

The Church, no longer the object of political passion, enjoyed its freedom without being compromised by any association with the regime, and the period between 1833 and 1840 was one of religious peace. Frenchmen began to forget the events associated with the Bourbon Restoration, as Roman Catholics adopted a more reserved attitude and the middle classes came to regard religion as a useful, if partial, antidote to the violence of the masses. The Concordat was applied in a more accommodating spirit and Minister of Religious Affairs sought the opinions of the bishops before making new choices for the French hierarchy. By 1838 anti-religious passions had declined and it was possible to restore crucifixes in the law courts. The King replied to the good wishes of the new Archbishop Affre of Paris by remarking that he regarded the promotion of religion as one of his first duties.

The religious revival in France during the years before 1848 was both genuine and real. Within three years the number of communicants in one of the less salubrious parishes of Paris rose from 720 to 9,950. Furthermore, the revival was common to all the Christian churches, Protestant as well as Catholic. However, there were limitations. The revival was most evident among the upper or middle classes; the working and peasant classes were hardly affected and the condemnation of Lamennais had seemed to identify the Church with the forces of reaction. Rationalism and anti-clericalism, materialism and indifference did not disappear after 1815, while those Frenchmen who were attracted by Liberal Catholicism were not necessarily prepared to endure clerical or ecclesiastical obscurantism. In 1844 Alexis de Tocqueville remarked:

> When I think of the attitude to religion shown by public opinion and the Press scarcely three years ago, and compare it with the attitude today, I cannot help seeing that the clergy must have committed huge blunders to reach their present position. By violent personalities and exaggerated accusations they have contrived to spoil an excellent cause. Instead of restricting themselves to common law and claiming their elementary rights, they have revealed their intention of dominating and even controlling all forms of education.

Napoleon had not united, but placed side by side, ecclesiastical and secular education. The bishops were allowed to open ecclesiastical secondary schools and by the end of the Empire they were teaching 18,000 pupils compared with 35,000 in the *lycées* and colleges. By the end of the Bourbon Restoration the ecclesiastical schools were educating a third of the secondary pupils, while two thirds were in the colleges run by the various communes. Catholic families sent their children to Church schools, while the rest went to the *lycées* and colleges; the division of Frenchmen into two hostile camps supporting the Church or the Revolution would be perpetuated in the educational system. Furthermore, the struggle between the Church and the University – the former anxious to secure a privileged position in the field of education and the latter determined to preserve the monopoly which it had acquired – paralleled the struggle between the Church and the Revolution. Some of the bishops indulged in offensive exaggerations in their campaign against the University, which was accused of turning children into foul animals and savage beasts, and of permitting teaching which allowed not only sensuality but even parricide. The supporters of the University and anti-clerical parliamentarians retaliated by attacking the Jesuits. Catholics were faced with the prospect of engaging in an unsuccessful and unhappy controversy as Montalembert tried to rally them on the more secure ground of the defence of liberty.

Montalembert called on French Catholics to follow the example of Belgian or Irish Catholics and to campaign for their rights through petitions, newspapers and elections. Although Catholics might not be able to form a parliamentary majority by themselves, they could either make a substantial contribution or seriously embarrass the Government. The advent of laymen like Montalembert into ecclesiastical politics was not always welcomed by the bishops: 'Laymen have no mission', said the Archbishop of Rouen. 'Their best course is to pray while the bishops make requests'. However, Montalembert himself fought for specific rights and liberties in the Chamber of Peers as well as through political action. He organized a 'Committee for the Defence of Religious Freedom' and political activities throughout the nation so that after the general election of 1846 over 140 deputies were pledged to the freedom of Catholic education. The atmosphere in Parliament dramatically changed and the Prime Minister, Guizot, was forced to recognize publicly that the rights of parents and of religious beliefs in education came before those of the State. A new education bill was introduced in 1847, but the subsequent controversy had not been settled when a revolution broke out in the following year.

Charles de Montalembert

Louis Veuillot

III: The election of Pius the Ninth and the year of revolutions

The pattern of papal elections during the nineteenth century helps to illustrate the somewhat ambivalent or ambiguous attitude adopted by the ecclesiastical authorities towards contemporary society. The election of a new Pope often seemed a reaction against the policies of the preceding Pope and reflected either a renewed hostility towards or a desire to come to better terms with secular society. Thus the conservative Leo XII was followed by the more progressive Pius VIII who was in turn followed by the conservative Gregory XVI. The cardinals who attended the conclave in 1846 appear to have felt the need for change. The conservative candidate was Lambruschini, while the liberal candidates included Feltrinelli and Gizzi. Mastai-Ferretti was the compromise candidate who won the votes of the moderates. Nevertheless his election was tantamount to a political programme. He took the name Pius, in memory of the Pope who had been imprisoned by Napoleon and who in 1797 had preached on the compatibility of democracy and republicanism with Christianity and Catholicism. The same Pope had befriended Mastai-Ferretti during his student days in Rome and, like himself, had also been Bishop of Imola.

Pio Nono would originally be adored by the Roman crowds and welcomed throughout Europe; even the Master of Balliol considered him to be 'a capital fellow'. But he would die condemned throughout the world and cursed by the Roman mob who threw mud at his coffin. As Bishop of Imola, he had freely criticized the Papal Government and when he received the red hat the Pope expressed the hope that in the future he would prove to be more devoted and faithful to the Holy See. However, Mastai-Ferretti continued to show a spirit of liberal independence which lost him the support of many of the upper classes and senior clergy. He was a frequent visitor to the house of the liberal Count Pasolini, where,

> in friendly conversations he was led to recognize the griefs and the shames of the present and the unavoidable necessities of the new age

> so that these walls heard him deplore the blindness of the governments, the secret sects, the foreign domination, and with tears implore from God a Church purified from worldly passions and an Italian fatherland free and well ordered'.

Here too, he was able to read the latest liberal publications. On the eve of the conclave, he wrote, 'the Pope will certainly not be myself, but tell your wife . . . that I have put in my bag those books which she gave me at Montericco and that I shall make the new Pope read them'.

French Liberal Ultramontanes believes that at last 'their' Pope had come. Ozanam predicted that Pius IX was 'truly sent by God to accomplish the main business of the nineteenth century – the alliance of religion and liberty', while Montalembert was delighted to learn that the new Pope had described him as a 'champion of the good cause'. In 1847 Ventura, who was very close to Pius IX, wrote to his old friend Lamennais:

> I have an overture to make to you; it is on behalf of the angel whom heaven has sent us, from Pius IX whom I saw this morning. He has charged me to tell you that he blesses you and awaits you to embrace you.

On the other hand, negotiations with Russia and relations with both Austria and Prussia were prejudiced by the advent of a liberal Pope. 'We had foreseen everything', remarked Metternich, 'except a liberal Pope'. Other Italian princes, conservative cardinals and even Anglican archdeacons were far from happy at the prospect: 'A pretty state we are in altogether', commented Robert Wilberforce in 1848, 'with a Radical Pope teaching all Europe rebellion', while other commentators described him as a 'pontifical Robespierre' and prophesied that he would suffer the same fate as Louis XVI.

At the time there was throughout Europe, and especially in Italy, a widespread and confident expectation of change. It was also hoped that conflicts could be resolved and reforms introduced without bloodshed. The Italian patriots themselves wanted internal political, constitutional and economic reforms, the expulsion of Austria and the union of Italy, though without necessarily abandoning the different traditions of the individual states or deposing their various rulers. The Pope himself seems to have shared these general hopes and was certainly convinced of the need to carry out reforms and to correct what was wrong. When Pius IX declared a political amnesty which brought about the release of more than a thousand prisoners and the return of hundreds of exiles, Italians became convinced that he was about to lead the movement towards constitutional democracy and national unity. Throughout the world, the amnesty was seen as a political change of heart; 'God never grants amnesties', Metternich remarked, 'God pardons'.

The amnesty was followed by a whole series of reforms. A commission on railways and an Agricultural Institute were established, gas lighting was planned and there were general reforms affecting education, tariffs, the criminal code, press censorship and even the Papal Government itself. Laymen were introduced into the Government of the Papal States and a Consultative Assembly was set up to help in the work of Government. However, many of these internal reforms turned out to be half measures, while the *Consulta* of twenty-four counsellors was, as the name itself indicates, restricted to the role of consultation. Pius IX was not prepared to endanger his political independence which he believed to be essential for fulfilling his spiritual office, by granting complete constitutional rights to the laity or by tolerating the development of their constitutional control either directly or indirectly over ecclesiastical affairs. The dual responsibilities of the Pope as a temporal and spiritual ruler meant that he could not become a constitutional monarch in the sense of limiting his sovereignty or allowing it to be controlled by an elective assembly.

It is sometimes said that Pio Nono was influenced by the writings of Gioberti, a priest who outlined a national programme of reform and political action. Gioberti argued that Italy must look to the Catholic Church and to the papacy for her regeneration as a nation. Italian princes must introduce popular representation, the different Italian states must then federate under the presidency of the Pope, while the King of Piedmont should provide the army which would be needed to drive the Austrians out of Italy. Ultimately, of course, Rome and Piedmont would conflict over the unification of Italy which would eventually be achieved by Piedmont alone. However, before 1860 the unification of Italy could only be conceived on federal lines because of the substantial differences between the various regions. Furthermore, it was taken for granted that the Papal States would form part of the new Italy and it was commonly suggested that the Pope himself might be its president.

At the beginning of his pontificate Pius IX did work towards some measure of Italian federation and he made an important move towards Italian unity by concluding a customs union with Tuscany and Piedmont.

However, he believed that the great powers would never allow the emergence of an Italian league with the Pope as its head and he declared, 'I will not do what Mazzini wants, and I cannot do what Gioberti wants'. The Pope was well aware that the support of radicals like Mazzini and Garibaldi put him in a false position. Even in his first encyclical, *Qui pluribus*, he pointed out that he was in fundamental agreement with his predecessor and had nothing in common with some of the political and philosophical 'liberals'. However, it became impossible for him to restrain the popular enthusiasm; 'We shall make him the fatted ox of politics', Mazzini cynically declared, 'we shall suffocate him with flowers'.

As a result, the Pope became identified with the forces of revolution and every demonstration or insurrection during 1847 and 1848 claimed his support. Mazzini himself told the Pope that he was the most powerful man in Italy and even in Europe. But Metternich who believed that a 'liberal' Pope, at least as a secular ruler, was quite impossible, was forming a very different impression:

> Each day the Pope shows himself more lacking in any practical sense . . . a good priest, he has never turned his mind towards matters of government. Warm of heart and weak of intellect, he has allowed himself to be taken and ensnared, since assuming the tiara, in a net from which he no longer knows how to disentangle himself, and if matters follow their natural course, he will be driven out of Rome.

The Pope also became involved in a quarrel with Austria over the occupation of Ferrara, and his bold stand against Metternich, who was eventually forced to withdraw, further fanned the flames of Italian nationalism. Pius IX, however, was merely defending his own territory in resisting the Austrians. He had no intention of merging the Papal States within a united Italy nor of declaring war on Catholic Austria. Furthermore, it was becoming increasingly clear that the ambitions of the 'liberal' revolutionaries were not necessarily compatible with the interests or even with the freedom of the Church. The seven Catholic cantons of Switzerland were being crushed by the 'liberal' and Protestant Federal Diet, while the King of Piedmont was more interested in extending the territory and influence of the House of Savoy than in federating the various Italian states.

A revolution in Sicily during 1848 spread to the Neapolitan mainland and when the north of Italy rose against the Austrians the Italian nationalists became convinced that joint military action would provide the best defence against the threat of Austrian retaliation. It was in this context that the Pope made a famous statement in which he pointed out that the Church could best be defended by Catholics throughout the world:

> A great gift from heaven is this: one of the many gifts which He has bestowed on Italy; that a bare three million of our subjects possess two hundred million brothers of every nation and every tongue. In times very different from these, when the whole Roman world was disordered, this fact remained the salvation of Rome. Owing to it, the ruin of Italy was never complete. And this will always be her protection so long as the Apostolic See stands in her midst. Therefore, O Lord God, bless Italy and preserve for her this most precious gift of all – the faith!

Unfortunately, this last remark was interpreted as the proclamation of a crusade and a condemnation of Austria, and the Bishop of Milan, for example, allowed his seminarians to volunteer for the Italian forces.

With the success of the revolutionary movements, Italian rulers began to grant constitutions and the Pope himself was forced to grant a constitution in Rome. When a revolution also broke out in Vienna and Metternich was forced to fly from the country, it seemed that the time had now come to drive the Austrians out of Italy. But for the Pope to have joined an Italian uprising would have involved identifying himself with republican revolutionaries as well as risking the danger of a schism in Austria. On 29 of April, therefore, in a papal allocution, Pius IX censured the extreme Italian nationalists, repudiated the Italian *Risorgimento* and made it clear that he would never declare war on Austria in the interests of Italian nationalism. The Italians were infuriated and the Pope's popularity immediately sank to the level of that of his predecessor. What came to be known as 'the Roman Question' had now been raised: if the Pope's role as an Italian secular ruler was incompatible with his spiritual office, should he not be expected to surrender his temporal power since this was harming the Italian nation as a whole?

The defeat of the Italians by the Austrians was followed by the return of disillusioned volunteers and regular troops to Rome. Nationalist extremists organized the murder of Rossi, the realistic and liberal premier of the Papal States, a revolution broke out and the Pope's cabinet resigned. The Pope himself, now without a Government, refused to accept democratic demands which would, in effect, have ended the Papal States. He became a prisoner of the revolution before escaping to Gaeta and going into exile. Meanwhile, republicans from all over Italy flocked to Rome where, on 9 February 1849, the Assembly voted to end the temporal power of the Pope and to establish a democratic Roman Republic.

The popular appeal of the Roman Republic in history and the criticisms of the reforms and policies of Pio Nono were not necessarily shared by the Pope's own contemporaries. Pius IX should not be judged at this time in the light of his later and more reactionary career. He had carried out large and important measures of social and political reform; few contemporary rulers had treated their subjects so well and he had the reputation of being the most lenient of monarchs. The Protestant ambassador of Holland claimed 'that never has a Sovereign, so worthy of the love and devotion of his subjects of all classes, found himself so basely and so completely abandoned as at the present time', while an English officer in Rome at the time of the Pope's flight spoke of 'the ingratitude of a cowardly and short-sighted people to a liberal-minded but weak prince'.

'The Year of Revolutions' began with unrest in Lombardy and an insurrection in Sicily. An agricultural crisis in 1846 had been followed by a financial crisis in 1847 which checked investment, limited credit and led to an industrial crisis. There was widespread famine in the spring of 1847 which caused food riots, while the economic crisis resulted in unemployment in industrial areas before the end of the year. In spite of inevitable differences, the revolutions in Europe during 1848 were simultaneous and often inspired by a common ideology. Lamennais and *L'Avenir* had provided one of the ideological influences and for a time it seemed that the whole of Europe was attempting to reorganize itself according to the principles of democracy and nationalism. But although the various revolutions achieved some social and political results, sooner or later in every country and in almost every respect, the revolutionaries were defeated as people rallied to conservatism.

On 10 February 1848 Lacordaire had preached a panegyric on Daniel O'Connell in Notre Dame and two weeks later the revolution broke out in France. The revolution of 1848 was as favourable to the Church in France as that of 1830 had been hostile and on the whole it was welcomed by Catholics, though Dupanloup and Montalembert had some reservations. The revolutionaries treated the clergy with great respect and it seemed that the Church would now secure the complete freedom which Catholics desired. Catholics had opposed the previous regime which refused them some of the liberties they demanded; and although many Catholics still hoped for a restoration of the Bourbons, they were prepared to settle for greater ecclesiastical freedom, especially since a Bourbon restoration was considered quite impossible at least for the time being.

Piux IX congratulated the people of Paris on the veneration which they had shown towards the Church and the Archbishop of Paris immediately accepted the new republic and gave his allegiance to the new government. Cardinal de Bonald rejoiced that France no longer needed to envy north America, while the Bishop of Langres who would later become a leading Ultramontane conservative now proclaimed that:

> There is nothing more profoundly – indeed, I would say more exclusively – Christian than these three words that are inscribed on the national flag: LIBERTY, EQUALITY, FRATERNITY. Far from repudiating these sublime words, Christianity claims them as its own work, its own creation: it is Christianity, and Christianity alone, that has introduced them, that has consecreated them, and caused them to be practised in the world.

Four bishops and thirty-two priests were on the electoral lists, three bishops and twenty priests were elected including Lacordaire who became a deputy for Marseilles and who took his seat in his Dominican habit on the extreme left, not far from Lamennais. Some of the clergy blessed newly planted trees of liberty, but few of them survived and their premature demise was later attributed by anti-clericals to poisoned holy water.

Liberal Catholics in their new periodical *Ère Nouvelle* maintained that there was no opposition in principle between Catholicism and Democracy, and they argued that the time had come for Catholics to follow the example of the Pope and accept democratic institutions. Even the Ultramontane Louis Veuillot in the *Univers* was condemning the divine right of kings as Gallican and arguing that Catholic theology supported the divine right of peoples:

> The Europe of the Middle Ages was a confederation of Christian democracies. The legislation of the popes and councils was a legislation of liberty. The whole history of the Christian world for ten centuries is nothing but the story of the struggles for Christian liberty represented by the Church against the reactions and enter prises of pagan despotism. What else is there to be seen all the way

from the cross of Jesus Christ to the throne of Pius IX . . .?

However, this appearance of unity amongst French Catholics was largely superficial and the French Church was ill-equipped to deal with the emerging crises. From the beginning of the century the Church in France had been faced with the need to reconstruct the Church and with political problems associated with relations between Church and State. At the beginning of the Second Republic the reconstruction of the French Church was far from complete and the political attitudes of French Catholics were not finally determined when a third problem, the social problem, seemed to emerge dramatically from the background.

The development of Social Catholicism was an attempt to deal with the massive problems created by industrialization, urbanization, pauperism and the stratification of classes. It was reported that workers at Lyons were stunted, emaciated, permanently ill and living in shocking hovels. At one time, less than a quarter of the children born to the working classes in Nantes survived. At Lille some 23,000 out of a population of 70,000 were destitute and 3,000 of these lived in cellars. The working classes who felt betrayed by the revolution of 1830 had rioted in Paris and Lyons during 1831 and 1834, but these riots were brutally suppressed. Social Catholics believed in the possibility and the moral necessity of improving social structures and relieving the victims of industrialism. Social Catholicism was a reaction against a situation too often seen in the light of the predominant economic doctrines of *laissez faire*. It was widely believed that Government intervention would obstruct the automatic and beneficent operation of economic laws and free competition. Liberal and Social Catholics were sometimes opposed because the former were frequently associated with the economic liberalism of *laissez faire*, whereas Social Catholics believed that liberty was of little use to men who were dying of hunger.

Both conservatives and socialists, right and left-wing Catholics, played their part in the origin and development of Social Catholicism. Chateaubriand expressed his indignation at the 'excessive inequality of conditions and fortunes', while de Bonald criticized the exclusive search for wealth and the growth of an industry 'which cannot nourish those whom it brings into the world'. D'Eckstein warned men of property against making 'the lower orders of society a beast of burden' and from 1826 repeated his warnings in his newspaper *Le Catholique*. The Society of St Joseph founded in Paris during 1822 is a good example of the work of conservative Catholics. This organization provided employers with a supply of good workers; it trained them, insured them against sickness and provided education and welfare services especially for immigrants from the provinces. Several branches were established in provincial towns to provide links with Paris. In spite of its considerable success, the society was dissolved in 1830 on the fall of the Bourbons, because it was discredited by its legitimist associations.

Other conservative Social Catholics attempted a fundamental criticism of the structure of industrial society and proposed specific reforms such as legislation regulating child labour, working hours or housing conditions. Vicomte Alban de Villeneuve-Bargemont who served under the Bourbons, advocated Government schemes to improve working conditions, housing and education. He opposed *laissez faire* and supported Government intervention in the hopes that industrial development in France might avoid the pauperism which had resulted in England. Count Armand de Melun founded an organization to study scientifically the best ways of serving the poor and improving their conditions. He began the *Annales de la Charité*, lectured on behalf of unfranchized workers, prepared factual information and made concrete proposals to Parliament for solving social problems. The Society of St Francis Xavier, many of whose members were legitimists, became a type of workers' association which provided medical treatment and assistance during illness, free legal aid and funeral benefits. An employment bureau was established and the *Revue du Travail* was published monthly. The society spread rapidly; in 1845, within five years of its foundation, there were 15,000 members in Paris and 3,000 in Lyons.

Some legitimists, restricted in the public activities in which they were allowed to engage, used the conditions of the working classes as arguments or propaganda against later political regimes. These political conservatives were often motivated by a genuine sense of charity but they also believed in the virtues of the *ancien régime*. They contrasted the benefits of historic institutions such as guilds and corporations with the evils which had resulted from the isolation of the working class and 'liberal' individualism. They were heirs to a social tradition that they sought to recommend and looked to the past for a solution to contemporary problems, whereas Catholics of the left looked forward to the construction of a new democratic or even a socialist order.

L'Avenir published several important contributions on social reform and supported political measures such as the extension of the franchise as a means of achieving reform. Lamennais himself condemned those who,

> regard the poor man as a mere machine from which the largest possible profit is to be obtained within a given time . . . You will soon see to what excesses contempt of man can lead. You will have industrial helots who will be forced to imprison themselves in factories in order to earn a crust of bread . . . Are those men free? Necessity makes them your slaves.

Frederic Ozanam founded the Society of St Vincent de Paul whose members visited and made friends with the poor, provided funds for the children of prisoners, trained apprentices and took care of domestic servants. By 1839 there were some forty conferences in France and by 1848 282 conferences in France and one hundred and six outside. When the society celebrated its centenary in 1933, its members were numbered in hundreds of thousands who worked in almost every area throughout the world where Catholics could be found. By establishing the 'SVP', Ozanam was instrumental in opening the eyes of many Catholics to social problems and arousing the social conscience of Catholics in every part of the world.

Some left wing Catholics became early Christian Socialists, convinced of the need to reconcile and combine Catholicism and Socialism. Some Catholics moved towards Socialism; others like Buchez were Socialists who were converted to Catholicism. Philippe Buchez was one of the first Christian Socialists; 'Christianity and revolution are one and the same thing', he said, 'and the Church's only fault is in not being revolutionary'. As early as 1829 Buchez denounced 'the exploitation of man' which resulted in vice 'no less among the exploiters than among the hapless exploited'. He condemned the length of working hours, the unsuitable employment of women and children. He rejected charity or policies of resignation and recommended the peaceful establishment of equality through association, the Workers' Productive Association, which would enable workers to become their own employers – the owners of the capital and the tools of their labour. Between 1840 and 1850 Buchez influenced a group of working men who published the journal *L'Atelier* which attacked capitalism, advocated a revival of the ecclesiastical condemnation of usury, supported the right of association, and criticized the St Vincent de Paul Society for concentrating too much on charity or alms and too little on the need for economic, social and political reform. One of the contributors to *L'Atelier* later became a secular priest and four others became Jesuits or Dominicans.

As a result of these various activities of right and left wing Social

Catholics, it is not surprising that in 1845 the Bishop of Annecy should have denounced the abuses of capitalism and demanded Government legislation to defend the working classes or that the Archbishop of Cambrai should have issued a pastoral letter on the 'Law of Labour' which manifested a real awareness of social problems and even foreshadowed the encyclical *Rerum Novarum* by Leo XIII. However, these bishops were exceptional and well in advance of the leadership or lack of it which was being offered by the popes in Rome. In the encyclical *Mirari vos* Gregory XVI had condemned all forms of liberalism except the one which was not even mentioned, economic liberalism, which left the working classes at the mercy of capitalism.

As a young priest, Mastai-Ferretti had supported the rights of the workers to share in the profits of their labours and his library included many books on the social problem and the need to reform working conditions. But, as Pope, he became totally preoccupied with political questions, and the Pope who so bitterly condemned liberalism and socialism failed to condemn social injustice. Similarly the French bishops as a whole proved to be ignorant to the point of being obtuse in dealing with social and economic problems and their example was followed by the majority of French Catholics who were either indifferent or ignorant when they were not simply reactionary. In 1842, the *Abbé* Luc published a book on the question of pauperism from the social and political point of view in which he maintained that,

> Poverty, considered as the necessary lot of the larger part of mankind, is by no means an evil . . . It serves as a basis for authority, increases courage, shows up merit, works marvels, and is useful and advantageous to government.

The prospect of social reform seemed to improve with the revolution of 1848 and a group of Social Catholics including Lacordaire and Ozanam founded a newspaper, *Ere Nouvelle*, of which Archbishop Affre was a patron. They effectively began the first Christian democrat movement in France as their prospectus declared:

> There are two forces only that still count – Jesus Christ and the people. An alliance between them will be the salvation of France and it is, therefore, the duty of Catholics to accept the Republic that comes from the people.

Ere Nouvelle was explicitly republican and democratic, it openly referred to a 'Christian economy' and 'Christian Socialism', and advocated a policy of social reorganization. The newspaper supported legislation to protect children, to provide for workers who were sick or old, advocated a reduction in working hours, demanded a more just distribution of wealth, suggested adopting a graduated income-tax instead of indirect taxation, recommended partnership and profit sharing, and supported compulsory arbitration in industrial disputes.

Ozanam once warned his supporters: 'Do not be afraid if wicked men of wealth treat you as communists', but the first number of *Ere Nouvelle* was immediately repudiated by leading Catholics including Dupanloup, Montalembert who described Lacordaire as a sycophantic demagogue, and Veuillot who dubbed the newspaper '*Erreur Nouvelle*'. Many Liberal Catholics were too concerned with political problems and too influenced by the theories of *laissez faire* to show much awareness of the social problems with which the writers of *Ere Nouvelle* were attempting to deal. Some of the Ultramontanes showed a greater awareness of social problems, but Veuillot, for example, who once supported the principle of freedom of association for all workers, eventually became simply conservative and filled French Catholics with a horror of Socialism. Originally, *Ere Nouvelle* enjoyed a circulation of about 20,000, but it would quickly become one of the casualties of the tragic events which were about to follow.

The revolution of 1848 was political rather than social; members of the Assembly were predominantly 'liberal' or 'conservative' and they proceeded to adopt conservative measures. The revolution had made an already bad economic situation even worse. Business stagnated, unemployment increased and, in an effort to ease the social problem of unemployment, the Government originally embarked on a policy of providing employment by initiating a series of public works. However, the increasing numbers employed in unproductive labour were not only expensive, but seemed to form an army of men ready for another revolution. The Government quickly changed its policy, cancelled the public works and conscripted all men under the age of twenty five into the army. There followed three days of mob violence as a violent proletarian insurrection broke out in Paris.

Monsignor Affre, the Archbishop of Paris, attempted to mediate between the two sides, but he was shot in the back by a stray bullet. The rebels carried him on a stretcher of interlocked rifles to a local presbytery where they assured him of their sorrow and their gratitude for his efforts. The Archbishop. for his part, expressed the hope that his would be the last blood to be shed, but he was to be disappointed. The insurrection was ruthlessly suppressed by the Government. There was no evidence that the Archbishop was killed by the rebels, in fact there was some evidence to the contrary. But the insurgents were held responsible since it was obvious that he would not have died if the rebellion had not broken out. His funeral was turned into a triumph and it was said that French people had never been so well disposed to the Church, but the nature of this support might well have disturbed Archbishop Affre.

Conservative forces throughout the country were appalled at the prospect of anarchy and the threat to property, law and order. The way was opening for the advent of a 'strong man', Louis Napoleon, the *coup d'etat* and the Second Empire. In the meantime even many non-Catholics and anti-clericals were turning to the Church as the institution which could best secure the obedience of the people. As Ozanam later remarked, 'There is not a Voltairian burdened with an income of a few thousand francs who is not anxious to send everybody to Mass, provided he doesn't have to go himself'. Renan described them as 'Christians by fear', acting on the recommendations of Voltaire who preferred his wife and servants to believe in God on the grounds that he would then be cuckolded and robbed less frequently. However, most Catholics and their priests willingly co-operated with the forces of law and order since they themselves belonged to those sections of society, nobility, bourgeoisie and peasantry, which had most to lose from any attack on or redistribution of property and had least knowledge of the problems caused by industrialization.

Few of the bishops understood the real causes of the revolution. The Bishop of Chartres issued a pastoral in which he stated:

> They say that the Republic dates from Calvary, and the revolution is Christianity. No, Jesus Christ never mentioned political liberty in his discourses. The word 'liberty' does not appear even once in the Gospel. Far from prescribing a form of government, he declared that his kingdom is not of this world . . . Likewise when St Paul said, 'My brethren, you are called to liberty', he meant liberty from the passions, not this unbridled liberty of the revolutionaries who, it seems, would like to see the terrible days of 1793 again, and who dare to say 'property is robbery' . . . What would become of France if she fell under the yoke of such rulers? But no! God will not allow her to be handed over defenceless and for ever to a horde of cannibals and to myriads of hangmen's assistants'.

The Archbishop of Rheims regarded democracy as 'the heresy of our time, more dangerous and more difficult to overcome than Jansenism'. The French bishops as a whole attributed the insurrection of 1848 to the subversive teachings of socialists and dangerous ideas instilled in the minds of the people, while the only 'solutions' which they were able to recommend included the revival of Catholic teaching, piety and private charity.

Ozanam tried to remind the forces of law and order that although they had 'crushed the revolt; you still have a foe in poverty'. But French Catholics almost unanimously joined with the party of order and the Altar was allied, not this time with the Throne, but with money and the social order. Clerical members of the Assembly remained silent as the socialist Pierre Leroux called on them to intercede on behalf of arrested insurgents. The Liberal Catholic periodical, *Le Correspondant,* declared: 'We are not the ones to stay the hands of justice out of a sentimentality that has nothing particularly Christian about it'. Veuillot maintained that society needed slaves and that poverty was part of the law of God; he roundly declared, 'We do not admit that the workers have a strict legal right to demand anything'. Even Montalembert believed that 'Nothing is really useful or fruitful except private charity' and he called on the poor to avoid covetousness, to resign themselves to their poverty and so to merit an eternal compensation and reward.

Ere Nouvelle continued to maintain its alliance with the forces of democracy and argued that fear of socialism should not be used to reject just social reforms. However, two months after the insurrection the discouraged Lacordaire gave up his connection with the newspaper. The bishops undermined its circulation by boycotting it and forbidding the clergy to read it. Circulation dropped to a mere 8,000 and it was eventually sold, passing out of the hands of democratic Social Catholics into the hands of a legitimist. This was not to be a happy period for Social Catholics. On the 29th of April 1849 a group of socialist priests organized a banquet in Paris where they toasted 'Jesus of Nazareth the father of socialism' and 'the union of democracy and Christianity'. But they were rejected by most of the faithful as well as their bishops; they indulged in quarrels amongst themselves and their movement as such came to an end with the *coup d'etat* of Louis Napoleon.

When Louis Napoleon stood for the presidency there were two issues of immediate interest to French Catholics, the freedom of education and the restoration of the Pope to Rome. Although Napoleon gave satisfaction on both points and was also being hailed as the saviour of the nation from anarchy and irreligion, Catholics were neither united nor consistent in supporting him, nor were they influenced by the same reasons. Archbishop Sibour of Paris supported the other principal contestant, Cavaignac, whereas Dupanloup urged Catholics to support Napoleon in the interest of secure government and because he had promised to meet their demands, though he later regretted this move. Montalembert also feared revolution and at first welcomed the dictatorship of Louis Napoleon, though he too quickly regretted his folly.

At the time of the June rising the whole of the middle class, monarchists as well as republicans, united against the insurgents. But when Frenchmen voted for their President in December, Catholics on the whole voted with the monarchists. In fact, the Catholic political party which emerged at the time refused to accept Catholic republicans and was no longer 'Catholic before everything', but primarily conservative and monarchist. This breach between Catholics and republicans had hardly been confirmed in the elections when the Roman Question turned it into a bitter conflict; in the summer of 1849, a French expeditionary force overthrew the Roman Republic and restored the papal monarchy.

The middle class reaction to the events of 1848 began that process of the 'Christianization' of the middle classes in France, though the mass of the people continued to be indifferent or hostile to the fate of the Catholic Church. The irreligious middle class of the 1830s were the grandparents and great-grandparents of the supporters of Catholic Action in the Fourth Republic. Nominal Catholics, Catholics by fear or by prudence, eventually gave way to a generation of devout Catholics and real Christians. Some historians, of course, have argued that the 'rechristianization' of the middle classes took place as the 'dechristianization' of the masses continued. But in order to understand the 'dechristianization' of European society, it is important to abandon the myth of an earlier 'Christian' epoch. The notion of a 'Christian Middle Ages', at least in so far as the essentially rural masses are concerned, is a legend which is increasingly being challenged by contemporary historians. 'Christian Europe' was a social-intellectual-cultural complex rather than a historical or geographical union of converted believers. It is even arguable that this majestic complex had to decline before the essential mission of Christianity, that of converting the world, could begin again; gregarious conformity had to be ended before it was possible to demand individual conversions.

Before it is possible to discuss the phenomenon of 'de-Christianization' in the modern world, it is also necessary to ask to what extent the mass of the people had in fact been christianized by the outbreak of the French Revolution and how far the Christianity which they had been taught was faithful to the spirit of the Gospel. The fact that the 'Christianity' of the *Ancien Régime* still included to the extent that it did, magic and superstition, constraint and conformity, as well as practices and doctrines which had little to do with the message of Christ, inevitably raises the question how far it is still possible to speak of the 'dechristianization' of the modern world. What seems to have emerged by the eve of the French Revolution was a divergence between a qualitative religion or a greater fidelity on the part of some Christians to a better appreciation of the Gospel message, and a quantitative adherence or general conformism which would later break under the pressure of events. In other words, the process of christianization was far from complete at the end of the eighteenth century when illiteracy was widespread and when political revolution, industrialization and urbanization were about to throw both clergy and laity into a state of total confusion.

Two other points might also be made. In the first place, dechristianization is 'news' for historians who too easily take for granted the many and unseen works of charity carried out on the parochial or the individual level. French Catholics not only supported the conferences of St Vincent de Paul or the diocesan associations of St Joseph at home, but they also provided personnel and money for the Lazarist schools in Constantinople and the Holy Land, for the hospitals of the Sisters of St Vincent de Paul in India, China and Korea, the establishments of the White Fathers in Algeria or the Franciscan Missionaries of Mary in China. Secondly, and as the Theophilanthropists had pointed out earlier, the 'Orthodox' were not always the best preachers of 'Christianity'. Claude Antoine Corbon who was to reject the Church because of its later identification with social and political reaction, declared in 1877:

> France is being decatholicized, as everyone can see . . . but it is not being dechristianized . . . Modern society, although it is not religious in your fashion, is more deeply, more generally Christian than that inspired by ultramontanism and Jesuitism.

The immediate impact of nominal Catholics or Catholics by fear on the French Church was somewhat mixed. They certainly contributed to the rapid improvement in the Church's financial position, though they delayed the development of Social Catholicism. However, their most significant service to the Church was the development of a secondary education outside the State system. The architect of this reform was the Minister of Education appointed by Louis Napoleon, the Vicomte de Falloux, a leading member of the Catholic party. The Church recognized the right of the University to control primary and secondary education, while the State allowed the Church to co-operate in running the University. Elementary school teachers were to be appointed by municipal councils and were subject to the supervision of mayors and parish priests. Secondary schools could be opened if the headmaster had the necessary qualifications and examinations were to be conducted by members of the University. However, the bishops themselves could appoint the assistant masters and there were no conditions about their competence. The University retained its monopoly over education, but the Higher Council for Public Education could henceforth include members of the hierarchy, while the clergy were also to be represented on education councils at departmental level.

The Falloux Law which was passed on the 15th of March 1850 would eventually play a great part in winning over an important part of the middle class to the Catholic Church. At the time, however, many Catholics including Veuillot and many of the bishops opposed the Law because it did not give complete freedom to the Church; after all, only sixty years before, the Church had enjoyed a monopoly in the field of education, while the rights of Truth could not be restricted by secular governments! Furthermore, Veuillot complained, the Falloux Law, which he condemned as 'Falloux *fallax*' had not been submitted to the Roman authorities for approval! However, the Pope himself later congratulated Montalembert and Falloux, and he instructed the French bishops to put the Law into operation.

The terrified middle classes who had supported the Falloux Law as a defence against social disorder also supported the political repression of socialists and radical democrats. Most Catholics joined the middle classes in their support for the dictatorship of Louis Napoleon who in turn offered to the Church a protection which it was not unwilling to accept. Napoleon gave seats in the Senate to French Cardinals, appointed chaplains to Government institutions and gave five million francs – from the property of the House of Orleans – to the poorer clergy. The police enforced Sunday observance, generals and prefects attended Mass in full uniform, hostile plays and publications were censored.

When civil liberties were restricted, the Pope himself congratulated the French Ambassador on the authoritarianism of the new regime; the

Monsignor Dupanloup, Bishop of Orleans

liberties of the French Church – freedom of press, speech and association – were, of course, maintained. The religious budget was increased regularly and rose from over thirty-nine million francs to some forty-eight million francs. These measures won the support of Catholics in spite of the fact that Napoleon had made no fundamental change in the position of the French Church. He simply wanted the support of the institution against revolutionary and socialist propaganda. As a result of Government support, however, the number of priests increased, old orders continued to revive and new ones were established, the numbers and percentage of children educated in Catholic schools increased, while respect for religion was inculcated even in State schools as hostile teachers were removed.

The result of this new union of Throne and Altar or, as Montalembert said later, 'of Bodyguard and Sacristy' was 'to identify the Church's cause with that of absolutism'. Left wing Social Catholicism tended to disappear until the emergence of Christian democrats towards the end of the century, and the development of Social Catholicism was again dominated by that of its conservative or right wing. Count Armand de Melun proved to be the most important conservative Social Catholic during this time. He secured the passing of valuable measures of social reform and he interested the wives of politicians in his society for the organization of charitable or social relief. His proposals embraced maternity-hospitals, day-nurseries, orphan asylums, popular education, vocational training, welfare associations, saving associations, housing improvements and the regulation of working hours.

As a member of the National Assembly, de Melun secured the appointment of a committee to study the question of public assistance for the poor which produced a series of reports and assisted in passing a body of legislation dealing with unhealthy housing, pension schemes, mutual aid societies, the education and protection of juvenile offenders, outdoor relief, medical services and sanitation. His recommendation that friendly societies might help to enable workers to cope with the hazards of an industrial system was adopted by Napoleon himself as one of his own social reforms. These societies were increasingly successful and by 1869 there were 6,000 societies with over 900,000 members. Payments were made in cases of sickness, injury and death, but not in cases of unemployment.

Frédéric Le Play was another influential figure of the Napoleonic regime. In 1864 he published a book on social reform which Montalembert described as 'the most powerful book of the age'. Le

Play was opposed to economic liberalism which destroyed the family and degraded men for the sake of profit. But he was equally opposed to socialism or State control. The ideal society, he maintained, should be 'monarchical in the family and in the State', but 'democratic in the commune and aristocratic in the province and in industry'; an organic and harmonious society based on order and justice. Such was the origin of Paternalism or Corporatism; an attempt to help the workers without consulting them or associating them with the decisions which governed their lives. Such an approach tended to divert those Catholics who adopted it from supporting other policies which were more in keeping with the social and political developments of the time.

By this time, most Catholic societies or organizations tended to suffer from a common defect of right wing or conservative social reformers, that of adopting a paternalist or patronizing attitude which simply alienated the more enterprising and increasingly secularist workers. Social Catholics were active in providing guilds or clubs for apprentices and workers, but these were mostly under clerical control and tended to be politically reactionary. Catholics were, on the whole, suspicious of workers' control and trades unions, which therefore developed independently of Christian influences and often became anti-clerical. With other writers who produced histories of the Church's charitable activities and who praised the institutions of the *ancien régime,* Charles Périn advocated the formation of guilds. Many of the workers, on the other hand, were justly suspicious of the past and the adoption of historical solutions for contemporary problems.

Almost all French Catholics and their bishops supported the establishment of Napoleon's Second Empire. On the day before the crucial plebiscite the Bishop of Arras recommended Catholics to:

> support this astonishing Prince who has dared to undertake the well nigh supernatural task of saving France. Of him we can say what the Holy Scriptures say of divine wisdom . . . She reacheth from one end of the world to the other with full strength, and ordereth all things graciously.

Another supporter of the new Emperor was the Bishop of Amiens who began life as a royalist, supported *L'Avenir* in 1830, returned to legitimism, though he was also prepared to request a bishopric from Louis Philippe, became a democratic republican in 1848, and finally supported the Napoleonic establishment as a bishop.

Bishops who had celebrated the union of the Church with the Republic in 1848, celebrated its union with the Empire in 1852. The new Emperor was praised in sermons and pastorals: he was a man at the right hand of God whose words were perhaps the most beautiful to fall from the mouth of any Christian prince; it was not enough to say that he was a great man because he was clearly the efficacious and glorious instrument of Him who alone is great. When the Emperor visited Britanny in 1858, Monsignor Brossais Saint-Marc told him that of all the kings since St Louis, he was the most devoted to the Church and to its mission of civilization and progress. The bishop was rewarded and became an archbishop, as Falloux put it, earning his tip like a cab-driver. Tocqueville wrote to Montalembert:

> There is nothing to suprise or pain me in the fact that the journalistic canaille (Veuillot, etc.,) should have thrown themselves at the feet of the new master; it is a natural evolution. But the black ingratitude towards liberty, so shameful a retraction, such base flattery on the part of the preceptors of morals, the guardians of dignity and of true greatness – that really is too much!

With the coming of the Second Empire, Veuillot had rediscovered the basic incompatibility between Catholicism and democracy. Originally Veuillot had been less than enthusiastic in support of Napoleon, but he quickly rallied to the new regime, attacked those who were suspected of being lukewarm and excluded from the ranks of true Catholics those who did not agree with him. Dupanloup, Montalembert and especially Lacordaire, who for a time stood entirely alone, were abused on every possible occasion. Veuillot neatly summarised his own position when he wrote:

> As regards liberty, we ask liberty for the Church, that is, liberty for what is good . . . We no longer consider, as we used to do till 1848, that liberty for good necessarily involves liberty for what is bad . . . Let what is good be free, but not what is bad: that is how we understand liberty.

As Montalembert remarked, Veuillot's tactics amounted to saying that when I am weaker, I ask for freedom because that is your principle, but when I am stronger, I take your liberty from you because that is my principle.

The pattern of events in France during the nineteenth century seemed at last to have crystallized. The Catholic Church was not on the side of the France of the left, of reform or of freedom; it was closely identified with the France of the right, of order and of authority. Catholics who believed in the myth of a Christian France destroyed by the Revolution would soon be opposed by a counter-myth of a Revolutionary France which was the standard bearer of liberty. According to Catholics, republicans interpreted freedom as freedom to subvert the Catholic Church. According to republicans, Ultramontane Catholics equated freedom with ecclesiastical and clerical domination. In the long term the spiritual depth of the French Church would guarantee its survival and the revival of its influence in a new form when the old trappings of prestige and wealth were finally taken away. In the meantime, however, the power and influence of the Church was exaggerated and in terms of democratic politics, deceptive; it could not translate the nominal allegiance of French Catholics into political support even at the most critical moments in its history.

French Liberal Catholics were more realistic and dreaded the unpopularity which the Church might suffer if a future Republican regime identified Catholicism with the forces of reaction or absolutism. They appreciated that for Catholics to support a dictatorship so quickly after welcoming a democracy would cause that bitter hostility and distrust among democrats and republicans which endured even into the twentieth century. Catholics who had just acclaimed a republic now seemed prepared to sacrifice personal freedom, democratic government and social reform for their own immediate political ends and this difference of attitude was one of the main factors which contributed towards the increasing divisions between French Catholics which would widen dramatically during the next few years.

'If another revolution broke out today', wrote Montalembert in 1863, 'one trembles at the thought of what the clergy would suffer'. By then, Lacordaire himself would be dead. More than anyone else, he had tried to persuade his fellow Frenchmen that Catholics respected the past without necessarily attempting to restore it; they simply wanted to secure their own rights and freedoms, while respecting those of others. Yet, between 1848 and 1861, Lacordaire saw clerical and lay extremists attempting to regain former privileges and successfully reviving old prejudices by denying personal liberties. Lacordaire himself would die a 'penitent Catholic and an impenitent liberal'; he was not one of those who, as he wrote on his deathbed,

having claimed 'liberty for all' – civil, political and religious liberty –

have unfurled the standard of the Inquisition, and of Philip II, shamelessly eaten their own words, taunted their old companions in arms with their steadfastness and fidelity, dishonoured the Church and hailed Caesar with acclamations that would have excited the scorn of Tiberius.

Bishop Dupanloup was not, like Lacordaire, a liberal by instinct. Originally, he had been totally opposed to *L'Avenir* and those supporters of Lamennais with whom he was later to identify himself. However, Dupanloup was a better judge of character than of political principles; he put the interests of the Church before his own inclinations and in due course became a liberal by conviction. This son of a seduced peasant girl had been a legitimist priest who once had three queens attending his catechism classes during the Bourbon Restoration. He was a brilliant student and, as Director of Studies, he turned his seminary into a leading centre of intellectual life. It was he who persuaded the dying Talleyrand to sign a retractation. He also realized that the young seminarian, Renan, was not simply suffering from intellectual difficulties but had actually lost his faith; Renan who was then persuaded to turn away from the priesthood remained grateful all his life to the *Abbé* Dupanloup.

Dupanloup was Bishop of Orleans from 1849 until 1878. He attempted to reform the education and the training of his clergy and embarked on a programme of 'rechristianizing' his diocese which showed some results between 1858 and 1862 before falling away after 1865. There were many reasons for this failure including the inability of the clergy to adapt; their social position, their intellectual approach, their previous training and their prejudices meant that it was almost impossible for them to appreciate the political and social transformations which were taking place. In any case, the prospect of a large scale 'rechristianization' was probably by now a romantic dream; a personal religion of commitment has probably been and always will be the privilege of the few who are chosen.

For some time Napoleon continued the policy of uniting his imperialism and Catholicism, though some Catholics like Lacordaire remained critical of the Second Empire and some of his Bonapartist supporters were hostile to the Catholic Church. Furthermore, when loyalty to the Pope clashed with loyalty to the Emperor, Veuillot deserted Napoleon and the *Univers* was suppressed. In the meantime, however, guided by Veuillot, French Ultramontanism became increasingly clerical and anti-democratic, rather than popular and anti-Gallican. It was perhaps typical of the man that Louis Veuillot should have been converted on a visit to Rome as a result of the influence of a Catholic family and that he did not bother to seek preliminary instructions before making up his mind. He was self-taught, unintellectual, simple and rough, in manner and appearance, with a very engaging personality. With the best of intentions, he was an optimistic moralist who defended the cause of absolute truth by cudgelling friends and opponents alike. Although he was clumsy and even cruel, he was a brilliant writer and a formidable polemicist.

Veuillot was the type of apologist who preserved the self-respect of Catholics by derisively destroying their anti-clerical opponents. He was the Christian advocate or the theological controversialist who could best explain the faith to unbelievers and correct the views of his fellow Catholics. Eventually, Veuillot spoke for a whole generation of French Catholics and came to be regarded by many non Catholics as an official representative of the Church, though some of his views, attitudes and expressions were later echoed by *Action Francaise*. He was a man who threw himself into obedience, assimilated every item of devotion, extended orthodoxy to cover every belief and defended every aspect of Catholic history; concessions or compromises were signs of weakness. Thus the Inquisition was a divine institution, the massacre of St Bartholomew's Day was a justifiable measure of rigour, Luther should have been burned and John Hus should have been burned sooner; unfortunately, no European prince at the time of the Reformation had sufficient piety and statesmanship to undertake a crusade against the infected countries.

The increasing influence and success of Veullot inevitably led to increasing divisions and bitterness among French Catholics. Veuillot supported the idea of a Catholic party, whereas Ozanam had warned, 'I should not like a *party* to be Catholic, because then the *nation* could not be'. Divisions among French Catholics had been manifested as early as 1845 when a committee including Lacordaire, Dupanloup and Montalembert had been appointed to moderate Veuillot's tone as editor of the *Univers.* At this time the divisions were largely over matters of method rather than of opinion. Following his experience with Lamennais, Lacordaire knew only too well that provocative language could divide rather than unite, might alienate rather than convert. However, Veuillot remained in effective and rumbustious control as the events of 1848 created further and deeper divisions.

Originally Liberal Catholicism in France should probably be seen as an attitude of mind, respecting the value of political liberty, for example, rather than as a theological position. In this sense, Liberal Catholics included democrats and liberals, Gallicans and Ultramontanes, and they won the support of some of the professional classes as well as some of the French bishops. At one time the French Academy almost became a Liberal Catholic club with Lacordaire and Montalembert, Dupanloup and Falloux, while their periodical, *Le Correspondant* became the most cultured and best informed religious review in the country. At first many of the Liberal Catholics might well have been united only by their opposition to Veuillot and the *Univers*. The Liberal Catholics and the supporters of Veuillot used various pretexts and issues in an effort to undermine each other, and appeals were frequently made to the Roman authorities who usually urged moderation. However, the Pope only once censured Veuillot's opinions and that in the case of the controversy with Dupanloup over Gaume's attack on the use of pagan classics in schools; Gaume recommended that they should be replaced with Christian classics such as the works of the Fathers of the Church.

1853 proved to be a decisive date in the quarrels between French Catholics. The Archbishop of Paris and Bishop Dupanloup condemned the *Univers* and Veuillot appealed to Rome. The Pope replied in the encyclical, *Inter Multiplices* in which, incidentally, he strongly approved of the adoption of the Roman liturgy throughout France and in which the French bishops were exhorted to be,

> generous in their encouragements, and to show their goodwill and their love towards those men who . . . devote the watches of the night to writing books and papers so that Catholic doctrine may be propagated and defended, so that the ancient rights of this Holy See and its acts may enjoy their full force, so that opinions and sentiments contrary to this Holy See may disappear, so that the darkness of error may be dissipated and the minds of men flooded with the blessed light of truth.

The bishops were forced to withdraw their condemnation with the best grace possible.

However, the most significant occasion on which the deep divisions among French Catholics were revealed was the Mortara case of 1858 which had profound repercussions throughout Europe. The Mortaras of Bologna were Jewish by race and by creed. One of their children was secretly baptized when he was seriously ill, but the child then recovered. According to Canon Law and the law of the Papal States, such a child was to be taken from his parents and placed in a Catholic school. Pope Benedict XIV had confirmed this rule in principle, though he had also expressed the opinion that it was harsh and that it would be better to leave the child with his family provided that they undertook not to put pressure on him. In 1858, however, the Holy Office took a different view. The child was snatched from his home and taken to Rome where he eventually became a religious. On behalf of Napoleon, the French Ambassador asked the Pope to return the child to his family. Pius IX expressed his regrets at the steps taken by the Holy Office but declined to interfere, while the *Giornale di Roma* declared that 'paternal authority and individual liberty are mere fancies'. It was now clear that the future of Liberal Catholicism was being increasingly jeopardized by the development of Ultramontanism. The Mortara case had once again raised the question of the temporal power and ecclesiastical autocracy. It also prepared French opinion for a shift in Napoleon's foreign policy as his Government became increasingly opposed to the growth of clericalism and Ultramontanism as well as irritated by the legitimism which was still widespread among French Catholics.

Giuseppe Garibaldi

IV: The triumph of Ultramontanism and the loss of the temporal power

The establishment of the Roman Republic in 1848 had been accompanied with manifestations of anti-Catholicism and anti-clericalism, mob violence and robberies, public immoralities and even murders. Public opinion throughout Europe, but especially in France, tended to favour the exiled Pope. Almost all governments offered to help and Queen Victoria sent a personal message of sympathy. Immediately before returning to Rome the Pope issued *Quibus Quantisque* in which he rejected any conditions of restrictions on his restored authority; he condemned the revolution and the notion that the Church might benefit from the loss of the temporal power. Pius IX refused to distinguish his spiritual and temporal power, but used the former to defend the latter. The Papal States were the Patrimony of St Peter, the material means given by God to defend the spiritual independence of the Pope.

The Papal States, the last theocracy in an increasingly nationalistic and anti-clerical age, became an international issue with the growth of Italian nationalism and as a result of the hostile propaganda of exiled revolutionary leaders especially in England. Many of these hostile criticisms of the papal regime were equally true of other repressive and secular regimes, but the fundamental issue involved in the case of the Holy See was unique. Furthermore, many of the contemporary opponents of the Pope's secular government were sincere Catholics who hoped to free the Church from its temporal preoccupations. The papal authorities, on the other hand, preferred to act from day to day in their efforts to preserve the temporal power and ignored the fundamental reforms which were needed. The plebiscite which ended the temporal power in 1870 was predictable, but revealing; only forty-six voters in Rome and 1,461 in the Papal States opposed the union with Italy, compared with 40,785 and 92,896 who favoured it.

Pio Nono himself was a man of deep personal and apostolic piety who, for example, showed himself to be devoted and industrious in working for the missionary expansion of the Church. However, he was politically inept and on his return from Gaeta he tried to save the

Church by restoring doctrinal 'orthodoxy' and imposing his own disciplinary authority. Priests or laymen who revealed their sympathies for new ideas usually found themselves condemned. Ventura was criticized for a speech which he made in praise of the Austrian revolutionaries, Rosmini's *Five Wounds of the Church* and Gioberti's works were put on the Index. On the other hand, the Pope positively encouraged his own supporters like Carlo Curci, a young Neapolitan Jesuit who founded the *Civilità Cattolica* which later played an important part in the success of Ultramontanism.

The Pope depended a great deal on his Secretary of State, Cardinal Giacomo Antonelli, who was only in minor orders, though this did not limit either his authority or his influence. Antonelli lacked both principles and intelligence; he could neither learn from the past nor anticipate the future, while what he lacked in political or theological insight, he made up for in his acquisitive instincts and luxurious living. A greedy man, Antonelli used his position to accumulate a large personal fortune for himself and his relations. He fiddled the papal finances and rigged the corn trade. When Cavour announced his abortive plan to solve the Roman Question in 1860, he made a secret agreement whereby Antonelli would receive three million lire compensation and his numerous brothers would retain their eminent positions. When the Cardinal died in 1876, his illegitimate daughter, lured on by that part of his fortune which so far had escaped her clutches, began a lawsuit which was rich in scandalous revelations.

Pius IX did not reject all reforms on his return to Rome in 1849. He continued to reform the political, juridical and administrative institutions of the state, to promote economic progress, expand trade and improve communications. The revolution in the Papal States during 1831 had been followed by a conference of foreign ambassadors in Rome who recommended the introduction of more laymen into higher administrative and judicial posts, greater independence for the municipalities, elected local councils and a partly elected central junta to control finances. All that happened at the time was the appointment of a committee of laymen to help the Papal Legate in governing the different provinces and the establishment of consultative and nominated provincial councils with some control over finances to express the wishes of the people. Pius IX, however, put the main provisions of the memorandum of 1831 into effect. A Council of State was established, elected provincial and municipal councils were restored, and far more laymen than clerics were employed in administrative positions, though the clergy tended to hold more of the higher posts.

After 1848, the Pope also became more cautious of offending friendly conservative powers like Austria and very careful not to encourage aggressive states like Piedmont or Italian revolutionaries for whom the 'separation' of Church and State simply meant the subordination of the Church to the State. The most significant examples of political reaction and the new alliance between Throne and Altar in Italy were to be found in the agreements made between Tuscany and the Holy See in 1851 and the concordat signed with Austria in 1855. The Austrian concordat in particular was bitterly condemned by European 'liberals'. The bishops were given complete freedom to communicate with Rome and they became the final arbiters in all religious matters. Ecclesiastical courts regained jurisdiction over matrimonial disputes and the Government enforced episcopal sanctions imposed on the clergy. Relations between the Papal States and the Kingdom of Sicilly were already very cordial, though a number of outstanding difficulties were settled. The close relations between the Pope and the reactionary rulers of Italy as well as his public expressions of approval for them inevitably alienated more liberal opinion both in Italy and throughout the world.

When the Pope fled to Gaeta in 1848 he had already become disillusioned with the obvious ambitions of Piedmont to create an independent Italian Kingdom in the north under the House of Savoy and he pointedly ignored Piedmont in his invitation to Catholic countries to restore his political authority. The Government in Piedmont became increasingly expansionist and secularist as it appreciated that the the movement towards Italian unity inevitably led to a conflict with the Holy See, whereas if Piedmont made an agreement with the Pope, such an agreement would have entailed a reconciliation with Austria. The Government of Piedmont was able to manifest its continuing devotion to the cause of Italian unity by adopting policies opposed to those adopted in the Papal States and other reactionary Italin States. Furthermore, since Piedmont had a parliament and enjoyed a free press, this was the only Italian State where it was possible to criticize papal policies.

In 1848 the Government in Piedmont passed laws which restricted the control of the Church over education and increased the power of the State. By 1849 the Church was being attacked in the popular press, anti-Catholic literature was being freely distributed, and hostile demonstrations were taking place. The King himself was subject to a Chamber of Deputies which was increasingly influenced by left wing anti-clericals even before Cavour came to power in 1852. Cavour effectively controlled developments in Piedmont until his death in 1861. He attacked the institutions as well as the property of Religious Orders and by identifying 'modern progress' and the *Risorgimento* with anti-Catholicism, he might be said to have prepared the way for the later papal reaction in the *Syllabus of Errors.*

Cavour's foreign policy was to extend the power of Piedmont over the whole of Italy. He hoped to win the support of France and Britain by supporting them in the Crimean War and he was bitterly disappointed when the question of Italy was not put on the agenda of the peace conference at Paris in 1856. Napoleon III himself attempted to balance the popular support for the Pope among French Catholics with the demands of his foreign and domestic policies, and the influence of left-wing or anti-clerical groups in France. He also had a personal affection for Pio Nono which again had to be balanced against a romantic sense of involvement in the Italian cause. During 1831 one of the insurgents, the future Napoleon III, accompanied by his mother, received hospitality from Archbishop Mastai-Ferretti who also provided them with papers which enabled them to cross the frontier into Switzerland.

In 1858 Cavour met Napoleon III at Plombières where he secured an alliance with France against Austria. The defence of the temporal power of the Pope was one of the few issues on which French Catholics could still be united. Consequently, when Napoleon III joined Cavour in an attempt to expel the Austrians from Italy, both Ultramontane and Liberal Catholics such as Dupanloup and Montalembert, and to some extent even Lacordaire, joined in the attack on the French Emperor in the interests of the freedom and independence of the Holy See. Once again, or so it seemed to non-Catholics, the Church in France was becoming even more firmly identified with the forces of reaction when it began to oppose Napoleon's foreign policy in the interests of papal theocracy after previously so enthusiastically supporting him.

Lacordaire himself had previously refused to defend the temporal power. He believed that the Pope could best fulfil his responsibilities with a small independent territory and a subscription collected from the Church throughout the world. In time the Roman Question became the infallible test of political conservatism both inside and outside the Church. When Lacordaire was first proposed as a member of the French Academy, it is said that François Guizot, a Protestant, and Adolphe Thiers, an atheist, had objected that he was not Roman enough to be reliable! Lacordaire continued to sympathize with the cause of the

Italians, but he later tried to show that the temporal power, properly and legitimately constituted, presented no real obstacle to Italian unity and he advocated the increasingly unrealistic notions of a liberal independent papacy within an Italian confederation.

Once war broke out, Napoleon had several reasons for wanting to end it and he quickly concluded an armistice at Villafranca. Nevertheless, although the war was short, it provided an opening for Piedmontese aggression and left the Pope totally dependent on France, the victor in the struggle between the two protecting Catholic powers. The retreat of the Austrians was followed by a revolution in the Legations where they had been providing a police force. A subsequent plebiscite invited King Victor Emmanuel to assume sovereignty over the Legations so that, as a result of the alliance between France and Piedmont, the Pope lost Umbria and the Marches as well as the Legations before the end of 1860.

A papal army was formed of Catholic volunteers from all over the world, but this was quite unable to deal with revolutions incited from outside, let alone recover the lost territories or defeat a Piedmontese invasion. The possibility that the Pope might be prepared to come to terms with the new situation in Italy was effectively destroyed by Cavour's policy of extending the anti-clerical laws of Turin to the rest of Italy and by the arrest an archbishop and a bishop who proved unsympathetic to the new regime. These incidents also contributed to the failure of yet another proposed agreement which attempted to safeguard the Pope's spiritual authority in return for his recognition of the loss of his temporal power.

Although Napoleon had deliberately allowed the Italians to overrun the Papal States which he was nominally defending, he could not allow the Pope to be expelled from Rome because of the interests of his own foreign policy as well as the demands of French Catholics at home. French Catholics were indignant, Austria and Spain had come out in support of the Pope, while England favoured the emergence of the new Italian Kingdom; this now included the whole of the peninsula, apart from Venetia and the Patrimony of St Peter, as a result of Garibaldi's success in the south – a consequence which Napoleon III had neither foreseen or intended. Napoleon became increasingly estranged from the Italian politicians, and, vacillating as ever, was again moving towards political conservatism and even clericalism. The French Emperor found himself in the unenviable position of having to maintain an army at Rome in support of the Pope, while at the same time incurring the hostility of Italian nationalists as well as Roman Catholics throughout the world.

In 1864 France and Italy agreed to the complete withdrawal of French troops from Rome within two years. The Government of Piedmont promised neither to attack nor to allow revolutionaries to attack the Papal States, to allow the formation of a papal army which might include foreigners, to bear a just proportion of the debts of the old Papal States and to remove the capital of Italy from Turin to another city of the Government's choice. Napoleon withdrew his army and allowed them to be replaced by volunteers. The Italians then allowed Garibaldi's volunteers to attack Rome, whereupon the French army was ordered back to Rome and Garibaldi was defeated. However, it was now evident to all that French troops and only French troops were once again guaranteeing the security of the Pope's last remaining dominions.

Liberal Catholics were faced with two main problems, the political problem of the temporal power of the Pope and the intellectual difficulties which resulted from the increasing divorce between the Church and contemporary scholarship. In France, for example, it seemed that as soon as Catholics gained power, their moral and intellectual influence began to decline. The alliance between the Church and the Second Empire coupled with such factors as liberal sympathy for the Italian nationalists or the growing intellectual obscurantism of the Ultramontanes contributed towards that identification of republicanism and Freemasonry, scholarship and anti-clericalism which became even more evident later. After all, Catholics themselves identified republicanism with anti-Christ, while the reactions of ecclesiastical authorities to intellectual developments meant that critical and independent scholars almost inevitably ignored or rejected the Church.

The Pope and the Ultramontanes, however, came to believe that there was an absolute dichotomy between Catholicism and the contemporary world, and they actually encouraged a Catholic withdrawal from modern society as well as modern thought. In 1850 the Roman clergy were ordered to wear the cassock instead of breeches and frock coat in order to distinguish the clergy more clearly from the 'men of the age, infected with revolutionary principles'. Donoso Cortès, one of the leading Spanish Ultramontanes, identified Catholicism with absolute good and modern civilization with absolute evil, while the Pope himself, as Wilfrid Ward remarked, 'took up the position that Christendom had apostatized. The appropriate action of Catholics was intense loyalty to the central power, unity among themselves, and separation from the outside world'.

The Ultramontanes emphasized the need for an increasing sense of dependence on the Holy See and not simply in matters of faith or morals. They manifested a strong personal attachment and loyalty to the person of the Holy Father, seeking his guidance and direction in all areas of human activity. New types of Catholic associations and publications contributed towards the development of Ultramontanism throughout the world and in 1860 the Pope himself encouraged the establishment of the *Osservatore Romano* in order that Catholics everywhere might be kept informed of the Holy Father's ideas and intentions.

One of the decisive factors in the rapid success of Ultramontanism was the character and personality of Pio Nono himself. When a priest visited Rome in 1842, he was surprised by the fact that no one even bothered to raise their hats when the Pope passed along the road. It was largely Piux IX who encouraged Ultramontanism and created that intense personal veneration for the Holy Father which was such an evident feature of later Catholicism. Pio Nono was not a saint; he had his weaknesses including a quick temper. But he conscientiously tried to fulfil the duties associated with his office. He was a man of deep and genuine piety who had a quiet confidence in God. He scrupulously made a daily meditation, delighted in saying his office on his knees and spent much time in prayer before the Blessed Sacrament. Furthermore, he was an attractive person, sympathetic and charming, intelligent and witty. He once blessed some Anglican clergymen with the words taken from the blessing of incense during High Mass: 'May you be blessed by Him in whose honour you shall be burnt'.

The Pope and the Ultramontanes increasingly emphasized the Roman aspect of the Catholic Church. The triumph of Ultramontanism was reflected not so much in the definition of papal infallibility as in the transformation of Catholicism within a generation. By establishing a Roman approach to devotion, discipline and theology throughout the Catholic Church, the Roman authorities were able to take over the leadership of the Church, while the first Vatican Council simply defined the structure of the Church in accordance with their understanding of it. The rapid improvement in communications during the nineteenth century not only enabled the Roman authorities to exert a more immediate and greater control over the Church, but increased the number of pilgrims going to Rome as well as the number of priests and seminarians attending Roman colleges. Roman authorities increasingly controlled or amended the decisions of provincial councils and encouraged the practice of consulting the Roman congregations on questions of worship, discipline or theology. Roman or Italian devotions such as perpetual adoration or the 'Forty Hours' were adopted throughout Europe, while the clergy were encouraged to wear Roman and clerical dress. The adoption of Roman policies was also reinforced by the distribution of Roman titles such as 'monsignor', the appointment of bishops and the creation of cardinals. Pius IX created more *monsignori* in thirty years than his predecessors had done in two centuries.

At the beginning of the nineteenth century almost all episcopal nominations outside the Papal States were under local patronage, usually that of the Crown. However, the authority of the Pope over episcopal appointments steadily increased from the rebellions in Latin America at the beginning of the century to the destruction of the power of the Hapsburgs during the first World War. The position of the Pope was also strengthened by the establishments of new hierarchies in Europe and America, and by the appointment of bishops in missionary territories where Crown patronage had never existed. Pius IX was inclined to make episcopal appointments himself and without reference to local factors such as the opinions of the clergy. Other considerations, usually Ultramontane considerations, such as whether the candidate had been educated in Rome or whether he would prove accommodating to the Roman curia were regarded as more important. The Pope supported the old national colleges in Rome as well as the establishment of new ones such as the Polish and French, Irish and American Colleges. The length of Pio Nono's reign enabled him to replace the entire episcopate. On the eve of the first Vatican Council, only eighty-one bishops had been appointed during the reign of his predecessor and hardly any of these had survived by the time of his death. Pius IX revived the practice of periodical *ad limina* visits and was able to summon independent bishops to Rome, though most of the bishops chosen were devoted to him and to the Holy See. Few ever complained if their decisions were overruled and some even took the initiative in submitting them for approval to the Pope.

Although the Curia still included a number of clerics who were not priests and several worldly *monsignori*, their number declined year by year. There were fewer political officials and more theologians or canonists whose behaviour was strictly controlled by the Pope himself. The Sacred College of Cardinals declined in importance. Individual cardinals might influence the Pope, but he frequently ignored their advice and they were never consulted as a body. The few consistories held during his reign were simply informed of the Pope's decisions. There was also an increase in the number of non-Italian cardinals which helped to increase the authority of the Pope over national episcopates as well as manifesting his determination to spread the Catholic Church throughout the world.

Apostolic nuncios, whose original duties had been to represent the Pope in foreign countries, now intervened in the internal affairs of the Church abroad, acting as intermediaries between Pope and bishops, and directly influencing episcopal appointments. The papal nuncio in France, Fornari, prevented the holding of a national council in 1849 and even stopped a provincial council which had been called without papal authorization. He successfully increased the number of Ultramontanes within the French hierarchy, defended French priests who resisted Gallican bishops and ensured that Gallican publications were put on the Index. His success is reflected in the fact that during 1852 a memorandum by fifteen bishops deploring the decline of Gallican traditions and the apparently unlimited extent of papal infallibility had to be printed and distributed anonymously.

The Holy See continued to extend its authority over the Church in France throughout the nineteenth century. The Roman authorities condemned treatises on theology and canon law published by the Sulpicians and so destroyed the traditional opinions and customary laws of the Gallican Church. Rome refused to recognize diplomas granted by State theological faculties and established a college for higher studies in Rome from which French priests returned with the opinions, the customs and even the dress of Italian priests. French priests who wished to circumvent their local bishops found it easy to apply to distant Roman congregations for dispensations. The Holy See also supported the regular clergy in their struggles with diocesan authorities. In 1871 there was a great scandal at Montpellier when a leading Ultramontane, *Père* Alzon, vicar general of Nîmes and founder of the Assumptionists, appeared in a parish church in violet stole – the symbol of extraordinary episcopal authority – to read a Roman decree cancelling measures taken by Bishop Le Courtier against a religious community within his diocese.

The victory of Ultramontanism over Gallicanism within the French Church can be illustrated by the careers of three former disciples of Lamennais. The *Abbè* Rohrbacher produced an Ultramontane history of the Church to replace the old Gallican history by Fleury. The *Abbé* Gousset adopted the moral theology of St Alphonsus Ligouri which was favoured in Rome to replace more rigid Jansenist moral theology which had previously been taught in French seminaries. Finally, the *Abbé* Prosper Guéranger, incidentally the only one of the three to meet any strong opposition, advocated the adoption of a uniform Roman liturgy to replace the excessive number of Gallican liturgies in France.

Guéranger believed that liturgical ceremonies should express the continuity of tradition and that the principle of liturgical unity should correspond to the visible unity of the Church. In 1840 he published *Liturgical Institutions* advocating a return to the unity of Roman liturgical practice. There followed an open controversy in which no less than sixty French bishops opposed Guéranger. During 1842 the Pope declared that it was deplorable to have a variety of liturgies, but only half a dozen bishops had adopted the Roman liturgy by 1848. Nevertheless Guéranger continued his campaign and between 1849 and 1851 several provincial councils came out in his support and Pius IX informed the French bishops of his wish that they should adopt the Roman liturgy. By 1864 eighty-one out of ninety-one dioceses had adopted the Roman liturgy and before Guéranger died all the French dioceses had adopted the liturgy of Rome.

However, far more dangerous developments were taking place in the Church at the time. When philosophical Traditonalism blundered into fideism, it was condemned by the Church authorities. However, many Catholics, particularly supporters of Ultramontanism, continued to regard tradition as a guarantee or justification for believing all kinds of ecclesiastical legends. While French Bollandists and German ecclesiastical historians were adopting more scientific and critical methods, other Catholics manifested an uncritical 'openness' and even credulity towards all things spiritual and mystical. Writers like the *Abbé* Gaume defended the legendary on the principle that anything which had been traditionally believed was to be accepted if it fostered piety. The same author produced a four-hundred page treatise on holy water and explained that the reason for the seven days of the week was that the Devil had designated them to the seven sub-devils who administered the seven deadly sins.

A passion for the Middle Ages spread among Romantic Catholics, who indulged in processions and pilgrimages, the veneration of relics and new devotions to Our Lady and the saints. Canonizations became more frequent during the nineteenth century and they were often carried out with impressive ceremonial. Pius IX himself took a personal interest in the rapidly expanding devotion to St Joseph who was proclaimed patron of the Universal Church in 1870. Even Lacordaire believed that Lazarus, Martha and Mary Magdalen had evangelized Provence and many Catholics believed that apostolic figures had established the principal French sees. Liberal Catholics such as Montalembert and Ozanam, as well as enthusiastic Ultramontanes such as F.W. Faber, set about compiling lives of the saints which were often uncritical, while it was Dupanloup's account of La Salette that originally gave credence to the reports of the vision. Liberal Catholics as well as Ultramontanes showed an alarming ignorance of historical and biblical criticism which was most clearly seen in their inability to respond to Renan's *Life of Jesus* published in 1863. 50,000 copies were sold in six months and the book was translated into six languages within a year. But angry pastoral letters denouncing 'the new Arius' or the ceremony of reparation ordered by the Pope were no substitute for critical scholarship in dealing with contemporary critical issues and the threat to the faith of educated and uneducated alike.

The growth of new devotions was often closely linked with politics. French legitimists, for example, adopted the cult of the Sacred Heart which signified the submission of political authority to that of Christ. After 1870 Catholic monarchists organized pilgrimages to Paray-le-Monial and the dedication of France to the Sacred Heart. French Catholics learned to sing the popular *Sauvez Rome et la France, au nom de Sacré-Coeur* and the French Government built the famous basilica on the heights of Montmartre. Similarly there were political sympathies for the monarchists and the temporal power of the Pope in the development of pilgrimages to Lourdes especially following the military defeat of 1871 when 'national pilgrimages' were organized to Lourdes and the Assumptionists gained special concessions from the railway companies. In a *Litany of Our Lady of Lourdes* printed in Dublin, two consecutive petitions read:

> Who wilt save Rome and our Holy Father the Pope . . .
> Who wilt save France.

A '*Memorare*' *of Our Lady of Lourdes* included the petition:

> Protect, with that hand which nothing can resist, the Holy See of Rome, which has recognized the truth of thy apparitions; protect

> France so tried and so repentant, whose people gather from all quarters to glorify thee, and to acknowledge thee as the dispenser of the gifts of thy Divine Son.

Meanwhile Veuillot used the miracles and visions which seem to have abounded in France during the nineteenth century as support for the policies of the Ultramontanes in general and of himself in particular. There were visions of Our Lady near Besançon in 1803, in Paris during 1830 and 1840, at Blangy on several occasions between 1840 and 1846, at La Salette in 1846 and, of course, the most famous of all, at Lourdes in 1858. Non-believers regarded these visions and reported miracles as further evidence of the credulity and superstitions of French Catholics, especially when many priests were themselves suspicious. One of the children who was supposed to have seen the vision at La Salette told St John Vianney that he had lied, though he later retracted under pressure.

Anti-clericals and opponents of the Church were provided with even better ammunition when priests were sued for libel by a woman whom they had accused of fraud or when priests accused local women of impersonating the Blessed Virgin. In the case of Lourdes, anti-clericals argued that a well-known local lady who had arranged an illicit rendezvous in the grotto had been surprised by Bernadette and saved her reputation by an impulsive feat of histrionics. 'Wherever miracles are believed in', wrote one hostile commentator,

> miracles occur. Wherever they are no longer believed in – and that is where they are most needed – no one sees any. The Blessed Virgin appears at Lourdes, but not in Paris; she shows herself to Bernadette, but not to the Academy of Science.

Such criticisms had little effect on the Ultramontanes, especially since several of the visions were explicitly linked with the doctrine of the Immaculate Conception, the definition of which was such an important stage in the development of Ultramontanism. When the 'Lady' told Bernadette Soubirous on 25 March 1858 'I am the Immaculate Conception', the Church at the time and subsequently treasured the words as a confirmation of the dogmatic definition of 1854. One of the first historians of Lourdes commented:

> No one could have guessed that Mary would step from her throne, place her feet on the earth and say to all Christians in the person of Bernadette: This word of the Roman Pope is the oracle of divine truth. I am indeed exactly as the Pope has defined, the Immaculate

> Conception, and till the end of time, here, in this place where I speak, countless miracles will bear witness alike to the actuality of my appearances, to my Immaculate Conception and to the Infallibility of the Pope.

This point was repeated when Bernadette was canonized in 1933:

> That which the Pope by virtue of his infallible teaching office defined, the Immaculate Virgin desired to confirm openly, through her own mouth, when soon after she proclaimed her identity in a famous appearance at the grotto of Massabielle.

In the centenary encyclical of 1958, Pope Pius XII remarked:

> Certainly the infallible word of the Pope, the authentic interpreter of revealed truth, required no endorsement from heaven to be valid for the faithful; but with what emotion did Christian people and their shepherds receive from the lips of Bernadette this answer which came from heaven.

The definition of the Immaculate Conception in 1854 manifested the growing strength of Ultramontanism, while the way in which the doctrine was defined was most significant in its future consequences. The original initiative came from ordinary Catholics in the Church, mostly from outside Italy, but the Pope himself had a deep personal devotion to Our Lady and he attributed his cure from epilepsy as well as his speedy return from exile to her intercession. The popular movement in France received a great impetus in 1830 when Catherine Laboure had a vision of the Blessed Virgin surrounded by the inscription, *'O Mary conceived without sin, pray for us who have recourse to you'*. The Pope himself was also influenced by the conversion of Alphonse-Marie Ratisbonne after seeing a vision of Our Lady surrounded by the words *'O Mary conceived without sin'*.

In 1848 the Pope appointed a theological commission to study the question and in the following year he issued an encyclical asking the bishops for their prayers and advice. The replies of the bishops might be seen as evidence that they were acting as an episcopal college in the exercise of ecclesiastical infallibility. But it has also been claimed that the bishops were merely giving moral support to the Pope influenced by his personal popularity and the Ultramontane climate of ecclesiastical opinion, rather than expressing their theological convictions. Only one or two of 603 replies took the line that the doctrine could not be defined, a few more thought it would be inopportune, but 546 replies were enthusiastic in their support for the definition.

From the point of view of future policy and procedure, as the Pope's secretary, Monsignor Talbot, appreciated at the time, the manner in which the dogma was defined was more important than the doctrine itself. A meeting of the bishops was called, but they were not asked whether they believed the Immaculate Conception, nor whether the definition might be opportune; they were simply asked to make any changes which they thought necessary in order to make the definition more acceptable to the world at large. The suggestion that the bishops might be associated with the Pope in the proclamation of the dogma was not accepted precisely on the grounds that if the Pope alone pronounced a definition to which the faithful spontaneously adhered, such a definition would be a practical demonstration of the sovereign doctrinal authority in the Church and of that infallibility with which Christ had invested his Vicar on earth.

Thus the dogma of the Immaculate Conception was pronounced on the sole authority of the Pope after 'consulting' bishops and theologians, but without a General Council. This was an important precedent as a practical manifestation of papal infallibility which influenced the form in which papal infallibility was defined and which was consciously followed again in the later definition of the Assumption. Pius IX acted 'by virtue of the authority of the holy Apostles Peter and Paul and of Our own authority' and effectively exercised the privilege of papal infallibility some sixteen years before it was actually defined. The definition of the Immaculate Conception immensely strengthened the position of the Pope within the Church and gave great encouragement to Ultramontanes everywhere.

In 1863 Liberal Catholics organized an international congress at Malines where Montalembert delivered two famous addresses criticizing those Catholics still devoted to the *ancien régime* and urging them to accept political and religious liberty. The alliance of Throne and Altar, he argued, compromised or weakened the Church by restricting its political and religious freedom; he condemned 'those Paradises of religious absolutism' which 'have become the scandal and the despair of all Catholic hearts' and he protested against those who had demanded universal liberty in 1848, but were content with freedom for Catholics in 1853. Quite deliberately, if somewhat tactlessly and carelessly, Montalembert adopted Cavour's famous formula, 'a free Church in a free State', 'which, though snatched from us and put into circulation by a very guilty man remains . . . the symbol of our convictions and our hopes'. Montalembert did not associate himself with the Piedmontese prime minister who, he maintained, favoured 'a despoiled Church in a spoliative State'. Furthermore, Montalembert did not recommend a complete divorce between Church and State, and he made an exception of the Papal States from his more general recommendations.

With similar qualifications, Montalembert quoted Dupanloup: 'We accept, we invoke, the principles and the liberties proclaimed in '89 . . . You made the revolution of 1789 without us and against us, but *for us*, God wishing it so in spite of you'. Once again, Montalembert did not simply advocate democracy which, as he recognized, at the time was often associated with extreme views, state monopolies and bureaucratic centralisation. On the contrary, he argued,

> The more one is a democrat the more it is necessary to be Christian; because the fervent and practical cult of God made man is the indispensable counter-weight of that perpetual tendency of democracy to establish the cult of man believing himself God.

Nevertheless, in spite of all these qualifications, conservative Catholics immediately attacked Montalembert, and without even reading him the Pope concluded that he was reflecting a dangerous trend. Pio Nono remarked,

> The Church will never concede it as a principle that error and heresy may be preached to Catholic peoples. The Pope certainly desires freedom of conscience in Sweden and Russia: but he does not desire it as a principle.

The subsequent condemnation of Montalembert, which Dupanloup tried so hard to prevent, was courteous, confidential and friendly, but it was virtually a condemnation of the causes to which the old man had devoted his life. Other policies were being adopted and moves in another direction were already being made by the Roman authorities.

In September 1863 another congress was held at Munich. Ignaz Döllinger had recently criticized German Ultramontanes and neo-scholastics, especially in 1861 when he condemned the way in which the Roman authorities and their German supporters were distorting problems of Church and State. The main theme of the Munich congress was the need for academic freedom and scientific investigation, the independence of reason, history and science in their relations with

Cardinal Antonelli

theology and the views of the ecclesiastical authorities. Döllinger offended Roman thelogians by criticizing the limitations of Italian scholarship and maintaining that an adequate theology depended on a proper understanding of history and philosophy such as was found in Germany.

The Pope's subsequent Brief to the Archbishop of Munich did not actually condemn Döllinger, but implicitly condemned his attitude towards academic freedom by insisting that scholarly research should be conducted with full deference to ecclesiastical authority. Catholic thought was to be guided by the ordinary *magisterium* of the Church, the decisions of the Roman congregations including that of the Index, the teaching of theologians as well as the dogmatic definitions of the Church. In effect, this meant that the scientific pursuit of truth must respect not only ecclesiastical dogmas but the Roman congregations and those contemporary theological opinions which were acceptable to the bishops.

It is sometimes said that the congresses at Malines and Munich, the convention providing for the withdrawal of French troops from Rome, or even the publication of Renan's *Life of Jesus* were the motives which prompted the Pope to publish the *Syllabus of Errors* and the encyclical *Quanta Cura* in December 1864. However, the publication of the *Syllabus of Errors* was a deliberate act which was being prepared for some thirteen years before it actually took place. The Pope apparently believed that his spiritual power to excommunicate or to condemn doctrinal errors and the policies of secular governments might still prove influential as it had been in the past. Events were to prove him wrong, but not before he had so used *Civiltà Cattolica*, issued the *Syllabus* of *Errors* and secured the definition of papal infallibility.

It was possibly Cardinal Pecci, the Bishop of Perugia and future Pope Leo XIII, who first suggested the idea of promulgating a collection of contemporary errors about ecclesiastical authority and property. Pio Nono entrusted the task to Cardinal Fornari, the former nuncio in Paris, and letters were sent to bishops and laymen throughout the world seeking their views on the principal errors and the state of contemporary society. The commission which had finished the preparatory work for the definition of the Immaculate Conception was then asked to prepare for publication the document on modern errors, but progress was slow and the work was delayed. On 23 July 1860 Bishop Gerbet of Perpignan published a pastoral letter on the errors of the modern age which included a catalogue enumerating them. The Pope decided to use this as the basis of a papal document and he gave it to a commission which both revised it and prepared the proper censures.

In 1862 the completed work containing sixty-one propositions was given to the Pope. In June the three hundred bishops present at the canonization of the Japanese martyrs were asked for their comments. In spite of the fact that the bishops were bound to secrecy, an Italian newspaper secured a copy of the document and printed the text in the following October. As a result of the storm which followed, the Pope decided to adopt yet another form in which to carry out his intentions. He appointed a commission to make extracts from his own publications and the final result was a *Syllabus* of eighty errors arranged in ten sections; it was an index of condemnations referring to the relevant allocutions, encyclicals or apostolic letters, listing 'errors' torn from their contexts.

The condemnation of heretical ideas or even those regarded as a threat to the Church or disruptive of stable society might well have been justified. It was hardly surprising that the Pope should have denounced the opinions that God was merely nature, that human reason was the sole arbiter of truth and falsehood, good and evil, that all religious truths were derived from human reason, that Christianity contradicted reason or that revelation hindered the perfection of man, that biblical miracles were poetic fictions and Christ himself was a myth. Contemporaries could not have been surprised that the encyclical condemned the opinion that human society should be governed without regard to religion, or that it defended the independence of the Church and asserted its sacred right to train consciences, especially of the young, or that it reasserted the fulness of papal authority even in areas 'which do not concern faith and morals'.

However, the *Syllabus* also condemned the following opinions: that every man was free to embrace or profess the religion he believed to be true guided by the light of reason; that all who were not at all in the true Church of Christ could entertain good hopes of eternal salvation; that men might achieve eternal salvation in the practice of any religion whatever; that Catholics might dispute on the compatibility of the Pope's temporal with his spiritual rule; that the Church could not use force or any direct or indirect temporal power; that the Church should be separated from the State and *vice versa*; that it was no longer necessary that the Catholic religion should be held as the only religion of the State to the exclusion of all others; that the Pope could and should reconcile himself to and agree with progress, liberalism and modern civilization.

Of course, Pio Nono was totally preoccupied with the situation in Italy and had published a *cri-de-coeur* against the religious and political attitudes of the Turin Government and the Roman Republic. The condemnation of those who taught that the Pope could and should accommodate himself to progress, liberalism and modern civilization, was taken from an encyclical denouncing the extension of the secularist laws of Piedmont to the territories recently united with the Kingdom of Italy and the Pope's subsequent refusal to negotiate with Cavour. The condemnation of the idea that the civil authorities enjoyed complete control over education and the appointment of teachers referred to an allocuation attacking the Piedmontese laws on education. The 'errors' of plebiscites were originally condemned when the Piedmontese justified their seizure of territory by plebiscites following the invasion of the Papal States in 1860. Unfortunately, not all Catholics were Italians and consequently they failed to see the 'errors' in terms of the dissolution of monasteries or the imposition of secular education. As the Duc de Broglie pointed out, the condemnation of progress, liberalism and modern civilization seemed to refer to the secular press, telegraph and railways, and other recent scientific developments such as street lighting.

'While believers were lost and baffled, the unbelievers raised a tremendous shout of triumph'. Liberal newspapers throughout Europe poured ridicule and abuse, scorn and derision on Catholicism. According to one French anti-clerical newspaper, the *Syllabus* was the 'last challenge flung at the modern world by an expiring papacy'. For the next generation, anti-clericals were able to contrast the spirit of the French Revolution expressed in the *Declaration of the Rights of Man* with the spirit of the Catholic counter-revolution in the *Syllabus of Errors*. On the whole, anti-clericals were only united in their opposition to absolute authority and blind submission, and the one document in which opponents of the Church found the clearest demand for blind submission was the *Syllabus of Errors*. In Naples and Palermo Freemasons publicly burnt the papal documents, while the Austrian Government would not have allowed them to be published, had this not conflicted with the terms of the concordat.

In Belgium secular liberals used the *Syllabus* in their attack on Belgian Catholics and questioned their loyalty to the constitution. A leading Belgian Social Catholic, François Huet, took this opportunity to leave the Church and to mount a bitter attack on the development of Ultramontanism which, he said,

> hates only liberty and its martyrs; it eulogizes only despotism and its executioners. It has made the venerable centre of Catholic unity the odious citadel of absolutism in Europe, and the successor of the apostles the ally of the kings against the emancipation of Christian people . . . The Christian pulpit no longer consoles the poor, and denounces the rich. The degradation of intelligence is accounted the perfection of the law. Spiritual worship is perishing beneath a mass of petty, puerile, and superstitious practices which St Paul would not have known how to condemn strongly enough.

Other Catholics, particularly in Germany and France, but also in England and America were surprised to learn that religious toleration or free speech were regarded as un-Catholic, especially when Veuillot added that the parliamentary system rested on an heretical principle. They had not realized that the Church authorities still maintained that the Church had the right to use force and to be regarded as the only religion of the State to the exclusion of all others.

'God is not obliged', remarked Cardinal Bernis on one occasion, 'to repair by miracles the imprudences of His Vicars'; this task usually fell to others and on this occasion to Bishop Dupanloup. Dupanloup himself expressed the fear that the Church would be outlawed throughout Europe for half a century if 'this senseless Romanism' was not checked and he set about the task of 'explanation'. The Bishop explained that only a *certain* type of progress or civilization was condemned and he distinguished between the thesis and the hypothesis, between the ideal rule of the Church and the lesser evils of the conditions of an imperfect world. *Quanta Cura* and the *Syllabus of Errors* were not meant to be outlines of practical politics; Protestants or Atheists, for example, were tolerated without being approved, or, as they said in Paris referring to the papal nuncio, 'The thesis is to burn M. de Rothschild: the hypothesis is to dine with him'.

Certainly, there was more than an element of speciousness about Dupanloup's interpretation: he argued that the Pope had no need to reconcile himself with what was good in modern civilization since he had never ceased promoting it. A member of the French Government remarked that the encyclical as presented by Dupanloup was not only quite acceptable, but no longer recognizable. Montalembert appreciated that the Bishop had accomplished a *tour de force*; his pamphlet was a 'first-class verbal vanishing trick'. Nevertheless, Dupanloup's approach was welcomed with a profound and widespread sense of relief. De Broglie commented, 'Society, which hardly dared to breathe, felt relieved, like a man being throttled when someone cuts the cord round his throat'. The Bishop received over 600 letters of congratulation from other bishops throughout the world.

Neither the Pope nor the Ultramontanes, however, were entirely satisfied with Dupanloup's interpretation. Veuillot accused the Bishop of altering the sense and purpose of the *Syllabus* and in this he was probably right because contemporary as well as subsequent interpretations such as Dupanloup's do seem to have obscured the Pope's original aims and intentions. In replying to Dupanloup, Veuillot encouraged his own followers to:

> gather round the Sovereign Pontiff, follow unflinching his inspired commands, affirm with him the truths which alone can save our souls and the world . . . Let us hurl ourselves into obedience. Obedience will give us the solidity of stone, and on this stone, *hanc petram*, truth will set her triumphant foot.

Although the Pope himself approved of Dupanloup's pamphlet, he also praised Veuillot's reply *L'Illusion Liberale*. But it is quite possible that if Dupanloup had not ingeniously combined his interpretation of the *Syllabus* with a denunciation of Napoleon III, he would never have received a letter of approval from the Pope. In any case, the papal letter was extremely guarded in congratulating Dupanloup for associating himself with those courageous bishops who 'reproved these errors in the sense in which we reproved them ourself', which was not quite what Dupanloup had done. The Pope's letter also concluded with an obvious sting:

> We therefore express to you the gratitude of our soul, persuaded by the zeal with which you have continued to defend the cause of religion and truth that you will explain to your people the true sense of our letters with a diligence and exactitude all the greater because of the vigour with which you have refuted the erroneous interpretations they have received.

Furthermore, the Pope himself did nothing more to calm the fears which the *Syllabus* aroused and he refused to encourage Antonelli's qualified approach to the encyclical, even when some Catholic theologians and curial officials as well as opponents of the Church claimed that the *Syllabus* was an example of papal infallibility.

It is, of course, impossible to ignore the historical background as well as the contemporary situation. Pius IX himself as well as two of his predecessors had personally suffered at the hands of revolutionary forces, while at the time, Erastianism and anti-clericalism seemed rampant in France and Belgium, Austria and Italy, Spain and Switzerland. Furthermore, the *Syllabus* which incidentally was signed by Antonelli and not by the Pope, was a technical document enumerating previous condemnations to be understood within their original contexts. However, the Pope chose to ignore the situation in the United States, for example, where religious toleration was proving a positive advantage to the Church, and by using universal terms and value judgments he provoked a hostile reaction throughout the world. A more conciliatory Pope would have acted differently, but the *Syllabus of Errors* went a great deal further in rejecting contemporary society than *Mirari vos*, without adding anything to the traditional or doctrinal teaching of the Church. Pius IX's language seemed to challenge the men of the age who could hardly have been expected to receive sympathetically such a condemnation of their most cherished beliefs.

As a manifestation of the Church's encounter with the nineteenth century, the *Syllabus* became symbolic; it was the clearest rejection of the age until then and perhaps the worst example of the Church's failure. Certain aspects of the spirit and the developments of the time were, as always, hostile to the teaching or even to the existence of the Church, but the completely negative manner of dealing with these in the *Syllabus* ignored other aspects of the age which might be new or strange, but were not hostile. The possibility of compromise, co-existence or even co-operation already existed; the Concordat of 1801 clearly implied that a compromise with modern society was not only possible but was part of papal policy. However, it was to be many years before the necessary accommodation would be allowed or attempted and consequently even longer before it could ever be realized.

Between 1864 and 1870, Catholics debated the dogmatic significance of the condemnations in the *Syllabus of Errors*. Although the *Syllabus* was not in fact an infallible statement, Ultramontanes certainly hoped to identify the necessity of the temporal power with dogmatic truth. As a result, the spiritual and temporal authority of the Pope, and relations between Church and State were the subject of frequent and intense debate during the late 1860s. However, the ultimate point at issue was probably the nature of the Church and in fact questions of ecclesiology quickly came to dominate the first Vatican

Council. The doctrine of papal infallibility was already tacitly accepted by most theologians and had been defended by Dupanloup as his doctrinal thesis in 1842. But the 'inopportunists', as they came to be known, were opposed to the possible consequences of a definition of papal infallibility which might further strengthen Ultramontanism within the Church, alienate secular governments and increase the divisions amongst Christians. In the event, the Council never had time to discuss the problems of religious and political liberty, the principles of 1789 or the temporal power of the Pope. The Council documents simply reaffirmed traditional teaching and, in some respects, even modified the tone and the terms of the *Syllabus of Errors.*

On the feast of the Immaculate Conception 1866 the Pope invited Catholic bishops to Rome to celebrate the eighteenth centenary of the martyrdoms of Saint Peter and Paul on 29 June 1867. It was suggested that the doctrine of papal infallibility might be proclaimed on this occasion as that of the Immaculate Conception had been on a similar occasion in 1854. Bishop Dupanloup, however, succeeded in removing the word *infallibilis* which appeared repeatedly in the bishops' address to the Pope and in limiting the scope of the papal *magisterium* by the formula *ad custodiendum depositum*. Pio Nono himself simply took the opportunity of announcing his intention of calling a General Council which formally opened on the feast of the Immaculate Conception 1869.

Most of the bishops who had been consulted were in favour of holding a council in order that the Church might cope more successfully with the difficulties raised by contemporary intellectual, social and political developments. Guizot, the Protestant statesman, believed that 'Pius IX has given proof of admirable wisdom in convoking this great assembly, whence will issue perhaps the saying of the world; for our societies are gravely sick, and for great evils great remedies are needed'. But whereas the Ultramontanes hoped that the Council would reinforce papal authority by the definition of papal infallibility, Liberal Catholics hoped that the Council might end the exaggerations of Ultramontanism. The continuing difficulty of the Liberal Catholics was how to be true liberals without becoming disobedient Catholics. Veuillot and his supporters were idenitifed as the only 'true' Catholics. Liberal Catholics, therefore, originally welcomed the prospect of a council as a balance to the growing papal autocracy, but they were quickly alienated by the activities of the Ultramontanes and the nature of their aspirations.

On 6 February 1869 an inspired article, based on reports from the nuncio in Paris and requested by the Secretary of State, appeared in *Civiltà Cattolica*, the semi-official Jesuit review which maintained that when the Pope thought, it was God who was thinking in him! The article, 'Matters Relating to the Future Council: Correspondence from France', included the following remarkable passage:

> Everyone knows that Catholics in France are divided into two parties, one simply Catholics, the other calling themselves Liberal Catholics. True Catholics believe that the Council will be very short. They hope that it will declare the doctrines of the Syllabus, that is, that the propositions there given in negative form will be expressed in positive formulations and with the necessary expansion. They will receive with joy the declaration of the dogmatic infallibility of the supreme bishop. No one finds it surprising that Pius IX, with a sentiment of proper reserve, does not wish to take the initiative himself for a proposition which seems to relate to him alone; but it is to be hoped that this definition will be made with acclamation by the unequivocal manifestation of the Holy Spirit through the mouth of the fathers of the Ecumenical Council.

Following indignant protests, the Roman authorities claimed that this article did not reflect the opinion of the Holy See, but the damage had been done. The article had implied that Liberal Catholics were not true Catholics, that the Council would define the *Syllabus* and had prejudged the issue, and almost the terms and the extent, of the definition of papal infallibility.

The *Civiltà* was supported by Veuillot who maintained that the Holy Spirit did not need time to debate or to formulate an opinion; 'It is worthy of note that in the Upper Room no discussion preceded the outpouring of the Holy Ghost'. His newspaper, *L'Univers*, organized lay and clerical petitions in favour of the definition and he accused opponents of ignorance, disloyalty or heresy. Veuillot himself substituted the name of the Pope in hymns or biblical quotations originally addressed to God the Father, Jesus Christ or the Holy Spirit. 'Pius' replaced 'Deus' in the hymn for None which was paraphrased,

> Rerum PIUS tenax vigor,
> Immotus in te permanens,
> Da verba vitae quae regant,
> Agnos, oves, et saeculum.

Verses of the *Veni Sante Spiritus* were addressed to the Pope:

> Come, thou Father of the poor,
> Come with treasures which endure;
> Come, thou light of all that live.

A verse from the *Epistle to the Hebrews* was applied to the Pope;

> To suit us, the ideal high priest would have to be holy, innocent and uncontaminated, beyond the influence of sinners, and raised up above the heavens.

The *Univers* once answered the question 'Who is the Pope?' with the reply 'He is Christ on earth'. Bishop Jean François Bertaud of Tulle once referred to the Pope as 'the Incarnate Word continuing Himself', while Bishop Gaspard Mermillod of Lausanne and a future cardinal preached on the three incarnations of the Son of God, 'in the womb of a virgin, in the Eucharist, and in the old man in the Vatican'.

From the opposing point of view, Döllinger wrote a series of hostile articles in *Allgemeine Zeitung* which were later published as *The Pope and the Council* under the pseudonym 'Janus'. The Pope and the Jesuits, he argued, were preparing for a revolution by imposing on the Church a definition of papal infallibility and primacy of jurisdiction in spite of the facts of history. Döllinger's opinions were to some extent shared by another great historian, Bishop Hefele of Rottenburg, who wrote to him that it was quite impossible 'To acknowledge as divinely revealed what is not in itself true'. Hefele also remarked in the same letter, 'I thought I was serving the Catholic Church, and I served the caricature which the Jesuits have made of it'. A majority of the German bishops meeting at Fulda in September thought that a definition would be inopportune, fourteen of them wrote to the Pope to express their fears, while a 'Layman's Address' was sent from Coblenz also opposing the definition.

In France, Archbishop Darboy of Paris maintained that a definition of papal infallibility would be opposed to the facts of history as well as common sense. Bishop Dupanloup publicly expressed his conviction that a definition was inopportune; the dogma itself was incapable of accurate definition and would simply alienate other Christians. Unfortunately, Dupanloup adopted such a public and bold stand that he could not become the dominant figure at the Council which otherwise might have been possible. The most damning criticism of all came from the dying Montalembert who had devoted his life to the cause of freedom and Ultramontanism. He now saw that the Ultramontanes rather than the Erastian secularists were threatening the freedom of the Church and that the earlier liberal pontificate of Pius IX had been replaced by the papal autocracy supported by the *Univers* and the *Civiltà*. 'Who could have foreseen', he wrote:

> the permanent triumph of those lay theologians of absolutism who have begun by making a sacrifice of all our liberties, of all our principles, of all our earlier ideas, before Napoleon III, in order, in due course, to offer up justice and truth, reason and history, as a holocaust to the idol which they are erecting at the Vatican.

The rise of papal autocracy coincided with developments in the secular world and in particular with the growth of centralization and imperialism. The Hegelian concept of the State as 'God walking on earth' influenced political developments in Bismarck's Prussia, public democracy had little part to play in the Bonapartist dictatorship of France or the 'enlightened despotism' of the Emperor Franz Josef in Austria. The United States reasserted its unity after the Civil War, while Great Britian was indulging in imperialism. Salvation in both Church and State seemed to depend on a strong centralized government dominating a unified and obedient people. However, in contrast with the Council of Trent, no secular government was represented at the Vatican Council. Although the Catholic powers were not invited, they were told that they could in fact take part. The fact that none of them did so was another sign of the growing divisions between the Church and secular governments, Catholic as well as non-Catholic.

In order to prevent any surprise or unexpected developments in the Council, the Roman authorities carefully prepared the ground. As early as October 1868, Dupanloup was complaining that Cardinal Barnabo wanted to drive the bishops like a herd of pigs. Another indication of the growing authority of the Pope within the Church was the fact that, again unlike former councils, he claimed the exclusive right to initiate the proposals which came before the Council. Furthermore, the decrees of the Council were introduced in a new and significant way: 'Pius, bishop, servant of the servants of God, with the approval of the sacred council'. This formula must be contrasted with that used at Trent: 'The sacred synod, lawfully assembled under the Holy Ghost, under the presidency of the legates of the Apostolic See, ordains . . . .'. Clearly the emphasis had moved from Council to Pope as the dominant authority in the Church.

At the opening of the Council, Pius IX emphasized his neutrality, but as the proceedings became prolonged, he grew irritated with the opponents of a definition. On hearing Montalembert's reference to the 'idol', the Pope accused the opponents of not believing that the Council was governed by the Holy Spirit:

> full of daring, folly, irrationality, imprudence, hatred, violence, they employ, in order to excite those of their faction, the means by the aid of which it is customary to catch votes in popular assemblies: they undertake to remake the divine Constitution of the Church and to adapt it to the modern forms of civil governments.

Having no personal doubts about his own infallibility, Pio Nono praised and congratulated whoever supported the definition, while making it perfectly clear that those who resisted the definition incurred his displeasure and jeopardized their future prospects. He told Guéranger:

> The adversaries of infallibility are men who, while boasting of their standing as Catholics, show themselves to be entirely imbued with corrupt principles: they reiterate cavils, calumnies and sophisms in order to lower the authority of the supreme head whom Christ has set above the Church and whose prerogatives they fear.

The *schema* on the Church originally only dealt with papal primacy and not with papal infallibility. However, the special deputation on the faith which received proposed amendments to the *schemata* was not the mixed tribunal which it should and which it was expected to have been. Archbishop Manning was apparently largely responsible for the disingenuous trickery by which opponents of the definition were deliberately excluded from being selected for this deputation. He secured a block vote for or against a list of twenty-four names chosen by himself and those who sympathized with him, and he is reported as saying that heretics came to a Council to be heard and condemned, not to participate in formulating doctrine! There was in fact one inopportunist on the deputation, but this was an accident because Archbishop Simor of Esztergom had altered his opinions after arriving in Rome.

The debates on the papacy centred on the primacy of jurisdiction as well as papal infallibility. The opposing minority argued that the Pope did not enjoy a universal primacy of jurisdiction since bishops within their own dioceses exercised ordinary jurisdiction and received their authority from God and not from the Pope. For the last two decades, however, Pius IX and his officials had encouraged appeals to

Rome and sometimes reversed the decisions of local bishops. The Pope now insisted that he possessed 'the full plenitude of this supreme power' and not simply 'the principal part'. This declaration was one of the most significant moves in the centralization of ecclesiastical authority in the hands of the Pope and the Holy See. It was the logical result of various victories over local hierarchies, sometimes as a consequence of concordats which limited the scope of episcopal power in favour of direct agreements between the Pope and secular governments. Bishops increasingly lost their independent authority and became little more than papal officials.

The Vatican Council defined papal primacy of jurisdiction without also defining the limits of that jurisdiction, though the Fathers recognized that primacy was not all-embracing or unlimited. The exercise of primacy was subject to definite limits, but these limits were not defined; they were left concealed in the mind of God and that of the Holy Father. It should be pointed out in defence of the bishops that, although some of them were aware of the danger of undue papal interference in the administration of their dioceses, few of them could have foreseen the transformation which would take place when the Pope and the Roman congregations, freed from their preoccupations with the temporal power and the routine administration of Canon Law, would be able to turn their attention to the smallest details of ecclesiastical administration anywhere in the world.

The Ultramontane majority grew impatient when it seemed that 'the Question' might not be discussed before the Council was adjourned for the summer. Having successfully petitioned in favour of putting the subject of infallibility on the agenda, the Ultramontanes then proposed that it should be moved up the agenda. Manning and his friends appealed directly to the Pope who instructed the Fathers to consider the issue of papal infallibility forthwith. On the other hand, the opposing minority of about two hundred bishops objected to the short time allowed for studying the texts on primacy and infallibility as well as to the practice adopted by the deputations of inserting new clauses at the last moment. The minority bishops were not allowed to discuss the historical objections against papal infallibility with the deputation on the faith. They were also unsuccessful in pleading that the role of the Fathers should receive greater emphasis, while that of the deputations and their spokesmen should be reduced.

The minority opposing bishops made several suggestions in order to be able to agree with the majority. Bishop Spalding suggested that the

Council should confine itself to indirect formulas such as condemning those who claimed the right to appeal from the Pope to a General Council. Cardinal Rauscher proposed that the Council should adopt the formula of St Antoninus of Florence according to which the Pope was infallible when he had taken the advice of the universal Church. Cardinal Guidi recommended speaking of the infallibility of the Pope's doctrinal decisions rather than of the infallibility of the Pope himself. 'The definition is infallible and irreformable, not the person, though to the person is given the assistance whereby he was the authority to issue such definitions'. Furthermore, Guidi argued, the Pope was obliged to use ordinary human industry such as prayer and study in coming to a decision, while 'the normal means was consultation with a greater or less number of bishops, according to the circumstances, the bishops being the witnesses to the belief of their churches'. When the Pope remonstrated with the Cardinal, the latter pointed out that he had simply maintained that bishops were witnesses of tradition; to which Pio Nono replied, '*I* am tradition'!

In the event, the minority failed to secure a formula which would demand a consultation of the Church before the Pope made a pronouncement. The deputation on the faith would never concede this and a modification in the opposite sense was actually introduced in the last few days in an attempt to maintain that papal definitions were irreformable in themselves and not as a result of the consent of the Church. This modification was added three days after the trial vote taken on 13 July which showed that four hundred and fifty-one Fathers were in favour of the definition, eighty-eight against, sixty-two in favour subject to certain conditions, while seventy-six bishops absented themselves. The minority, led by Archbishop Darboy, still tried to secure a final compromise. They promised to vote with the majority if it was made clear, for example, that the Church and the bishops were not excluded from papal pronouncements and if the clause – also introduced at the last minute – claiming full plenitude of Papal primacy or authority was removed. However, the Pope, strongly supported by Manning and his friends, refused and the final clause was added to the formula which then read:

> the Roman Pontiff, when he speaks *ex cathedra*, that is, when, as Shepherd and Teacher of all Christians, by virtue of his supreme apostolic authority he defines that a doctrine on faith or morals must be held by the Universal Church, enjoys, by the divine

> assistance promised to him in the person of Blessed Peter, that infallibility which the divine Redeemer intended His Church to possess when defining doctrine concerning faith and morals; and therefore such definitions of the Roman Pontiff are unalterable in themselves and not by virtue of the assent of the Church.

Just over a thousand ecclesiastics were entitled to take part in the Council, but only seven hundred were present at the opening session and never more than eight hundred actually attended the Council. Some eighty per cent of the membership was Italian and the deputations were almost entirely composed of supporters of the definition which was finally passed by five hundred and thirty-three votes to two, the dissenting bishops being those of Cajazzo and Little Rock. Only just over half the eligible membership actually voted and some eighty bishops absented themselves. However, it is an indication of the triumph of Ultramontanism that none of the bishops who opposed the definition refused to accept it; the last two bishops to submit were Bishops McHale and Moriarty at the Synod of Maynooth in 1875. It is also significant that the decisions of the Fathers undoubtedly reflected the opinions of the great majority of Catholics through the world. The attitude of Catholics to the opposing bishops was sometimes very hostile. When Bishop de Marguerye of Autun tried to explain his position to the clergy of his diocese, they shuffled their feet in opposition and he felt obliged to resign. Furthermore, unlike the sixteenth century, only small minorities rejected the definition and left the Church, and even these, at least originally, attempted to preserve their Catholic character.

As the definition was passed, thunder rolled, the clouds burst and the rains came down. Some opponents of the definition interpreted this unusual storm as a sign of the protests of heaven, whereas supporters of the definition recalled that on Mount Sinai Moses had received the Ten Commandments amid the sound of thunder! The definition of papal infallibility also coincided with the outbreak of the Franco-Prussian War. Napoleon III was forced to withdraw his troops from Rome, leaving the city at the mercy of the Italians. The Council which had discussed only six out of fifty-one *schemata*, was postponed until more propitious times. The Italians occupied Rome and the infallible Pope became the prisoner of the Vatican.

The proclamation of papal infallibility and the apparent weakness of the Church at the time occasioned several bitter attacks on the

Church by secular governments. The Church itself must accept some of the responsibility for creating the conditions which resulted in Bismarck's *Kulturkampf* or the anti-clericalism of French and Italian Governments. However, this was also a period of nationalistic imperialism and jingoistic racism, the age of Bismarck and the French dream of revenge, the 'scramble for Africa' and the Italian invasion of Libya, the Boer War and the Spanish American War. The greatest nationalist politicians such as Bismarck, Clemenceau or Crispi were often the most anti-clerical and hostile to the Church. Secularization and anti-catholic policies were widely adopted even in supposedly Catholic countries from Bavaria or Württemberg in South Germany to the new republics of Latin America. In 1869 the Austrian Government subjected Catholic schools and junior seminaries to the control of the State. In the following year the Emperor protested against the definition of papal infallibility. He refused to allow the dogma to be proclaimed and declared that the Concordat was null and void. The Austrian Government later recognized the Kingdom of Italy and encouraged the schismatic Old Catholic movement.

The internal life of the Church seemed unnaturally calm after the definition of papal infallibility; no new or vigorous policies were adopted, while the Church appeared to be necessarily committed to the obscurantist policies of Pius IX. As the Pope himself became older, he lost the vitality of his earlier years and closed his pontificate as the Prisoner of the Vatican. Although he could rejoice in the enthusiasm and success of Ultramontanism, enjoy a personal popularity without parallel in the history of the modern papacy and be consoled by the missionary expansion of the Church, he left Catholicism facing grave and unsolved problems. Following the early promise of his liberal days, he had shown little understanding of political realities, social or economic trends and the intellectual developments of the age.

During the pontificate of Pius IX, the Church was politically allied with forces of legitimism and reaction which were about to be defeated. The Church had failed to win the support or respect of either the employers or the new urban industrial working classes. Meanwhile, intellectual difficulties had become more rather than less pressing, and not simply as a result of developments in knowledge, but because of ecclesiastical actions and attitudes. Ecclesiastical pronouncements in the realm of thought commanded little respect except from Catholics. In general, by 1878, Christianity and Catholicism seemed at best too idealistic and at worst positively obscurantist; the Church appeared to be moribund, unable to offer any solution for contemporary difficulties.

By 1876, even Cardinal Manning had become depressed by the isolation, the inactivity or even what he called the 'stagnation' of Rome. 'Six years have passed over the Holy See since 1870, and its organization has been dying out year after year'. Unprepared and disunited, the Roman authorities ignored the everchanging world; 'All this darkness, confusion, depression, with inactivity and illness, made me understand the *Tristis est anima mea usque ad mortem*'. Shortly before his death, Pius IX himself is reported to have confessed:

> I hope my successor will be as much attached to the Church as I have been and will have as keen a desire to do good: beyond that, I can see that everything has changed; my system and my policies have had their day, but I am too old to change my course; that will be the task of my successor.

Dr J. J. I. von Döllinger

V: Church and State in Germany and Italy

The history of the Church in France during the nineteenth century must inevitably be written in the light of political developments. The history of the Church in Germany, on the other hand, where the Revolution was cultural, social or intellectual rather than political, provides a welcome corrective to this political over-emphasis in the history of the Church in the modern world. Of course, the Revolution destroyed political structures in Germany as well as in France, but without dividing the nation or violently interrupting its political development. The destruction of the old German ecclesiastical structures, the suppression of monasteries and universities, the confiscation of Church property and the abolition of ecclesiastical privileges, the disorganization of the hierarchy and the absence of an established ecclesiastical order for almost twenty years had thrown German Catholics on to their spiritual resources and enabled them to face the future unencumbered with organizations established during the *ancien régime*.

German Catholics accepted the new situation, the abolition of the prince-bishoprics and the secularization of church property, and did not fight to restore the past. They did not react against the political revolution as they attempted to cope with their new mission of evangelization and to bring about a spiritual and intellectual revival within the Church itself. Furthermore, it was not without significance that with the possible exceptions of Austria and Bavaria, German kingdoms tended to be predominantly Protestant so that German Catholics were never tempted to identify the interests of the Throne and the Altar. German Catholics also showed a greater awareness of social and economic problems, and attempted to adopt a more positive approach to intellectual difficulties than the Catholics of some other countries.

The process of secularization freed the Church in Germany from the political associations of the *ancien régime*, while the German Enlightenment had been led by prince-bishops, devout theologians and reforming pastors, and not by rationalists or materialists, *philosophes* or *libertins*, and former pupils of the Jesuits in revolt against their old masters as had so often been the case in France. During the last quarter of the eighteenth century there had been a Catholic revival throughout Germany associated with names like Fürstenberg and Overberg in Münster, Sailer in Dillingen and Munich, Dalberg in Aschaffenburg and his coadjuter Wessenberg in Constance. Francis von Fürstenberg was vicar general of Münster for some fifty years. The Church in Münster was closely integrated with society at large and its clergy were famous for their intellectual openness as well as their social and pastoral concern. In the summer of 1779 the Princess Amalie Gallitzin had been deeply impressed on a visit to Münster and was formally reconciled with the Church in 1786. Princess Gallitzin, the daughter of a Prussian Field-Marshal and the wife of the cultural attaché at the Russian Embassy in Paris, was a friend of philosophers like Diderot and soon became the centre of the social, intellectual and even the religious life of Münster. This Münster circle with its contacts with leading contemporary intellectual figures played an important part in the conversion of several leading German intellectuals; Leopold Graf zu Stolberg, for example, a friend of Goethe, was received into the Church in 1800.

During the eighteenth century theologians had tried to support the declining authority of the prince bishops either by opposing the authority of Rome or associating them with it, either by Febronianism or Ultramontanism. Legal claims, however, could not replace theology in providing a coherent and valid understanding or justification of the Church. The need to replace the structures and organizations swept away by secularization was accompanied with a greater appreciation of the Church as the vehicle of Catholic life, tradition and doctrine. It has been said that the study of ecclesiology in the nineteenth century first began when John Michael Sailer revived the Pauline notion of the Church as the Body of Christ, a community of grace, embracing heaven and earth.

Sailer himself was a link between the Enlightenment and the Romantic Movement, and was in fact the first of the Catholic romantics. He interpreted the growth and development of the Church in organic terms and revived the notion of the Church as the mystical body of Christ. It was largely due to him that theologians in the nineteenth century were able to rediscover a more spiritual conception of the Church as opposed to the legal understanding of the Church which tended to dominate the controversies after the Reformation and during the Enlightenment. Sailer himself was opposed to the policies of increasing centralization which were adopted by the Roman authorities during the nineteenth century and he showed little sympathy for those Catholics who supported closer administrative ties with the Holy See. As a result, he was opposed by the German Jesuits and suspected by Roman officials. His first book was put on the Index and he became a bishop only in 1830.

John Joseph von Görres was another leading figure in the German Catholic revival. Görres had been an enthusiastic supporter of the French Revolution before he became dissillusioned and began to work for the freedom of Germany and the establishment of democracy. He founded the first great German newspaper, *Die Rheinische Merkur*, which won the admiration and then the displeasure of Napoleon as well as the hostility of reactionary German rulers. It was suppressed in 1816. As a result of his liberal convictions, Görres sympathized with Pope Pius VI and fought for the rights of the Catholic Church in the new German states. After fleeing from Germany in order to avoid arrest, he became increasingly disillusioned with German politics and concluded that the Catholic Church, an institution which was older than all political regimes, was the only power which could survive the forces of revolution. In 1824 he was formally reconciled with the Church and in 1827 became a professor at Munich university and the centre of a group of Catholic scholars which included John Adam Möhler and John Joseph Ignatius von Döllinger. Görres and Döllinger tried to reconcile traditional Catholic teaching with the findings of modern research and to provide a more effective Catholic apologetic for their contemporaries. They also advocated the separation of Church and State.

Members of the famous Tübingen School associated with Möhler were also forced to study history for apologetic purposes and they came to a greater appreciation of the historical aspects of Catholic doctrine and teaching. Incidentally, one of the later professors at Tübingen was the famous church historian Karl Joseph Hefele who opposed the definition of papal infallibility at the Vatican Council. Möhler's early work on *Unity in the Church* published in 1825 was clearly influenced by Schleiermacher's understanding of the Church as the external expression of spiritual Christianity. But the book also revealed for the first time the influence of patristic sources on Catholicism during the Romantic period. In time Möhler became preoccupied with the importance of tradition: the objective historical Church in which and through which the individual acted and was freed from the dangers of mere subjectivism. Möhler and the Tübingen School played a crucial part in reviving the long forgotten tradition of the Church as Christ living on in history. Tradition was dynamic and organic, 'the word of God living eternally in the body of the faithful'.

Möhler's most famous work, *Symbolism*, was an exposition of the doctrinal differences between Christians, but it was not written in that spirit of extreme polemic which so often marred the apologetic of the time. Möhler insisted that Christ established a visible society, the Church, which corresponded to human needs and aspirations. 'Jesus Christ has made visible the superior world; the Church is its image and likeness, for it is in her and through her that what he meant to represent has been given reality'. In order to retain its unity, the Church must have a head, instituted by Christ, the successor of St Peter. However, the Pope enjoyed 'essential' rights which were permanent and unchanging and these had to be distinguished from his 'accidental' powers which varied from time to time and might even become outdated.

Döllinger would later testify to the fact that for a whole generation of Catholics Möhler rediscovered the spiritual or mystical Church behind the structures of the legal or institutional Church. He also revived St Cyprian's formula, 'the church in the bishop'. As a result, German Catholics were able to appreciate the religious dimension of hierarchical and ecclesiastical government; they could respect the episcopacy, while avoiding the Erastian implications of Gallicanism and recognize the position of the Pope as the centre of unity without becoming dominated by Ultramontanism.

Although there were some Ultramontanes in Germany, particularly in Bavaria, most German Catholics tended to ignore or oppose the writings of French Ultramontanes. The *Tübingen Theological Quarterly*, for example, described Maistre's work as 'the foolish declamations of a dilettante'. Furthermore, German Catholics generally were opposed to the policy of trying to safeguard the position of the Church by political means. Schlegel's remarks on Lamennais' *Essay on Indifference* are very revealing:

> To come to the point, it is through becoming a party that the French clergy are losing the best part of the influence they might otherwise have. There is no greater desecration of God's matter than to treat it as a party affair. The book you praise so highly I regard as one of the most pernicious and destructive books which have appeared for a long time; and I am busy refuting it.

Möhler himself believed that,

> the Church, as the visible expression of Christ's way of salvation, should be defended on its own grounds and with its own means, and never used or misused as a foil or buttress for political doctrines. Political leaders must fend for themselves and make out as best they can with their Absolutism or Constitutionalism, their Monarchism or Republicanism. It is a poor service to our Church to involve it in struggles in which, as we see every day alas, the political mistakes, all the necessary or unnecessary reaction, and all the sins of misgovernment recoil upon her as the supposed propagator of these doctrines, while the sacred interests of man are forgotten. As a result even the honest champions fall, without noticing it, into the company of those who want to buttress their political wisdom with the prestige of the Church, without genuinely honouring it, or increasing its good name by the holiness of their lives.

Other German writers such as Francis von Baader were even more critical of the development of Ultramontanism and in 1844 John Ronge wrote his notorious article on 'German Catholicism'. Ronge had resented the way in which his bishop, Count Sedlnitzky of Breslau, had been forced to resign on the grounds that he had not identified himself sufficiently with some German bishops who had been arrested. In the summer of 1844 more than a million pilgrims from Belgium and Luxembourg as well as from Germany itself went to Trier where the Sacred and Seamless Robe of Christ was reputed to be kept. Ronge, who had been suspended and had renounced his priesthood, took the opportunity to condemn the Bishop of Trier; 'Already the historian is reaching for his pen and is holding up your name, Arnoldi, to the scorn of generations, present and future, calling you the Tetzel of the nineteenth century'. Ronge's letter created a sensation and, following his excommunication, he called for the establishment of a German Church independent of Rome. However, in spite of widespread discontent among the younger clergy, the support of political liberals opposed to the policies of Gregory XVI and a few remaining Josephinists, the new 'German Catholic Church' almost inevitably failed and in so doing contributed to the development of Ultramontanism in Germany.

It is significant that the writings of the French Ultramontanes received the greatest support from a magazine like *Der Katholik* of Mainz where German Catholics had shared the experiences and the reactions of their French co-religionists. Bishop Joseph Ludwig Colmar refused to sign the Civil Constitution of the Clergy and during the Terror he lived in hiding, ministering to his flock. He had been appointed bishop by Napoleon and he organized his famous diocesan seminary according to the recommendations of the Council of Trent. Like Colmar, Bishop Räss of Strasbourg who founded *Der Katholik* in 1820 had also suffered persecution during the French Revolution. Räss himself was a rather narrow critic and was notorious for denouncing the errors of others. Through the pages of *Der Katholik*, he introduced German Catholics to the ideas and the controversies of French Catholics and to the eccentric theories of writers like Veuillot. In later years attempts were even made with the support of the Roman authorities to align the Church in Germany with that of France.

The Church in Mainz seemed to combine a narrow theological approach with a genuine pastoral and social concern, and a flair for organization. Mainz was the first centre in Germany to support the revival of scholasticism as German theologians began to reflect Roman opinions. The Romantic movement had removed former prejudices against scholasticism in Germany even before Italian neo-scholasticism made any impact. The neo-scholastics were first successful in Naples where they later enjoyed the support of the influential Jesuit periodical, *Civiltà Cattolica*. Matthew Liberatore's *Institutiones Philosophicae* was one of the first modern syntheses of Thomist philosophy, but it was largely through Joseph Kleutgen, a Jesuit professor at the Gregorian University and the author of *The Theology of the past* and *The Philosophy of the past*, that neo-scholasticism began to influence German theologians.

In 1848 the aims of the German theologians at Tübingen and Mainz seemed to be identical: to free the Church from Erastian bureaucrats and to enable German Catholics to resist the forces of anti-Catholicism. The theologians at Mainz, however, tended to be more clerical and Roman, and they refused to support theological faculties affiliated to secular universities. Döllinger, on the other hand, considered that it was dangerous to isolate Catholics from secular universities, especially when trying to reconcile the teaching of the Church with contemporary intellectual developments. For their part, the Ultramontanes generally denied the possibility of reconciling the Church with the modern world and were very critical of those university professors who, in their opinion, ignored the significance of the *Magisterium Petri*. Suspicions and denunciations poisoned relations between the Ultramontanes and their opponents, and between German theologians and Roman officials.

Most of the denunciations came from German ecclesiastics and neo-scholastics, and were circulated by the nuncio in Munich. Those denunciations which came before the Congregation of the Index were examined in a less than impartial way by Kleutgen, who was one of the consultants.

Between 1835 and 1861 three important philosophical systems were condemned – condemnations which ensured the success of neo-scholasticism. The publication of David Friedrich Strauss' *Life of Jesus* in 1835 helped to reinforce the conservative fears of those who rejected contemporary scientific methods, and in the same year the ideas of George Hermes, who had attempted to reconcile the philosophy of Kant with the doctrines of Catholicism, were condemned in the Brief *Dum acerbissimus*. In 1857 the scholastics gained another success when the works of Anton Günther, who attempted to interpret Catholic sacramentalism in terms of contemporary idealism, were placed on the Index. Günther's violent attacks on neo-scholasticism probably contributed to his condemnation, which was the first occasion on which official papal approval was given to scholasticism. Encouraged by their success, the neo-scholastics secured the appointment of Denzinger to the chair of dogmatics at the university of Würzburg. His *Enchiridion symbolorum definitionum et declarationum* was intended to inform theologians of the definitive interpretation of the *Magisterium Petri*.

The Roman authorities found scholasticism attractive because of its generally conservative and traditional character, while the fact that none of the Roman theologians held any of the alternative theological or philosophical systems increased their suspicions of those who did. Furthermore, it was possible to find 'nationalist' overtones among some of the theological opponents of scholasticism. Gioberti, a leading Ontologist, was also an important figure in the Italian *Risorgimento*, while Döllinger openly referred to the superiority of German scholarship and theology over that of other nations and schools. At the Munich Congress, he accused the Roman scholastics of using arguments which had failed at the time of the Reformation and claimed that they were defending the faith with bows and arrows, while German theologians were using guns.

The fact that scholasticism was both conservative and the only theological system common throughout the Church reflected the increasing traditionalism and centralization within the Roman curia. The definition of papal infallibility, which was mainly supported by the Jesuits and scholastics, finally decided the outcome. The defeat of those bishops and theologians who were opposed to the definition coupled with the dominating position of the papacy in the teaching office of the Church ensured the triumph of scholasticism, though this had no actual connexion with the Pope's teaching office. After 1870 the Holy See became the only source of theological decisions and new theological developments were impossible without the approval of the Roman authorities.

The theological authority of the curia and Vatican officials also increased as agents of an infallible papacy. It was clearly impossible for the Pope himself to supervize personally every aspect of ecclesiastical administration and he depended a great deal on his advisers and officials. But, as with all civil servants, these officials tended to be anonymous in sharing the authority of their superior. Theologians throughout the world became subject to the 'infallible' authority as well as the secrecy and anonymity of the curia, and some of the Roman authorities themselves undoubtedly went out of their way to secure denunciations and condemnations.

The political and religious situation in Germany had been transformed by the Revolution and the subsequent secularization. After 1803 there were no longer any completely Catholic states in Germany. Catholic Bavaria incorporated Ansbach and Bayreuth, while Württemberg incorporated half a dozen abbeys and Catholic principalities, and the predominantly Catholic Rhineland became part of Prussia. Furthermore, the rulers of Prussia tried to unite the whole of Germany under their own leadership and attempts to subject the Catholic Church to the governments of various German states were frequently accompanied by efforts to spread Protestantism, especially when Protestantism became explicitly linked with German nationalism. These Erastian and proselytizing tendencies reinforced the development of German Ultramontanism; the support of the papacy might prevent the German Church from being controlled or exploited by secular authorities, while the German bishops increasingly associated their authority with that of the Pope as their own local influence declined. The Government of Württemberg appointed parish priests, cancelled holidays of obligation, forbade the exposition of relics and even changed the practice of confession. The authorities in Badan would not allow the Archbishop of Freiburg to publish pastoral letters without permission and appointed sixty of the eighty parish priests in his diocese. This Erastian and 'Protestant' campaign was waged most systematically and energetically in Prussia where the conflict came to a head over the question of mixed marriages.

As Prussia incorporated predominantly Catholic territories, Protestant officials married into Catholic families and tended to object to the restrictions imposed on them by the Church's regulations on mixed marriages. In 1825 King Friedrich William III extended the application of an earlier royal declaration whereby children were to be educated in their fathers' religion. This measure favoured Protestants at the expense of Catholics since more Protestant men married Catholic women than *vice versa*. Leading Catholic families however wanted to protect their property and positions from the consequences of marriages with Protestant Prussians. Consequently, Catholics accused the King of breaking a royal promise made in 1815 to protect the Catholic religion and began to apply the rules on mixed marriages more strictly.

In 1830 a papal brief ordered priests simply to attend weddings without giving a blessing in those cases where promises to safeguard the Catholic education of children had not been given. However, the German bishops were only able to communicate with Rome through Berlin and the Prussian Government refused to allow this brief to be published. The Government then coerced a few of the bishops into making an agreement which effectively annulled the provisions of the brief. Parish priests were not obliged to demand the promises and must only refuse the blessing if they knew that arrangements had actually been made to educate children outside the Church. The Roman authorities themselves who were anxious to avoid a quarrel quietly accepted the 'explanations' subsequently offered by the Prussian ambassador in Rome.

In 1835 the Prussian authorities requested that Archbishop Clemens August Freiherr Droste zu Vischering should be elected to the see of Cologne. The new archbishop, who had fallen under the influence of Princess Galitzin in his native Münster, ordered his clergy to enforce the provisions of the papal brief and on 20 November 1837 he was arrested and imprisoned, as was Archbishop Martin von Dunin of Gnesen-Posen. The Roman authorities issued a vigorous protest, public opinion throughout Europe was scandalized and even Lamennais, who had just left the Church, joined with Montalembert and Döllinger in protesting against the arrest of the Archbishop. Görres reacted by publishing *Athanasius* and *Triarier*, which not only aroused German Catholics to the defence of their Church but indirectly contributed to the growing Catholic revival as well as enabling Catholics in Germany to become conscious of their strength.

Peace was restored when Frederick William IV who had a romantic admiration of Catholicism came to the throne. He established a Catholic department at the Ministry of Culture and allowed bishops to exercise authority over mixed marriages. In 1848 the King promulgated a constitution which guaranteed Catholic freedom of worship, complete autonomy in ecclesiastical appointments, freedom of communication with Rome, the right of association and the right to open schools. However, whether to curb the Archbishop himself or in an effort not to alienate the Prussians further, Droste-Vischering found to his annoyance that Gregory XVI had appointed a coadjuter to administer the diocese of Cologne in his place.

The imprisonment of the Archbishop of Cologne was a turning point in the career of a Prussian civil servant, William Emmanuel von Ketteler, who not only devoted himself to the service of the Church but identified himself with the needs of working people. German Catholics like Adam Muller, Friedrich Schlegel and Francis von Baader had opposed the economic notions of liberal capitalism during the earlier years of the century and several German priests and laymen had criticized industrial abuses and demanded protective legislation. Ketteler himself had been impressed with Father Adolph Kolping's efforts to organize workers along Christian lines and used Kolping's organizations to circulate his own ideas on the Church's attitude towards work and labour. In the 1840s Kolping had begun to organize the *Gesellenverein*; these organizations consisted of young journeymen and master workmen directed by a chaplain who tried to assist the moral and intellectual development as well as to improve the economic conditions of their members. Discussion of political issues was forbidden. Kolping's original aims were spiritual and charitable, but he later fought to defend the rights of labour. Furthermore, by leaving the initiatives to his young members rather than to their chaplains, he avoided the paternalism and clericalism associated with so many Catholic societies. In 1855 the *Kolpingfamilie* consisted of 104 branches with 12,000 members. A central organization was established in 1858 and when the founder died in 1865 there were more than 100,000 members. The movement eventually had its own newspapers and periodicals, libraries and infirmaries, and a membership of over half a million by 1901.

Ketteler gave his patrimony to the poor and during 1848 and 1849 he delivered a series of addresses in the cathedral at Mainz on 'The Great Social Questions of our Age'. Ketteler condemned economic liberalism and socialism, and demanded social justice:

> You have taken God from the heart of man, and now man has made an idol of his property. The world lies crushed beneath a mountain of injustice; the rich man squanders and dissipates his wealth, leaving his poor brethren to waste away through lack of the most necessary goods. He steals what God intended for all men.

After the elections which took place in 1848, there were about forty clerical deputies including Ketteler and three bishops at the parliament in Frankfurt.

Ketteler advocated the right of workers to form trade unions in order to achieve the reforms he considered necessary. He supported demands for higher wages and better holidays, and legislation to improve working hours and conditions and to prohibit or control the work of women and children. He insisted on the necessity of Government inspection and the need to protect wives and mothers who did not go out to work. Through his seminary and his periodicals, he encouraged the formation of priests who were socially trained and concerned. He initiated the national conferences of German bishops, the second of which took place in 1869 when he formulated a statement on the Church and social questions for the other bishops. Ketteler drew up a programme for German Catholics, which became the basis of the social policies of the Centre Party. His influence also extended to Social Catholics in other countries; he directly influenced Albert de Mun and the Bishop of Perugia who, as Pope Leo XIII described him as 'Our great precursor'.

In 1862, Baron von Schorlemer established associations of peasants to defend their economic interests and to enable them to live good Catholic lives. He maintained that:

> . . . the large-scale proprietor should live as a Christian; that is to say, he should differ from those who consider a great estate as a useful investment for their capital or as a means of avoiding the summer heat. We ought to share the people's sufferings as well as its joys . . . Rich or poor, we are all unprofitable servants before God, a truth which affords no grounds for a real social hierarchy.

Until the first World War, every German province had a *Bauernverein* with its house and newspaper, laboratory and fertilizer stores, cooperative bank and insurance society.

As a result of the social and pastoral concern shown by German Catholics, the German people were able to recognize in the Church a

Christian social order in reality, while Catholic congresses and organizations under the leadership of laymen helped to identify the German laity more closely with the Church and the clergy. The first meeting of a national assembly of German Catholics, the *Katholikentag*, had taken place in Mainz during 1848. This congress had opposed the last remnants of Josephinism or any movements towards establishing a national Church in Germany, while demanding the freedom 'to implant Catholic principles in life as a whole and to work for a solution to the social problem'. German Catholics at the time were becoming more conscious of their rights and their strength and more Ultramontane, but not more clerical. The *Katholikentag*, which eventually met annually, provided an obvious forum for the discussion of social issues and this emphasis on social problems was further stimulated by the formation of the *Volksverein* or meetings of Catholic workers.

This was the beginning of a 'Catholic Action' or a 'Catholic Party' out of which would later emerge the powerful Centre Party. In fact, the progressive social policies adopted by the Centre Party were regarded as dangerous by 'liberal' as well as conservative politicians and was one of the subsidiary reasons for their hostility to Catholicism revealed during Bismarck's *Kulturkampf*. On the other hand, Bismarck's attack on the Church ultimately failed largely because the Church was so firmly rooted in the life of the nation and especially in the lives of the working classes. As one recent historian has remarked, 'Bismarck was compelled to recognize that his struggle against Catholicism and its political influence merely paved the way to revolution and threatened to undermine the social order on which his Empire was founded'.

The development of Ultramontanism was accompanied with a change in German attitudes towards Catholicism as old Protestant and Erastian attitudes gave way to more nationalistic criticism of the 'foreign' authority of the Pope and the Catholic Church. As early as 1848 one German historian had claimed that 'Ultramontanism and German patriotism are mutually exclusive' and in 1854 the octogenarian Archbishop of Freiburg was imprisoned during one of those disputes between Church and State which became quite common in Germany. In 1866 Prussia defeated Austria and then defeated France some four years later. These two wars brought about the unification of Germany or, more correctly, the creation of the Prussian Empire. The victory of Prussia was regarded as a Protestant victory in spite of Ketteler's efforts to associate Catholics with the national struggle and to deny any confessional significance to the movement towards national unity. Most Catholics would have preferred a united Germany based on Austria and even Ketteler himself described the Prussian victory at Sedan as a German defeat. At the time German nationalism was rampant and historians like Gregorovius and Mommsen declared that this was the moment to complete the work of the Reformation. At the celebration in honour of Martin Luther which took place at Worms in 1868, one of the speakers proclaimed that 'We Protestants taking our stand on the Christian spirit, on German patriotism and on civilization, reject all hierarchic and dogmatic claims intended to lead us back towards Rome'.

But equally significant in the subsequent pattern of events was the national and international situation which faced the new Germany. After 1870 the only internal or external forces resisting Bismarck happened to be Catholics. A third of the new Germany was Catholic, but the German Catholics lived in precisely those former Polish, French or South German territories which had only recently been acquired and which did not owe a tradition of allegiance to Berlin. Similarly, Germany's external enemies were the Catholic powers of Austria and France, and some French Ultramontanes were particularly prominent among those Frenchmen who were demanding a war of revenge. Other Catholics also supported the notion of fighting a crusade to restore the Pope to Rome and if this was successful, similar moves might be made against the new Germany.

Bismarck was able to use the decrees of the Vatican Council to justify his attack on the Church. The Council seemed to have implemented the teachings of the *Syllabus of Errors* as well as proclaiming that the Pope was the absolute ruler of the Catholic Church throughout the world. Many politicians in other countries feared the threat from a political Catholicism, doctrinally and politically united under an infallible Pope, while the atmosphere was further poisoned by almost incredible suspicions. Gladstone, the Liberal Prime Minister, felt obliged to attack *The Vatican Decrees in their Bearing on Civil Allegience*, while Acton, the distinguished English opponent of Ultramontanism, actually feared for his life in Rome. As late as 1896, the Chancellor, Prince Chlodwig zu Hohenlohe-Schillingsfürst, still believed that the death of his brother the Cardinal had at least been hastened by the Jesuits.

In Switzerland a bishop who had suspended two priests who opposed the definition of papal infallibility was 'deposed' and expelled by the secular authorities. Swiss Catholics began to organize themselves, particularly in the Bernese Jura where they gave the freedom of the city to bishops suffering at the hands of the secular authorities. The civil authorities retaliated by passing a law giving them power to control parish priests, and some three-quarters of the parishes in the area were suppressed. The subsequent explosion of popular fury was such that the Government had to occupy the Jura with troops. In Geneva the authorities refused to recognize the episcopal rights of Bishop Mermillod after the Vatican Council and then banished him, even though he was a citizen of Geneva. The Bishop, however, continued to rule his diocese from across the border in France where hundreds of Swiss Catholics came to visit him. The Grand Council of Geneva then passed a 'Law for the Reorganization of the Catholic Church' which gave the civil authorities the right to create or to suppress parishes and to prohibit the publication of episcopal or papal documents. Churches were confiscated from exiled priests and handed over to the 'Old Catholics', though the movement eventually proved as ineffective in Switzerland as elsewhere. Some of the anti-Catholic laws passed in Switzerland at the time restricting the establishment of religious houses are still in force.

It is possible that the conflict in Germany was possibly precipitated by Catholic Bavaria where an anti-clerical Government supported the Old Catholic movement and prohibited the publication of the Vatican decrees. In Germany the political struggle became associated with a cultural struggle between the 'liberal' Protestant north and the Ultramontane Catholic south, where political and theological conservatives accepted the *Syllabus of Errors* and even supported the restoration of the temporal power of the Pope. Many German Catholics felt a sense of relief at the outbreak of hostilities, partly at least because this would justify their hatred of modern society. Conflict with the liberal world seemed but the normal condition for an Ultramontane Church militant. Professor Moufang declared in *Der Katholik* that his ideal bishop was one in chains and when the young Ludwig Pastor heard of the arrest of the Bishop of Trier, 'A heartfelt *Gott sei dank* unwittingly escaped me'.

Bismarck for his part proclaimed in 1875:

> At the head of this state within the state . . . stands the Pope, with his autocratic powers. This monarch is in our midst at the head of a closed party which elects and votes according to his will. Through his semi-official press in Prussia, the Pope has the power to have his decrees publicly proclaimed and to declare the laws of our country

> null and void! Furthermore, he keeps on our soil an army of priests, he collects taxes, he has cast about us a net of associations and congregations which have a great deal of influence – in short, since we have had our constitution, there has scarcely been anyone so powerful in Prussia as this lofty Italian prelate, surrounded by his Council of Italian clerics. In itself, such a position would be highly dangerous and would scarcely be tolerated by the state, even if it were held by and restricted to a subject. But here it belongs to a foreigner.

However, if the *Kulturkampf* originally meant the conflict between the Catholic Church and the German State, it later simply described the persecution of the Church by the State.

Bismarck began by giving legal support to the 'Old Catholics', who refused to accept papal infallibility and who had appealed to the German Government for protection against the attacks made on them by 'Roman' Catholics. In June 1871 the Government ordered the German bishops not to prevent Old Catholic professors from continuing their work in the universities. In July the Catholic department in the Prussian Ministry of Religion was abolished on the grounds that it had interfered in Polish affairs. In December the rights of clerics to discuss affairs of state were suppressed and political criticism in the pulpit was punishable by law. The Pulpit Law threatened any cleric who criticized the new Germany or its constitution with heavy fines or imprisonment; the Old Catholics were considered part of the constitution.

In 1872 Bismarck appointed the Bavarian Cardinal Hohenlohe, a personal friend of Döllinger and a close associate of the Old Catholics, as the new German ambassador to the Holy See. Since the Cardinal was already a member of the Papal Court, he could not properly act as the representative of a foreign power and the Pope used this fact as the reason for refusing to accept him. Bismarck broke off diplomatic relations and a press campaign in Germany united Protestants, Liberals and Socialists in a concerted attack on the Catholic Church.

In February 1872 Dr Falk, the new minister of religion in Prussia, issued the first of his infamous laws and initiated a programme to bring education under the direct control of the State instead of operating as before through the Evangelical and Roman Catholic Churches. All education including religious instruction was subject to State inspection and religious congregations were forbidden to teach or to give religious instruction. In July 1872 the Jesuits – who were blamed by Bismarck for the Pope's refusal to accept Hohenlohe – and other 'affiliated'

Otto von Bismarck

bodies such as the Lazarists and the Redemptorists were expelled from Germany. In April 1873 the Prussian constitution was amended and both Catholic and Protestant Churches were subjected to the laws of the State and to the supervision of the State as defined by law. The State then assumed control over the appointment and dismissal of the clergy.

The Falk or May Laws of 1873 put clerical training under the control of the State. Seminarians had to study in a university or seminary recognized by the State and were examined by Government officials at the end of their courses. Seminaries were subject to Government inspection and could be closed by the Government which also controlled student discipline. Episcopal appointments had to be submitted to the civil authorities who could veto them. All religious instruction had to be given in German and only Germans could hold positions of authority within the German Church. The civil courts had the final voice in all appeals from the ecclesiastical courts or from the German bishops.

Further penal laws were passed including the imposition of an oath of unconditional obedience on the Germany bishops, putting ecclesiastical property under the control of lay committees, insisting on the necessity of civil marriage in Prussia and closing Church schools in Alsace. In 1874 recalcitrant priests were interned or expelled from the country. In April 1875 the State ceased to give financial support to the Catholic clergy and in the following month all orders and congregations except those engaged in nursing were expelled from Prussia. Finally, in June 1875 three paragraphs safeguarding the position of the Catholic Church in the Prussian constitution were removed. The laws passed in Germany roughly corresponded to the legislation passed in France during the 1880s and in 1905, though they were never so rigidly enforced, and some of them actually remained on the Statute book until 1918. Furthermore, the *Kulturkampf* was not conducted with the same ferocity throughout Germany. Prussia was the obvious centre of the storm and the pressure was also severe in Bavaria and Baden, Hesse-Darmstadt and Alsace-Lorraine, but Württemberg and Oldenburg, for example, were only slightly affected.

Bismarck's policy was an attempt to make the German bishops independent of the papacy, the clergy of the bishops, the laity of the clergy, and to make the Catholic Church totally dependent on the State. However, the German bishops, clergy and laity simply refused to accept the legislation. Bishops and priests were fined or imprisoned, exiled and deposed. Sees and parishes remained vacant as Catholics were deprived of the sacraments. Those priests who were allowed to remain were forbidden to administer the sacraments outside their own parishes. Seminaries were closed, professorships fell vacant and the training of priests practically ceased. As a final indignity, the small number of Old Catholics were given priority in the use of churches and the Government actually established a new bishopric for their leader.

Bismarck had once declared, 'To Canossa we will not go', but he was eventually forced to recognize that his attack on the Church had failed. In spite of their former differences, Catholics in the German empire had united under the political leadership of Ludwig Windhorst. Physically, Windhorst was a diminutive figure with a huge head and bandy legs, but he had a sharp mind and was an able debator and a superb tactician. The Centre Party was not originally conceived as a Catholic Party, but was intended to unite all those who were opposed to the uniformity which the Prussian politicians wished to impose on Germany and to the militarism on which that uniformity was based. An important element in the Party's programme was a detailed policy of social reform, particularly with regard to the organization of labour, which won a great deal of support. However, the strength of the Party was based on the union of persecuted Catholics and a Catholic vote which included the particularists of southern Germany, the Polish Catholics of Posen and the French Catholics of Alsace-Lorraine. French and Polish, conservative and liberal Catholics supported the Centre Party, and through it German Catholics, unlike their French co-religionists, were able to play an important and constructive part in the development of parliamentary democracy.

The Centre Party continued to grow in spite of, or perhaps because of, Bismarck's persecution. After three years' persecution the Party almost doubled its representation in the Prussian Diet and the German Reichstag, while in July 1878 the number of its representatives increased from ninety-five to one hundred and three in a Reichstag of three hundred and ninety-seven. The persecution of the Church by Bismarck not only reinforced the strength of Catholicism in southern Germany, but also created a new sense of solidarity with the Holy See, and many of the Old Catholics returned to the Church. The *Kulturkampf* also created a practical partnership of political co-operation between the Centre Party and the Socialists in opposition to Bismarck, a partnership which was reinforced by the social awareness of German Catholics and later by the social policies of Leo XIII.

Meanwhile Bismarck himself ceased to be haunted by the sceptre of a European Catholic alliance and began to want the support of Catholics and the Centre Party to defeat, as he saw it, the rising menace of socialism. In May 1878 his first bill against the Socialists had been defeated by a combination of the National Liberals and the Centre Party, and by 1884 it was clear that his measures against socialism and in favour of social reform were dependent on the support of Catholic deputies and consequently on ending the *Kulturkampf*. Furthermore, in February 1878, the new Pope Leo XIII had announced his accession to the Emperor William I of Germany in mild and courteous terms in which he expressed his anxieties over the conflict and made an appeal on behalf of German Catholics. The Emperor replied reservedly but deferentially and so began a friendly correspondence which prepared the way for an improvement in relations between the two powers. The Emperor himself had always doubted the wisdom of Bismarck's religious policies which were also distasteful to many of the Chancellor's political colleagues.

Bismarck opened negotiations with the Belgian nuncio in Bavaria during 1878. At one stage, he remarked:

> I am ready to give you much and *also to make you a little Canossa* . . . already it is being said that I am on the way and that if I have not gone to Canossa, it has come to me.

When it was later reported in 1886 that Bismarck was making concessions on the education of the Catholic clergy in his negotiations with the Jesuit General, an Italian periodical remarked that the Chancellor was not only preparing to go to Canossa but even to Loyola. In 1879 Dr Falk was asked to resign and in 1881 Germany re-established diplomatic relations with the Holy See. In the following year the Prussian Government resumed the payment of ecclesiastical salaries and abolished the State examinations of priests. In 1883 bishops were no longer required to submit the appointment of parish priests to the secular authorities. In 1886 the Royal Tribunal of Ecclesiastical Affairs was abolished, full episcopal authority over the clergy was restored and the process of revising the May Laws began. The Bishop of Fulda was appointed to the House of Peers, while the Pope asked a couple of bishops who had proved most hostile to Bismarck to resign in the interests of the Church. By 1887 the most offensive legislation had been withdrawn and the Pope was able to claim that the *Kulturkampf* had been brought to an end.

Windhorst himself, however, wanted to secure the complete freedom of the Church and the restoration of all its former rights. He was convinced of the possibility of achieving these aims and did not approve of working for or being content with particular concessions. At one stage Windhorst even believed that Bismarck was trying to destroy the Centre Party by engaging in negotiations rather than attempting to bring the *Kulturkampf* to an end. The Pope, on the other hand, was not vindictive and was prepared to go further than Windhorst in reaching an accommodation with Bismarck. Leo had already embarrassed German Catholics by decorating Bismarck with the Order of Christ in 1885, the first occasion on which a Protestant had received this decoration, when the Chancellor had accepted papal arbitration in a colonial dispute with Spain.

Two years later the Pope asked the Centre Party to support Bismarck's military budget in order to safeguard the improving relations between Germany and the Holy See. The President of the Party replied that this was not a religious issue and that he and many of his colleagues would resign rather than support the budget. The fact that Bismarck was able to publish this confidential correspondence was a further embarrassment for German Catholics. Nevertheless, on this occasion, the Centre Party refused to support Bismarck and he had to call new elections. However, Windhorst had earlier pledged that the Centre Party would accept any religious agreement which was approved by the Pope and, in spite of his own opposition, it was becoming increasingly clear that the Holy See was prepared to make greater concessions than he was himself in return for a general modification of the *Kulturkampf*. Consequently, the Centre Party felt obliged to obey the Pope and would later join the conservative politicians in supporting German military budgets against the opposition of the Social Democratic and Progressive Parties.

In attempting to come to terms with the contemporary world, Leo XIII was prepared to adopt different policies in dealing with different states. He also recognized the 'legitimacy' of the secular authority of the State and the significance of popular support for secular governments. He was therefore willing to work with a Lutheran monarchy in Germany, a constitutional monarchy in Belgium or a democratic republic in France. It is sometimes said that the success of his policy can be seen in the defeat of the *Kulturkampf* in Germany and the *klein Kulturkampf* in Switzerland, in the re-establishment of diplomatic relations with Russia and the withdrawal of anti-clerical legislation in Spain. Certainly, the new prestige which the papacy enjoyed under Leo XIII can be seen in the fact that several governments invited him to arbitrate in their disputes and in the visits paid to him by King Edward VII of Great Britain and the Kaiser William II of Germany on no less than three occasions.

The Pope for his part was no stranger to the arts of 'diplomacy'. In addressing William II during 1903, Leo XIII declared:

> I would add without wishing to flatter you, that only one sovereign has acted as you have thought and done: Charlemagne. He was the great monarch who, so to say, made the civilized world bow to the Cross on behalf of God, a mission with which he had been charged by Leo III. Now, reflecting upon your speech, I dreamed that you, the actual Emperor of Germany, had received from me, Pope Leo XIII, the mission to combat socialistic and atheistic ideas, and to recall Europe to Christianity.

However, it is only fair to add that the Pope might have been hoping to win German support in his efforts to secure a solution to the Italian Question.

In spite of the fact that Leo XIII urged French Catholics to adopt a policy of political neutrality and his request to the German Catholics in favour of supporting Bismarck's military budget, the Pope continued the policy of opposing the forces of democracy and nationalism in Italy. However changed might be the position of the papacy within the Church or in the world at large, the Roman Question and the issue of the temporal power continued to jeopardize relations between the Holy See and the new Kingdom of Italy. The Pope's failure to recognize the strength of Italian nationalism and to solve the Italian Question was probably the greatest weakness of Leo XIII's pontificate and certainly contributed to the development of anti-clerical and hostile forces in Italy itself.

In 1871 the Italian Parliament had attempted to settle the Question unilaterally by passing the Law of Guarantees which has been described as 'Italy's truly great achievement in the field of legislation' and which 'had world-wide and lasting repercussions';

> It was, indeed, thanks to this law and to the regime which it inaugurated that not only the world at large, but also the Papacy itself, became convinced that the temporal power had been too heavy a burden for the Holy See to bear, and that the latter's prestige, its

ability to rule the Church effectively and to work for the diffusion of Catholicism throughout the world, had been materially increased by the loss of that power.

The Pope was deprived of his sovereign rights, while retaining ownership of the villa of Castel Gandolfo as well as of the Lateran and Vatican palaces. He was given the honours of a sovereign and the same protection as the Italian Head of State, rights of precedence and diplomatic privileges, legal immunity and independence, the right to maintain his traditional armed forces and an annual allowance of over three million lire.

However, the Pope rejected the Law of Guarantees on the grounds that it did not sufficiently guarantee the independence of the Holy See. The Law of Guarantees offered a personal sovereignty to the Pope himself, but only gave extra-territorial status to his temporal possessions, while the various peace offers made by the Italians to the Pope never included an acre of Roman territory, the only gift which might have made them acceptable. After 1870 the Papacy, at least in theory, felt at the mercy of the Italian Government and therefore open to the charge that it had lost its moral independence. The Vatican therefore refused to recognize the new Italian nation, partly in case other governments chose to regard the Pope as subject to Italian influence and used this as an excuse for ignoring him when dealing with the Church in their own countries.

In any case, the Law of Guarantees was merely an internal Italian measure which was subject to the whims of future Italian parliaments and the Italian Government of the day seemed offensively anti-clerical and anti-Catholic. The Government refused to confirm the election of Italian bishops and some twenty sees were left vacant. Protestants were allowed to build churches in Rome and the Government encouraged a pathetic Old Catholic movement which sprang up in Naples and Sicily. Property owned by the Congregation of Propaganda was confiscated and paid for with Government stock. Convents and colleges were expropriated and during 1873 there were seventy religious houses in Rome whose communities had been dispersed. The anti-clerical forces of the Left won the elections of 1876 and proceeded to abolish the catechism in primary schools, ban religious processions, suppress religious orders, conscript priests into the army, dissolve Catholic congresses and pass a law threatening to punish any priest who ventured 'to make a public attack on State institutions or governmental decisions'. The secularist laws of Piedmont governing education and marriage were later extended throughout Italy.

It could well be that an open reconciliation between the Kingdom of Italy and the Holy See was virtually impossible at this time; the new nation was too jealous of its rights and the Pope was too committed to his supporters. Pius IX himself adopted a policy of *non possumus*: Catholics were forbidden to acknowledge the permanent existence of the Kingdom of Italy or to take part in Italian politics either by standing for election or voting in elections. This ban on Catholic political activity was intended to undermine the stability of the new Italian State. However, in practice it did more damage to the Church and to the process of democratic government by preventing Catholics from participating in the political life of the country. This political 'abdication' also prevented the development of Social Catholicism in Italy, while the divisions between those Catholics who supported a possible compromise and those who were opposed to the new nation prevented their effective cooperation in other spheres.

With the election of Leo XIII, which was almost universally welcomed, even by Italian Freemasons, there were hopes of an immediate reconciliation, but these rapidly faded and left behind a legacy of bitterness. The fact that the new Pope did not give his blessing from the balcony overlooking St Peter's was publicly interpreted as a sign that he intended to remain the Prisoner of the Vatican. This sense of disappointment was reinforced by the Pope's first encyclical *Inscrutabile Dei* in which he denounced the excesses of liberalism and the abandonment of Christian values; he emphasized the importance of ecclesiastical authority and described modern civilization as 'a phantom of civilization'. The moderate journal *Riforma* commented:

> The new Pope does not resort to imprecations, he does not curse, he does not, so to speak, threaten, and in this there is a perceptible (and perhaps the only) difference from the former. But as to the condemnation of all the conquests of the modern spirit, he is absolute, decided, inexorable, almost cruel, quite as the one he succeeded . . . The form is sweet but the substance is absolute, hard, intransigent.

At the same time, the liberal tone and kindly spirit which the new Pope always adopted offended Catholic intransigents. One of them quoted Pius IX as saying, 'Dying is a small matter; what worries me is that I shall have as my successor Cardinal Pecci who would ruin the Church, if that were possible, by his statemanship and diplomacy'; to which another added, 'To hope to win by inertia and meekness is a frivolity of mind unworthy of the least respect . . . a confidence which presupposes treason rather than ignorance'.

At times Leo XIII seems to have hoped for the total restoration of the temporal power through the efforts, never fully explained, of the Governments of France or Germany. At other times the Pope apparently expressed his willingness to be satisfied with a small parcel of territory large enough to ensure his independence from which he might exercise his spiritual authority. The need to guarantee his independence was illustrated when an Italian court claimed jurisdiction in a dispute involving members of the papal household. Furthermore, demonstrations against some French pilgrims and on the occasion when the body of Pio Nono was being taken to a new resting-place, seemed to show that the Italian Government was either unwilling or unable to provide proper protection for the Holy See.

Certainly, Leo XIII was more pre-occupied with the Roman Question than either his predecessor or his successor. This was partly a result of the fact that he was more of a diplomat than the other two popes, partly in an effort to convince other nations that the Vatican was not subject to Italian influence, but partly because the Pope does seem to have become somewhat obsessed with the issue. He made over sixty formal protests against the Italian usurpation of his authority and spoke with great emotion and anger about the Italian 'occupation' of Rome. The gulf between the Italian Government and the Holy See widened to such an extent at one stage that Leo XIII thought of seeking political asylum in Austria. Even at the end of his life when he was ninety-two years of age he continued to entertain unrealistic hopes for the restoration of his temporal power.

The policies adopted by Leo XIII in Italy inevitably identified the Catholic Church with the privileged classes and the forces of the right, strengthened the socialists and the anti-clericals, prevented the development of Social Catholicism or the progress of genuine reform and indirectly weakened the democratic movement as well as the consolidation of the nation. Italian political and social problems could not be solved without the intervention of Catholics, some of whom participated in politics in spite of the *non expedit.* Even after the publication of *Rerum novarum*, however, intransigent Catholics still regarded the solution of the Roman Question as more significant than the social or political problems facing the Italian people and the working classes were forced to turn more and more to the socialists.

The Pope's preoccupation with the temporal power also delayed the development of Catholic Action in Italy. He consistently refused to allow Italian Christian Democrats to engage in political and social action. When he approved of the formation of a Catholic political party which was somewhat analogous to the British Conservative Party, its members were still not allowed to take part in elections. When some of the opinions expressed in the encyclical *Libertas praestantissimum* seemed to encourage Catholics to become involved with political activities, he again repeated that he was not lifting the ban imposed in Italy. Apparently, what might be praiseworthy for Catholics elsewhere was not to be applied to Catholics in Italy.

Of course, the Italian Governments of the time would not have welcomed Catholics into the political arena. In 1898 political gatherings in churches were restricted 'as capable of disturbing the public peace', while clerical associations were 'considered and treated as subversive'. One moderate Italian politician remarked:

> The Roman Question, the eternal Roman Question, which short-sighted politicians foolishly believed so easy to combat . . . is at the bottom of all the present difficulties of Italy. Until it is resolved we shall never have internal peace . . . it is a question of life or death for the nation . . . The greater part of my compatriots will tell you that the papal question . . . has been and is still, the cancer of Italy . . . [The clerical party] cannot be viewed simply as a religious party, as it would be in France or any other country; its anti-dynastic and anti-unitary principles tend to make it regarded by the government as a political enemy . . . [and yet] the papacy has never been more powerful that at the present hour.

On the whole, however, both during and after the *Risorgimento*, Catholics were deliberately tormented and ridiculed rather than persecuted by Italian anti-clericals. Catholics were taunted that their loyalty to the Pope could not be reconciled with loyalty to Italy and minor civil servants took pleasure in banning Catholic meetings and processions, while left-wing anti-clericals enjoyed themselves dispersing Catholic meetings or raiding Catholic clubs. Some anti-clerical freemasons were responsible for appointing many nonentities to academic or political positions, though there is apparently no evidence that any Catholic of significance was actually excluded from an official position because of his religious convictions. Historical celebrations such as the anniversaries of Galileo, Voltaire or Garibaldi were given an anti-clerical twist even at the expense of historical facts. In 1882 the sixth centenary of the Sicilian Vespers provided an opportunity for anti-papal demonstrations since Pope Martin IV had supported the French. In 1888 the year of the Pope's Golden Jubilee, the civil authorities erected a statute of the former Dominican and atheist, Giordano Bruno, on the Campo dei Fiori. The Church authorities retaliated by using ecclesiastical celebrations and foreign pilgramages, especially during the Holy Year of 1900, to embarrass the Italian Government.

Italian Catholics, constantly irritated by anti-clericals, increasingly felt that the Church authorities should recognize the facts of the situation and by removing the *non expedit* enable the Italian laity to secure the reform of anti-Catholic legislation. They appreciated that, although some of the issues between Church and State were not subject to negotiation, some of the other political and economic, charitable and educational demands of Catholics could be achieved. Younger Catholics in particular were less concerned with the solution of historical issues than with the new situation in which the Italian Church found itself, particularly after the rise of socialism. There was, in any case, a growing divorce between religion and politics, and an increasing indifference towards former divisive issues; politicians showed themselves to be less concerned about internal religious questions, while there was nothing particularly 'Catholic' about such issues as tariff reform.

Consequently, there was inevitably some easing of tension if only as a result of the passage of time. The Kingdom of Italy became an established fact and it was obviously unrealistic to hope for a restoration of the position which had existed in 1859. It also became impossible for the anti-clericals to envisage expelling the Pope from the Vatican into a monastery, let alone exiling him from Italy. The tone of papal protests changed with the passage of time, while Vatican officials began to consider the advantages offered by the Law of Guarantees. Certainly, there was consternation whenever it seemed possible that the Italian Government might be having second thoughts about the law. Furthermore, the Government controlled all ecclesiastical appointments and the use of ecclesiastical or educational property in Italy. The opinions of the Roman authorities could not be made known officially and so unofficial channels had to be opened in order that the Holy See might express its preferences about ecclesiastical appointments.

The extent of the differences between Pius IX, Leo XIII and Pius X on the Roman Question should not be exaggerated. Merry del Val is reported as saying:

> When Pius IX proclaimed the *non expedit*, he meant that Catholic participation in Italian political elections was inopportune. It was Leo XIII who later transformed this into an outright prohibition. When I was Leo's Private Chamberlain, His Holiness told me that a day would come when his successor would have to remove this prohibition. Besides, if Pius IX had been able to see that the situation . . . would last so long, he would certainly not have proclaimed the *non expedit*.

Nevertheless, the pontificate of Pius X substantially changed Vatican attitudes to the Roman Question and eased relations with the Kingdom of Italy. Neither the Pope nor his Secretary of State, Merry del Val, shared the Roman nostalgia for the temporal power and although papal claims could not be renounced until papal independence had been secured, official Vatican thinking apparently became less specifically territorial. Merry del Val himself seems to have thought that the best solution would be to improve the Vatican's international standing and he therefore attempted, unsuccessfully in the event, to secure representatives of the Holy See on the various international conferences which took place at the time.

Although Pius X paid lip service to his predecessors' policies, the threat of Socialism and the dangers of Catholic isolation forced the Holy See into closer collaboration with the 'liberal' and previously hostile Italian State. Pius X continued to protest and remained the Prisoner of the Vatican, but this was simply a formal gesture and mark of respect for the traditions established by his predecessors. As Bishop of Mantua and Patriarch of Venice, he had beenable to appreciate the value of strong and vigorous Catholic organizations in areas where Catholics controlled municipal councils and public life. He also recognized the impatience which so many Italian Catholics felt as a result of their inability to enter public life. The Vatican's rapprochement with Italy should also be seen as a manifestation of an increasing awareness of the need for a conservative political alliance against the rising forces of the left. Not only would Pius X, unlike his predecessors, have been horrified by a violent restoration of the temporal power, but he even envisaged the possibility of Catholics dominating the Italian Parliament in the reasonably near future. During the general elections of 1904, 1909 and 1913, therefore, the Pope either sanctioned by dispensation or simply ignored the increasing infringement of the *non expedit* which was finally abolished by Benedict XV in 1919.

At the same time, Pius X rejected attempts to establish an Italian Catholic Conservative Party because he was concerned to maintain clerical control over the laity. The Roman authorities eventually became suspicious of the emergence of Catholic political parties because these were frequently forced to accept the implications of the new situation in which the Church found itself within a pluralist society. The new political parties might intervene in questions affecting relations between Church and State, whereas Vatican officials preferred to control all diplomatic negotiations directly. In some ways the position of the new parties seemed too analogous to that of the old episcopates in threatening the increasing concentration and centralization of ecclesiastical authority in the hands of papal officials. How far such Ultamontane and clerical attitudes were to influence subsequent developments in Germany as well as Italy, it is, of course, impossible to say.

Pope Leo XIII

VI: The Catholic Church under Pope Leo XIII

Joachim Pecci was apparently a widely-read and successful student. Cardinal Sala, the liberal critic of the political policies adopted in the Papal States, had been a formative influence in his early life, while Giambattista Pianciani, the Jesuit scientist in the Papal States who tried to reconcile the biblical account of creation with contemporary scientific discoveries, had been one of his teachers. Pecci made his first and not entirely successful contacts with a liberal and secular Government as papal nuncio in Belgium before being appointed Bishop of Perugia in the Papal States. Like Bishop Mastai Ferretti of Imola, Bishop Pecci did not have to deal personally with revolutionary activities since his people were not oppressed and did not join the revolutionary movement. It is also significant that the Bishop of Perugia was not on good terms with Cardinal Antonelli.

However, as one historian has put it, 'In his reform activities Bishop Pecci was liberal; in his support of the prerogatives of the Bishop of Rome he was conservative'. It is said that the Bishop of Perugia played a leading part in the preparation of the *Syllabus of Errors* as well as the definitions of the Immaculate Conception and papal infallibility, and that he was one of the thirty-four bishops consulted by Pio Nono before he called the first Vatican Council. In many ways, Leo's policies as Pope developed along the lines adopted by his predecessor. He continued the policies of educating future bishops and leaders of the Church in Rome, of centralizing ecclesiastical administration and of supporting the adoption of Thomism. Totally committed to the teachings of the Church, Leo XIII constantly reminded the world of those teachings and did not hesitate to condemn what seemed contrary to them. He condemned Rosmini, whereas Pio Nono had not. Pius IX had also been unwilling to denounce Curci's pamphlet on the '*Royal Vatican*'. The founder of *Civiltà Cattolica* had criticized the Holy See, demanded reforms and argued that the Church must come to terms with the modern world. Leo XIII forced him to retract.

However, although Leo's encyclical on the Church and Civilization,

Inscrutabile Dei published in 1878, hardly differed in principle from the allocutions of Pius IX, he was more moderate and calm, positive and constructive. If Leo wanted the Church to be more outward-looking and to modify the citadel mentality fostered by his predecessor, he preferred a dramatic to a revolutionary change. He did not adopt a simple or monolithic approach, but was prepared to adapt his policies to different situations. He tried to conciliate where this could be done without compromising anything fundamental or essential and he was even willing to suggest positive programmes to meet some of the needs of the age. Politically, he proved to be an able leader and a clear-minded statesman in trying to improve relations with individual government and removing political obstacles that did not involve basic principles. It is significant that in spite of his favourable attitude to the separation of the Church and State in non-Catholic countries, he was not necessarily in favour of disestablishment in Catholic countries.

The Pope's ambiguity or ambivalence was revealed most clearly in his attitude towards scholarship and in particular in his attitude towards Thomism. Leo XIII was well aware of the need for an intellectual revival in Catholicism and he endorsed the establishment of pontifical universities in Washington and Ottowa, in Lyons and Toulouse. He himself was personally interested in science and literature; he helped to improve the training of priests by emphasizing the importance of studying history, philosophy and science as well as theology. He also promoted the study of astronomy and provided the Vatican Observatory with modern instruments. On the 4th of August 1879 the new Pope launched his campaign to revive Thomism in the encyclical *Aeterni patris*, which was followed by practical directives in an apostolic letter *Cum hoc sit* issued during the following year. Pius IX had supported the Thomist movement in the *Syllabus of Errors* by condemning the proposition that the principles of the schoolmen were not in accordance with the needs of the time or the progress of science. Leo XIII, however, went much further and encouraged the supporters of Thomism to prepare for its triumph under Pius X. Whatever the virtues of the Thomistic system, the methods and the motives of some of those who introduced it and supported it might well be questioned.

Leo XIII instructed seminary teachers to use Thomism as the basis for the education of priests. The text-books and even some of the professors in the Roman universities and seminaries were replaced. Thomists were appointed to chairs in the College of Propaganda and the Gregorian University. The Dominicans were entrusted with the task of preparing a new and complete edition of the works of Aquinas and an academy for the interpretation and defence of Thomism was established in Rome. Not unnaturally there was some opposition to the directives of the Pope and those of his Jesuit brother, Giuseppe Pecci, the Cardinal Prefect of the Congregation of Studies and the Director of the Academy of St Thomas in Rome. However, in 1892 the Pope again wrote to all Catholic professors repeating his insistence on the need for contemporary scholarship to be 'in harmony' with the opinions of St Thomas.

The Pope did not seem to understand that philosophy was the result of rational processes and he was apparently unaware of the history and pluralism of scholastician. Leo seems to have regarded scholasticism as an instrument of apologetics to be imposed by authority if necessary; Catholics were ordered to adopt a system of philosophy by decree. The secular newspapers were not impressed and one periodical commented:

> [Philosophy] has no native land, does not depend on any sect or any religion. There can no more be a Christian philosophy than a Christian mathematics or physics, or chemistry, a Christian, Jew, or Protestant biology. Students then are being taught – by Catholic faculties – a Christian philosophy such as Dr Thomas Aquinas taught in the Middle Ages. In the light of Leo's reputation for liberalism the encyclical seems strange.

Nevertheless, the Pope's call to apply the thought of one of the most outstanding minds in history to contemporary problems undoubtedly promoted a great deal of serious philosophical reflection which was an improvement on the eclectic approach previously adopted in ecclesiastical academic institutions. Furthermore, some Thomists embraced scholastic principles not because they were ordered or taught to do so, but because they were convinced of their validity and these writers attempted to apply Thomist principles in a positive and constructive way to the problems of the day. The intellectual eminence and integrity of Désiré Joseph Mercier, Jacques Maritain or Étienne Gilson cannot be denied. On the other hand, the papal endorsement of Thomism unfortunately encouraged the establishment of a kind of philosophical orthodoxy, especially in seminaries and other clerical establishments. Philosophy was subordinated to clerical theological interests; in time, more rigid and narrow Thomists would be reinforced in their suspicions of and hostility to such original and independent thinkers as Maurice Blondel.

Leo XIII's attitude to history seems to have been much more open than his attitude to philosophy or theology. He established a historical library as well as a school of palaeography and comparative history. However, his most important move was to open the Vatican Archives to competent research students. The Pope himself observed that,

> *the first law of history is not ever to dare to falsify; the second, not to fear to tell the truth,* nor ever to lend onself in the slightest to *flattery or animosity*. . . . Truth, in spite of the persevering efforts against it, will break through and triumph; it may be obscured for a moment, but never extinguished.

His encyclical on biblical studies, however, was more restricted and was the occasion on which some Catholic scholars retracted earlier opinions or even left the Church. To some extent, *Providentissimus Deus* encouraged the use of contemporary methods in the study of scripture, but its definition of inspiration seemed unnecessarily narrow. Leo also appointed a Biblical Commission of comparatively liberal members, but such a commission was both unsuitable and incapable of acting as a sort of supreme tribunal to decide disputed questions or as a means of guiding and supervising scholars. During the pontificate of Pius X, the Commission almost inevitably became a second Congregation of the Index, though Leo's basic encouragement of academic research was not completely destroyed during this later period of anti-Modernist reaction.

Leo XIII was less ambiguous in his approach to social or economic problems and in promoting the development of Social Catholicism. He himself had first experienced the evils of industrialization as nuncio in Belgium, where Catholics supported measures to alleviate social and economic problems to a greater extent than Catholics in some other countries. Edouard Ducpetiaux, the Inspector General of Prisons and Charitable Institutions, was a Christian Socialist before 1850. Ducpetiaux argued that production should be for man, not man for production; society should be re-ordered on a co-operative rather than a competitive basis. He supported compulsory education and parliamentary reform, the regulation of child labour and Government inspection of factories.

On the whole, however, Social Catholicism in Belgium was originally paternalist and was restricted to providing moral or religious help and charitable relief through the formation of guilds. The policies of Belgian Catholics were neither radical nor socialist, but followed the conservative line of Charles Périn who was opposed to the theories of *laissez faire* on the one hand and the aims of revolutionary socialism on the other. Périn advocated social legislation, the formation of voluntary Christian guilds and the education of employers in Christian ideals. The Archconfraternity of St Francis Xavier founded in 1854, worked for the conversion of sinners, organized pilgrimages, distributed good books and destroyed bad ones, formed libraries and established night schools. The confraternity was much more successful in the small towns than in large industrial conurbations, but similar societies were established and their members began to appreciate the need to provide social, recreational, educational services and savings clubs as well as charitable relief.

In due course, Belgian Catholics began to realize that workers must be allowed to organize themselves, that the Government must reform industrial structures and that workers had rights in justice as well as claims on Christian charity. This was especially true after the elections of 1857 when the Liberals broke with Catholics and campaigned on the slogan 'Down with the priests'. Younger Catholics began to advocate more reforming and progressive policies. They launched a new journal *L'Universel* with policies similar to those of *L'Avenir*, but which went further in supporting the rights of trade unions and universal suffrage. At the Malines Congresses of 1863 and 1864, they attempted to secure recognition for the principle of a living wage. In short, they prepared the way for the advent of Christian Democracy, and Catholic governments in Belgium later introduced old-age pensions, subsidized mutual aid societies, saving banks, building societies and technical education. Legislation was passed regulating wages and the working conditions of women and children. Councils of labour and industry were formed and in 1895 the Social Department of Labour was created.

Leo XIII had experienced the poverty of the old agricultural society as a bishop in Italy. The growth of Italian Social Catholicism was largely a reaction against the development of Socialism. When a couple of former supporters of Garibaldi began a campaign of agitation amongst the agricultural labourers, Bishop Bonomelli of Cremona issued his famous pastoral on *Property and Socialism* denouncing the great landowners who failed to set a Christian example, ignored the needs of their workers, and subjected them to iniquitous contracts. Two of the most illustrious Social Catholics in Italy were Alessandro Rossi, a factory owner who turned his business into a 'Christian corporation', and Giuseppe Toniolo, great grandson of Joseph de Maistre, student of Aquinas and professor of political economy at the University of Pisa, who advocated social reform in programmes and publications, congresses and movements. Archbishop Joachim Pecci of Perugia was one of the few clerics in Italy to show any interest in social problems, not only because of his experience in Belgium, but as a result of studying the writings of Lamennais and Ozanam, Balmes and Ketteler as well as St Thomas Aquinas. The Archbishop issued a pastoral demanding a return to the principles of Christianity and the protection of Government legislation to protect the interests of the poor and the weak; he denounced their exploitation in the interests of profit, condemned excessive hours of labour and deplored the flagrant disregard of man's real needs.

In some ways the 1870s marked a turning point in the history of Social Catholicism. By 1870 Social Catholics had not achieved any lasting or fundamental effect and French Catholics were no nearer to providing answers to social questions than they had been in 1820. The few left-wing Social Catholics were too doctrinaire and utopian. while more conservative Catholics were often too afraid of democratic Socialism and too optimistic in hoping for positive reactions from those who enjoyed wealth, power and privilege. Neither side received adequate support from other Catholics in general or from their bishops in particular, who failed to appreciate the situation as a result of ignorance or indifference. When Bishop Mermillod preached on the dramatic contrast between the wealth of the upper classes and the poverty of their workers in 1869, he created a public scandal. In 1872 the French National Assembly appointed a commission to inquire into the conditions of the workers. All the members of this commission were practising Catholics who reported that working conditions were on the whole all that they might be expected to be and that practically nothing could be done about them.

Of course, economic developments were moving far too rapidly, while political developments further prejudiced support for the work of reform. Conservative fears were reinforced by the murder of a number of priests including the Archbishop of Paris during the Commune of 1871. Furthermore, as relations between the French Government and the Church grew worse, Catholic organizations, especially the Society of St Vincent de Paul, came under attack. Its general council was dissolved and local conferences were ordered to secure legal recognition. Meanwhile, over 400 conferences dominated by monarchists went into voluntary dissolution. Only the Social Catholicism of the right seemed to survive in France. Count Albert de Mun and Count René de la Tour du Pin for example boasted of their Ultramontane support for the *Syllabus of Errors*, their allegiance to the monarchy and their opposition to the French Republic. Du Pin even refused to abandon the royalist cause when Leo XIII later ordered French Catholics to 'rally' to the Republic.

Nevertheless, the events associated with the Franco-Prussian War helped to stimulate a sense of Christian charity and social concern. As prisoners of war, de Mun and du Pin had become familiar with developments in Germany. During the siege of Paris, Catholic committees had been formed to support pastoral and charitable work, while the strong desire for national renovation which followed the war led to an increase in the number and scope of these committees. Even the violence of the Commune revealed that the social and economic forces demanding reform could not be indefinitely contained. It was becoming increasingly obvious that if the Church failed to act on behalf of the workers, communists and socialists would not hesitate to do so. Consequently, some Catholics were beginning to appreciate more clearly that social reform was a matter of justice and not merely of charity, that the Gospel and the traditions of the Church preached a social morality and fianlly that, although the exposition of social principles was the task of theologians, the application of those principles was the responsibility of the laity.

During their investigation into the outbreak of revolutionary violence in 1872 de Mun and du Pin fell under the influence of Maurice Maignen who conceived of the idea of forming associations in which adult workers might attempt to rechristianize the proletariat and improve their working conditions. Du Mun himself established an Association of Workingmen's Clubs to bring together employers and workers under the guidance of the ruling class. The committee resembled the mastership of the old guilds, while the workers in graduated orders of full members and candidates were similar to the masters and apprentices of the medieval system. De Mun hoped to establish a new corporate social order and to provide recreation as well as assistance for its members. A very definite religious atmosphere was fostered by the presence of a chaplain, daily prayers and religious services. Its Ultramontane spirit was revealed in devotions to the Immaculate Conception and support for the *Syllabus of Errors*, while Leo XIII himself recognized its 'clerical' character when he wrote in 1881:

We approve especially, and this will contribute notably to harmony

> and prosperity in the Association, that you submit all your projects and works to the pastors of the churches whom you wish to have as presidents. It is, in fact, divinely ordained by the Church that it is the right and duty of the bishops to dictate the rules and to march at the head through doctrine and example, while it is the part of the faithful to follow the footsteps of the pastors, to obey with docility their precepts and to witness to them their filial love while giving them in abundance their practical assistance.

More liberal Catholics became critical of the political as well as the religious conservatism of de Mun's Association, which became politically reactionary and restricted in its development. It is perhaps significant that, although the gentry and the middle classes willingly cooperated, there was only a limited response from the working classes themselves. Originally, workers and their families might be flattered by the interest of their 'betters' and amused by the dramatic performances and lectures which were put on for their benefit. But they would quickly resent the regimentation and restrictions imposed by respectable society. The workers themselves were not given positions of responsibility in the Association and usually tended to come from the smaller rather than the larger industrial concerns.

Nevertheless, De Mun himself who broke with the monarchists and rallied to the Republic in 1885 was far more advanced in his social and economic outlook than many contemporary 'liberals' and most republicans. He became convinced of the need for other forms of Catholic social action including the need for political action. He supported an eight hour day, a shorter day for working women, the right to compensation for injured workers and the right to form trade unions. However, his support for medieval guilds seemed to favour the *ancien régime* which the workers associated with poverty and exploitation. De Mun believed that the Christian working classes were still hostile to the spirit of 1789, whereas they tended at the time to support the Revolution. In 1875, three years after the establishment of the Association, there were some 18,000 members and over 60,000 members by 1900, but the early enthusiasm had largely disappeared by then and the Association quickly declined during the twentieth century.

Leon Harmel was the Social Catholic who finally succeeded in crossing the dividing line between the left and the right, the liberal and the conservative, and who made the most valuable contribution to the development of Christian Democracy. Harmel, the owner of a spinning factory at Val-de-Bois, gave his workers genuine responsibility and partnership in the industry. He developed the whole working community into a model Christian town and into a worshipping as well as a working community. He attempted to establish a Catholic industrial democracy in practice and to work out a pattern of social relations which could be followed elsewhere. Each worker had his own house and garden, there was a system of family allowances controlled by workers' representatives, free medical services, assistance for the sick and the aged, 4 per cent interest was given on savings and elected representatives met every fortnight to consider every aspect of factory business. Strikes were unknown. Harmel tried to persuade other employers to adopt his methods and he took a group of industrialists to Rome in order to win the encouragement and support of Leo XIII who was obviously impressed. This was followed by larger pilgrimages of workers and employers which became one of the factors leading to the proclamation of *Rerum novarum*, a watershed in the history of Social Catholicism.

However, perhaps the Fribourg Union contributed even more to the preparation of the Pope's encyclical. This Union was made up of a group of Social Catholic leaders who met every year to study the implications of a Christian social order. Their deliberations were sent to the Vatican. The Union prepared a charter for industry as well as proposals for international agreements which included the recognition of a man's right to work and a worker's right to a living wage. The union also advocated the insurance of workers against sickness, accident or unemployment. In 1888 the Pope discussed their proposals with some of the members. He then asked for a memorandum which seems to have served as the basis for his own encyclical published in 1891.

Rerum novarum strongly attacked unrestricted capitalism, individualistic liberalism and revolutionary socialism. The Pope declared that private property was the right of all men and that the family was the primary social unit, prior to the State. The Pope also approved of the intervention of governments to safeguard the spiritual and material interests of the working classes. Workers must receive a family living wage which must not be affected by the pressures of economic laws. Workers also had the right to form associations and Catholics should be encouraged to form Catholic trade unions and workers' organizations. Papal pronouncements on social and economic questions which are to be accepted by all shades of opinion within the Church and which are vested with at least an aura of infallibility are of necessity somewhat cautious documents. *Rerum novarum* was a condemnation of extremes, could be interpreted in very different ways and was rather limited in its approach. Nevertheless, although Leo XIII was a genuine social reformer, rather than a radical, his encyclical was a landmark in the history of Catholic social thought and proved to be revolutionary in its future implications.

The encyclical was widely welcomed throughout Europe, even by liberal and left-wing periodicals, though some left-wing journals were rather sceptical and some right-wing periodicals were even critical. The German Socialist newspaper *Vorwärts* congratulated the Pope on having 'stolen a march on secular governments'. In France, the Catholic newspapers *La Croix* and *L'Univers* were reserved, while other Catholic periodicals virtually ignored the encyclical. One of the more moderate secular journals commented:

> One used to consider Catholicism an exceedingly conservative force, placing in opposition to each other the Church and the Revolution as two irreconcilable enemies, in spite of the Gospel showing itself favourable to ideas of social equality, in spite of the communist character which the Christian society showed in the early years. This antagonism was in all its violence at the moment when the Commune of Paris resolutely attacked the clergy and religion. Things have changed since that epoch.

In 1892, de Mun reminded one of his audiences:

> Do you remember the tremendous surprise the encyclical caused to all who like to look on the Church as only a sort of gendarme in the service of *bourgeois* society, and to all the comfortably-off who were scandalized when they heard the highest authority in the world sanction ideas and doctrines which hitherto they had regarded as fatally subversive? – and then the even greater emotion that was caused among all the workers, the men of the people, who for so long had been repeatedly told that they could expect nothing from Rome but an arm raised to condemn them, and behold instead they suddenly saw a fatherly hand stretched out to bless them.

Certainly, *Rerum novarum* marked a new phase in the history of Social Catholicism and Christian Democracy; Catholics were now bound in conscience to show a social and active concern in attempting to deal with the problems of the time. With all its caution, the encyclical defended the rights of workers as a matter of justice and not simply of charity; it also recognized the need for the workers to fight their own battles and to control their own organizations. These two principles of justice and autonomy were the basis of a new and fruitful, if shortlived, movement of Christian Democracy. Social Catholics were now able to speak of the Church's duty to transform society, while some Christian Democrats even made hesitant suggestions about beginning the transformation with the Church itself, modifying its hierarchical structures, simplifying its liturgy, encouraging priests to work in the world and co-operating with other Christians or even with virtuous humanists. *Rerum novarum* gave a strong impetus to the growth of the early Christian Democratic movements in Italy and Belgium, and to the development of Social Catholicism in France. However, the Pope's later encyclical, *Graves de communi*, published in 1901 was apparently directed against what Leo considered to be some of the exaggerations of left-wing Social Catholicism and Christian Democracy which were being adopted in Italy and in France.

The strengths and weaknesses of Leo's approach to the contemporary world were starkly revealed in his attitude to the Church in the United States, though the immediate failure of his policies in France might help to explain the change or ambiguity of his later attitude towards Catholicism in America. Throughout their short history Catholics in the United States had to justify their ecclesiastical and political stand to 'liberal' Protestants at home and Ultramontane Catholics abroad. Bishop John Carroll's original attempt to unite rural American Catholics in support of the liberal principles of the new democratic republic had been superseded by waves of immigrants, who transformed the Catholic Church in America into a predominantly urban and 'foreign' community. As an immigrant community formed from distinct national origins, it was obviously important for American Catholics to identify themselves with their new country.

However this process of adaptation was complicated by the increasing Romanization of Catholic practice and administration, by the divisions between those Catholics who were prepared to go further than others in adapting themselves to their new situation and by the ethnic divisions between themselves, which were such an obvious feature of the Catholic community. In 1844 Isaac Thomas Hecker was converted to Catholicism and joined the Redemptorists. However, he became dissatisfied with the Order's failure to adapt itself to the American way of life and in 1858 he received the approval of Pius IX to form a new congregation, the Society of Missionary Priests of St Paul the Apostle or

Cardinal James Gibbons

the Paulists. Hecker's dream of Americanizing Catholicism and attracting American Protestants was not very successful at the time but coincided with and to some extent influenced a third and perhaps the most important attempt to solve the dilemma of being an American Catholic.

Denis J. O'Connell, the Rector of the North American College and agent of the American bishops in Rome, was a flamboyant and extrovert American patriot who could never bring himself to admit that he had been born in Ireland. O'Connell supported the more liberal American bishops like Cardinal James Gibbons of Baltimore, Archbishop John Ireland of St Paul and Bishop John J. Keane, the first Rector of the Catholic University. There were strong personal links between the four ecclesiastics who worked closely together. Gibbons was originally O'Connell's patron and bishop, while at one time Keane had been O'Connell's ordinary and Gibbons' suffragan. However, O'Connell not only identified himself with the liberal bishops, but he has been described as 'Machiavellian' in the tactics which he used on their behalf. He was apparently so biased and partisan in his support that he alienated some of his own friends as well as more conservative members of the American hierarchy.

Recent writers have argued that 'Americanism' was a liberal Catholic reform movement which originated in the United States; a specifically American reaction to the historical developments which were taking place at the end of the nineteenth century, filling the void left by the decline of European Liberal Catholicism. Several influential thinkers had long regarded America as the hope of the future and it is hardly surprising that as Europeans looked to the United States for the solution of contemporary political and social problems, Catholics should have also looked to America for the salvation of Christianity and the Church.

Ireland, Keane and O'Connell believed that under divine providence a new and radically different age was about to be born and that America embodied this new age of democracy and individualism, initiative and activity, social concern, participation in government, involvement in civil and ecclesiastical affairs. The Catholic Church could not survive without adapting itself to this new age and American Catholics, living in and understanding the country embodying the new age, would guide the Catholic Church throughout the world in making the necessary adaptations. The Americanists had a vision of a reformed Church modelled on their own experience, a Church which was a friend of the people, which accepted scientific progress and which was reconciled with the spirit of the age.

Americanism was not simply the result of American patriotism or 'manifest destiny', but resulted from the desire to establish a truly American Catholicism in the belief that Roman Catholicism could adapt itself to any culture or any civilization and that the Church might find one of its finest expressions in America. Americanism was not simply a programme to demonstrate that good Catholics could be good Americans, but a campaign in favour of certain policies; the separation of Church and State was beneficial because it allowed the Church to exercise its own authority in freedom; the Anglo-Saxon common-law tradition might well be adopted by the Church because it more closely approximated to the natural law than did Roman private law which was incorporated into canon law; the Church should adapt itself to the modern age and introduce democratic procedures into ecclesiastical administration.

When Gibbons took possession of his titular Church, Santa Maria in Trastevere, he delivered an address in praise of the American Republic and quoted Leo's encyclical, *Immortale Dei*, in support of his claim that the Church was not committed to any particular form of government, but could adapt itself to all. He then contrasted the situation in America, where the Government protected all churches and religions without any interference, with the dangers in other countries where Governments restricted or hindered the mission of the Church. During the consistory, Gibbons stayed with O'Connell at the American College, where Ireland and Keane had been staying since the end of 1886 seeking approval for the proposed Catholic University. There can be little doubt that the four men took the opportunity to discuss matters of common interest. Catholicism was being accepted in America and the liberal bishops were concerned to secure even greater reconciliation between the Church and American society and to ensure that the Roman authorities did nothing to arouse American suspicions of 'foreign' domination. Relations between the American hierarchy and the Holy See were complicated by the fact that the papacy still maintained its claims to the temporal power as well as its diplomatic contacts with other secular powers. The Roman authorities tended to see America as an area for immigration rather than as an independent nation and, since American Catholics were still subject to Propaganda, the American Church was usually regarded as a missionary Church.

The attempt to create a distinctly American Church inevitably involved O'Connell and the liberal bishops in the various controversial issues which plagued American Catholicism. One of the most difficult issues was the claim by German-American Catholics that the Irish clergy deprived them of their rights in the Church. The Irish were not only more numerous, but were more easily assimilated into American society because many of them spoke English and some, like O'Connell himself, could even pretend to be native-born Americans. German immigrants, on the other hand, often came as communities with their own priests and nuns, and tried to preserve these communities within the new world. Their attitude irritated other American Catholics who argued that it hindered the development of American Catholicism. German Catholics replied by condemning American culture as liberal, materialistic or even irreligious. Irish Catholics also dominated the episcopate except in St Louis, Milwaukee and Cincinnati. Consequently, German immigrants tried to establish their own parishes for German-speaking Catholics independent of English-speaking parishes, to secure the appointment of additional German vicars-general in areas with large German populations or even the appointment of German bishops. On this issue, the more conservative American bishops supported their liberal colleagues in opposing the German claims and in due course, the Roman authorities came out on the side of the American hierarchy.

However, the attempt to avoid giving the impression of being a 'foreign' institution was only the negative aspect of the Americanists' programme. Their more positive policies involved adapting the Church to American society, policies which were opposed by the more conservative members of the American hierarchy, German and non-German alike. German Catholics claimed that two of the reasons why so many Catholic immigrants lapsed from the faith were the lack of Catholic societies to protect the Catholic working classes and the existence of public schools. Their claims were an implicit attack on the attitudes which the liberal bishops adopted on the Knights of Labor and the schools question, and this attack found support among some of the conservative members of the American hierarchy.

Most Catholic immigrants were labourers and many of them joined the Knights of Labor, an organization which engaged in collective bargaining in an effort to secure social and economic benefits. Some Catholics reached prominent positions within the organization and one of them, Terence V. Powderly, was elected Mayor of Scranton 1878 and Grand Master Workman of the Knights of Labor during the following year. The Knights took a pledge of secrecy and used ceremonial which was similar to that of the masons. The question was therefore raised whether this organization as well as the increasing number of other American secret societies had not been condemned by the Church. In 1884, as a result of the situation in Europe and at the instigation of the Archbishop of Quebec, the Holy Office declared that the Knights were a forbidden society and an American bishop in a neighbouring dioceses excluded them from the sacraments.

The liberal bishops came to the support of the Knights. Keane and Ireland wrote a defence submitted by Gibbons which emphasized the need for the Church to be allied with the people rather than with kings or princes. As a result of the efforts of the liberal bishops, the Holy Office decided in 1888 that the Knights could be 'tolerated'. This concession seems to have convinced Keane and Ireland that the Pope shared their vision of America as the pattern for the future. In 1893, however, the American bishops were again divided on their attitude towards secret societies and the case was sent to Rome. On this occasion, Leo's belief that secret societies tended to Socialism resulted in the condemnation of the three secret societies involved.

In 1879 Henry George published *Progress and Poverty* in which he argued that every man had the right to land, and he proposed to remove inequalities in landownership by taxing the 'unearned increment' of land values which resulted from economic developments or favourable locations. He also proposed to abolish economic rents and all other contributions to Government and to replace them with a land tax. When George decided to run for Mayor of New York in 1886 he won the support of Edward McGlynn, an intelligent and socially concerned priest, who was suspended by Archbishop Corrigan for his political activities. George was also supported by Terence Powderly. At the time when O'Connell and his friends were trying to avert the condemnation of the Knights of Labor, with whom both George and McGlynn were associated, Propaganda was asked to examine *Progress and Poverty*. The result was another compromise. In February 1889 George's works were put on the Index, but the Holy Office also declared that the condemnation need not be published.

Few issues divided the Catholic Church in America more widely than the controversy over the public school system which came to a head in the early 1890s. The development of education throughout the English-speaking world was frequently hindered and even jeopardized by the conflicting interests of Christian denominations. The Catholic Church in particular tended to emphasize its rights over education and wherever it was possible, tried to unite the secular and the religious education of Catholic children in parochial schools. The increasing numbers of Catholic immigrants, especially from Ireland and Germany, forced the American hierarchy to provide for the education of Catholic children, and in 1884 the third plenary Council of Baltimore decreed that each parish should establish its own Catholic school.

Originally, Catholic immigrants were deprived of formal education or forced to attend schools supported by the State. Protestant denominations in America had solved the problems caused by their sectarian divisions by restricting religious education to a non-denominational form of biblical teaching. This solution, however, was unacceptable to Catholics for whom the study of the King James version of the Bible without comment seemed to symbolize the basic anti-Catholicism of Protestant America. On the other hand, attempts to obtain public funds for Catholic schools inevitably aroused Protestant suspicions and prejudices, and had been met with the claim that any grant of public money to Catholic schools would be unconstitutional and contrary to the principle of separation of Church and State.

The political and religious controversies which took place in New York as a result of Catholic demands helped to convince the civil authorities of the value of the principle of separation and in due course led to the conclusion that the State was properly responsible only for secular education; religious instruction should be provided in the Church or in the home. This policy, of course, also implied that more extreme or prejudiced Protestant opinions must be excluded from the public schools, but many Protestants were prepared to accept this since 'neutral' State schools seemed preferable to giving State aid to Catholic schools. As a result of making these 'concessions', some Protestants became angry when Catholics continued to demand financial help for their parochial schools and these Protestants began to suspect that the Catholic demands were a plot to destroy the public school system.

The increasing numbers of Catholic immigrants had already aroused Protestant fears of Catholic domination; American institutions and ideals were being threatened by an alien and un-American religion. Secularists as well as Protestants came to believe that there was a great Catholic conspiracy, directed from the centre, which was intent on destroying the separation of Church and State. They believed that this conspiracy could be seen in Catholic attempts to secure financial assistance for their parochial schools and charitable institutions. Consequently, in the 1880s and 1890s Protestants reacted by opposing public aid for sectarian charities and public grants to sectarian schools.

The more prominence the Catholic hierarchy gave to the issue by exhorting the faithful to provide parochial schools for Catholic children or by issuing statements from the Vatican authorities emphasizing the moral dangers of secular education, the more convinced Protestants became of the existence of a Catholic plot. Their fears were reinforced by a former Catholic who warned that 'the order has gone out from the Vatican, and a war upon the public school system has begun'. *The National League for the Protection of American Institutions* won the support of many influential professional, political and commercial leaders in its attempt to pass an amendment to the Federal Constitution prohibiting the individual States from giving money to 'any church, religious denomination or religious society, or any institution, society, or undertaking, which is wholly, or in part, under sectarian or ecclesiastical control'.

Paradoxically, these attacks on Catholic designs came just at the time when the American hierarchy was most deeply divided over Americanism in general and the issue of the schools in particular. Archbishop Michael Corrigan of New York and Bishop Bernard McQuaid of Rochester were among the leading spokesmen for the conservative point of view, which was also supported by the Jesuits as well as the German and Irish clergy. For these Catholics, the right of Catholic education was a matter of religious principle. They were opposed to the secularization of education, insisted on the rights of Catholic parents and objected to the unjust tax burden imposed on Catholics who had to support both parochial and public schools. Ideally, Bishop McQuaid would have liked to replace public schools with publicly financed denominational schools.

Liberal Catholics, on the other hand, argued that the financial and educational burdens were too great to be able to establish Catholic schools throughout the United States. They pointed out that the American public schools system was far better than that in France or Italy, where the ecclesiastical authorities did not demand that Catholic children should be educated in Catholic schools. In 1890 Archbishop Ireland praised the public schools in America and simply complained that religion had been excluded from the courses which they offered. It was in this context that the 'Poughkeepsie Plan', which had been devised some time before in the Archbishop's own province, occasioned alarm and criticism both inside and outside the Church.

Several Catholic parishes in the 1870s had quietly made arrangements to secure public assistance for their schools. In 1873 the Pastor of St Peter's Church in Poughkeepsie had arranged to lease two parochial schools to the city for a nominal rent of a dollar each. The civil authorities undertook to pay the teachers and to maintain the buildings; students of all faiths could attend the schools and the board of education had the right to examine the schools and to appoint teachers. No religious instruction was to be allowed during regular school hours, but the priest retained control of the school premises outside school hours. As a result, Catholic pupils received religious instruction before the school officially opened, during the lunch break and after the school officially closed, while the teachers hired by the civil authorities were invariably nuns from the order which had previously provided staff for the school. This system was later adopted in several other counties.

Conservative Catholics objected to the Poughkeepsie plan because it seemed to imply that Catholics were willing to settle for less than their full rights and to tolerate a public schools system which was not only Protestant and secular, but even godless. In 1891 a German Catholic Congress officially condemned the Poughkeepsie compromise, but the Pastor of St Peter's immediately replied that the plan had worked admirably for eighteen years:

> It satisfies all intelligent people. But those who do not understand it condemn it. It is safe to say that not one of those foreign priests ever visited our schools. Some of them cannot comprehend the lessons in the first English reader. Their condemnation is a eulogy.

However, the opponents of the Catholic claims who were to used to the idea of a monolithic Church, failed to appreciate these internal divisions. When the Pope sent Archbishop Francis Satolli to settle the issue, Leo XIII was accused of planning to assume personal command of the Catholic attack on the public schools.

Archbishop Ireland who had made several proposals similar to the Poughkeepsie compromise was delated to Rome by more conservative Catholics. When he actually succeeded in putting some of his ideas into practice, he was opposed by Protestants who thought that the civil authorities had given too much and by Catholics who believed that he himself had made too many concessions. In 1892 Propaganda supported the legislation adopted at the third plenacy Council of Baltimore, while 'tolerating' the situation which existed in Ireland's diocese. This decision, however, simply intensified the controversy in America and it was also one of the reasons why Ireland was not made a cardinal at this time. In 1894 even Archbishop Corrigan himself was forced to compromise, but he shrewedly achieved what was possible and sacrificed only the impossible.

By 1894 the conservative bishops recognized that it had become politically impossible to gain public support for parochial schools. They still refused to compromise on anything less than full public support, but – ostensibly in the interests of public peace – decided that 'Justice must sometimes wait'. They expressed their willingness to accept a constitutional prohibition on public aid for parochial schools – which incidentally would prevent any future Poughkeepsie compromises – and successfully fought instead to retain public aid for sectarian charities. This was in New York a significant achievement. In 1866 the legislature had given over 129,000 dollars to sectarian charities of which barely 4,000 went to Protestant or Jewish institutions. Between 1869 and 1871 a politically motivated city Government supported by Catholic votes had given over one and a quarter million dollars to Catholic charities and only 300,000 to Protestant, Jewish or other charities.

As part of the effort to adapt Catholic immigrants to their new country, the Americanists not only opposed anything that might appear 'foreign' to their fellow countrymen, but attempted to improve relations with other religions by adopting a more ecumenical approach. Keane in particular manifested an interest in the reunion of Christians which was unusual at the time and took the lead in associating American Catholics with the interdenominational and interreligious World Parliament of Religions. At the Parliament of Religions held in Chicago during 1892, Cardinal Gibbons participated with Chief Moderator of the Presbyterian Church in an exhibition which illustrated the basic unity of man's religious belief shared by all the great religions of the world.

It was proposed to hold a similar Parliament at the Paris Exhibition of 1900. The idea was supported by a *Père* Charbonnel, opposed by the Archbishop of Paris and condemned by Leo XIII. Charbonnel later became an anti-clerical Protestant and he described Americanism as a sort of neo-Protestantism. This accusation reinforced the suspicions of conservative Catholics in both Europe and America who were already beginning to ask whether the policies of the liberal American bishops could not be identified with the liberalism and the indifferentism condemned in the *Syllabus of Errors*. By now, accusations of liberalism or even of heresy were becoming quite common in Europe as well as in the

United States.

The Americanists originally regarded Leo XIII as 'the Pontiff of the Age', who understood the unique situation of American Catholics and whose progressive attitude was in harmony with their own ecclesiastical hopes and aspirations. And to some extent, the hopes of the Americanists do seem to have been shared by the Pope as he revealed in private and public audiences, as well as by his Secretary of State, Cardinal Rampolla and Cardinal Parocchi, Vicar of Rome. However, none of the decisions of the Roman authorities had yet gone entirely in favour of the Americanists. Furthermore, within two years of his return to the United States in 1887, Keane had been called to the Holy Office to explain some of his writings which had appeared in the European press.

The tensions within the American Church and the frequent denunciations and delations made to Rome eventually induced to the Holy See to appoint an apostolic delegate, a move which the American hierarchy had so long tried to avoid. The American bishops were sensitive about the interventions of the Roman authorities because of the suspicions of American Protestants and also because they regarded themselves as competent to deal with their own affairs. For the first six years of his appointment as agent in Rome, O'Connell had resisted attempts to appoint an apostolic delegate. However, by 1891, O'Connell realized that the Pope intended to appoint a delegate and he therefore attempted to use the appointment in the interests of his liberal friends and their policies as well as to secure independence from Propaganda. Ironically, O'Connell's moves helped to bring about the destruction of the liberal party. The attitudes of Satolli, who was appointed in 1893, like the attitudes increasingly being adopted by the Roman authorities, were more sympathetic to the conservative than to the liberal forces within American Catholicism.

By 1895 Leo XIII had apparently become suspicious of or even frightened by developments within American Catholicism. His encyclical, *Longinqua Oceani*, praised the American Church, but again criticized secret societies and warned against the notion that the separation of Church and State in America was a suitable pattern for the rest of the world to follow. In summer of the same year O'Connell was asked to resign as Rector of the American College. This was largely as a result of the fact that his support for the liberal bishops had alienated German Catholics and conservative bishops as well as the Jesuits and the conservative forces within Propaganda itself. O'Connell was also accused of repeating the Italian gossip that Satolli was the illegitimate son of Leo

XIII. There were unjustified complaints about O'Connell's administration of the College and even more unjustified suggestions about his personal relations with Virginia Mactavish, the great granddaughter of Charles Carroll of Carrollton. However, Cardinal Gibbons immediately retaliated by appointing O'Connell as vicar of his titular Church in order that he might remain in Rome.

In America the Apostolic Delegate publicly reversed his earlier opinions by strongly praising the German Catholics and asking the Pope to condemn the Parliaments of Religion. *Civiltà Cattolica* interpreted this condemnation and that of the secret societies as a check on the liberals and accused the Americanists of a form of Pelagianism and separatism. In 1896 Satolli became a cardinal and in September of the same year Keane was asked by the Pope to resign as Rector of the Catholic University; Keane became a titular archbishop residing in Rome. Controversies continued throughout 1897 as Gibbons, Ireland and Keane were accused of liberalism, disloyalty and heresy. Ireland was even forced to answer his criticis from the pulpit of St Patrick's Washington, where he accused his American conservative opponents of being *réfractaires*, the word which Leo XIII had used to describe opponents of *ralliement*.

As the liberals faced increasing opposition in America and at Rome, they tried to broaden the basis of their support and continued to spread their ideas abroad. Many American publications were translated into European languages, American churchmen gave lecture tours in Europe and formed loose alliances with European supporters. In 1892 Archbishop Ireland himself had supported the *ralliement* in Paris, advocated co-operation between the Church and American democracy, and urged French priests to leave their sacristies and to go out and work among their people. In the following year, *Abbé* Félix Klein of the *Institut Catholique* had translated and published some of Ireland's speeches.

O'Connell himself was accused of trying to win over the Vatican by helping one of his friends who was a cardinal to canvass for votes at the next conclave. O'Connell's apartment in Rome became known as 'Liberty Hall' and was the meeting place for the 'Club' or the 'Lodge', a group of friends dedicated to the work of reforming and modernizing the Church. These included a couple of cardinals in favour of reconciling Italy and the Holy See, the distinguished scholars Louis Duchesne and Friedrich von Hügel, and John A. Zahm, the Holy See Cross Father. A number of other leading French and German intellectuals such as Alfred Loisy and Félix Klein were on the fringe of the group. Although the significance of the obvious links with future 'Modernists' should not be exaggerated, it would be wrong to ignore the fact that Ireland, for example, congratulated Hermann Schell on his criticisms of the Jesuits.

In 1891 the publication of Fr Walter Elliott's *Life of Father Hecker* had aroused little attention and no controversy. However, Félix Klein was asked to adapt a translation to the French situation and in his preface published in 1898 Klein described Hecker as the ideal new priest who could reconcile the Church with contemporary developments. Hecker's spirituality, Klein argued, was in conformity with the modern trends towards independence and freedom, and was based on an interior direction of the Holy Spirit responding to the active virtues of the new saints of the market place, not to the more passive virtues of monks and hermits. Klein's remarks immediately occasioned a controversy over Fr Hecker's alleged 'Americanism', though it was far from clear what exactly was meant by this term.

O'Connell himself had taken up the theme of 'Americanism' in an address, 'A New Idea in the Life of Father Hecker', which he gave to the International Catholic Scientific Congress held in Fribourg during 1897. He first spoke of 'Political Americanism', which was derived from the Declaration of Independence and the Anglo-Saxon tradition of common law; he made a mild attack on canon law and implied that the Church would be well advised to replace Roman law with common law and to adopt the American system. O'Connell then turned to 'Ecclesiastical Americanism', the unique relations which existed between Church and State in America. He explicitly introduced into his argument the famous interpretation of the *Syllabus of Errors* by Bishop Dupanloup. O'Connell defended the American 'hypothesis' and criticized the practical results of the 'thesis' or the union between Church and State.

Fr Charles Maignen, a French monarchist opposed to the *ralliement*, wrote a series of critical articles and reviews in the Catholic press associating O'Connell's address with Montalembert's famous speech to the Congress of Malines in 1863. Maignen argued that the doctrines of 'Americanism' had been condemned in the *Syllabus of Errors*. When Maignen wanted to include some of his articles in a book, Cardinal F.M. Richard of Paris refused to give an *imprimatur*, but Maignen secured an *imprimatur* from the Master of the Sacred Palace, Albert Lepidi, which seemed to imply papal approval. Maignen accused the Americanists of trying to create an 'American' Rome and he claimed that the United

States' Government had used the American Church for its own ends during the Spanish-American War. When the Congregation of the Index condemned John Zahm's *Evolution and Dogma* in 1898, this was interpreted as an attack on Americanism, but the real condemnation came in the encyclical *Testem Benevolentiae* which was published in January of the following year.

The Pope's encyclical distinguished between religious and political Americanism and condemned the notion of adapting the doctrines, though not the practices, of the Church to the needs of modern society. The extent of individual liberty was strictly defined and the claim that external spiritual guidance had been superseded by the more abundant graces of the Holy Spirit was also condemned. Leo rebuked those Catholics who preferred 'active' to 'passive' virtues and who emphasized natural virtues and an active external life at the expense of supernatural virtues or an internal life; such a way of life, the Pope claimed, would lead to secularism and indifferentism.

Reactions to the encyclical were so varied that new controversies immediately began over its interpretation. Some of the conservative American bishops thanked the Holy Father for saving their people from heresy, whereas Gibbons and Ireland, Keane and Klein accepted the encyclical while denying that they or indeed any educated American had ever held the doctrines which had been condemned. These denials were at least to some extent accepted in Rome. The Pope himself never claimed that any particular individual held the condemned doctrines and he maintained that his condemnation was not intended to refer to the characteristic qualities of the American people. Leo also admitted that the condemnation had been necessary to clarify French rather than American opinion.

Consequently, it was later argued that the 'phantom heresy', as Klein called it, never really existed, but was a European 'invention' of those conservative, monarchist and Ultramontane Catholics in their continuing campaign against more liberal Catholics. Certainly, the hostility of Maignen, one of the leading opponents of the Americanists, seems to have been based on his hatred of republicanism. Nevertheless, Maignen's accusations were reflected in *Testem Benevolentiae*, which questioned some of the opinions of the Americanists as well as the basis of their ecclesiology. The Church under Leo XIII was apparently not yet prepared to follow the policies advocated by the liberal bishops in the United States. Ireland and O'Connell ceased to advocate the 'Americanization' of the Church, and when Keane was appointed to the see of

Dubuque, the Pope actually reminded him of the encyclical on Americanism. But perhaps even more significant and ominous for the future were the circumstances surrounding the condemnation. Is it not possible that in the condemnation of Americanism, as in the case of Modernism, an approach or attitude of mind was elevated into an ideological system of belief, which as such did not exist? And would *Testem Benevolentiae* really have been necessary, had there been a thorough and impartial investigation of those who were to be 'condemned'?

The execution by soldiers of the Commune of the Archbishop of Paris and four other hostages

VII: The Church in France after 1870

The Ralliement

After the fall of Napoleon III, France once against became a republic, but a republic dominated by political conservatives. Monarchist deputies most of whom were Catholics outnumbered genuine republicans who tended to be sceptical free thinkers by two to one. Several factors help to explain the election of this Catholic and monarchist majority to the National Assembly in February 1871. In the first place, republicans were associated with the policy of continuing a hopeless war against Prussia. The confusion and disorganization which were widespread at the time favoured the election of local notables, while the collapse of the Empire prompted those who had something to lose to turn to those who were regarded as obvious supporters of conservatism. Finally, the Church was at least for the moment very popular.

During the war, priests had distinguished themselves as chaplains or unpaid hospital orderlies, while the Catholic gentry had provided some of the most heroic officers in the army. Seminarians had been encouraged to serve in the forces and some of the French soldiers who had previously served in the papal armies distinguished themselves fighting for France. Catholic colleges and seminaries were handed over for use as hospitals. In those provinces annexed by Prussia, priests were elected to the Reichstag and 'Jesuitism' became a new form of French patriotism. Bishops used their influence with the German authorities to moderate the severity of the occupation. They denounced German demands for hostages and the Archbishop of Rheims insisted on being the first to be put on a train as one of the hostages against the threat of derailment.

However, the authority of the National Assembly was almost immediately challenged by a revolutionary Commune in Paris. The capital which had been the centre of republican opposition to Napoleon was cut off from the rest of the country for four months towards the end of the war. The Parisians, most of them unemployed and many of them drunk, rebelled against the Assembly and established a Commune dominated by the lower middle classes. For almost a century, many of the lower middle classes had not regarded themselves as Christians and they bitterly resented the Church and the monarchy. Nevertheless most of the *communards* were on the whole worthy citizens who were not responsible for the atrocities committed by those undesirable members of society who often seem to dominate the events of a revolution.

The *communards* suppressed the Religious Budget and dis-established the Church. The inventories demanded by this legislation provided occasions for ridiculous and sometimes appalling scenes of violence reminiscent of the Revolution of 1789. These sudden vicious outbursts against the Church were part of the price which Catholics had to pay for their close alliance with Napoleon's Empire as well as their indifference to the economic and social problems of the time. Thirty out of the sixty-seven churches in Paris were turned into armouries or guard rooms, food stores or club rooms, though the rest remained open for worship. At the same time, *Père* Ollivier preached a course of lenten sermons in Notre Dame as if nothing had happened and at least one of the leaders of the Commune was seen taking his children to a catechism class.

Government troops shot any of the insurgents who fell into their hands and the *communards* retaliated by arresting hostages including 'citizen Darboy, calling himself Archbishop of Paris' and 120 other priests. The *communards* suggested that the Archbishop might be exchanged for one of their leaders, but the Government refused. The struggle was fought bitterly and indiscriminately. In one terrible week Government forces executed over 15,000 *communards* without trial. The *communards* executed seventy-four hostages including twenty-four priests and Archbishop Darboy, who was shot by a firing squad wearing the cross of Archbishop Affre who had died at the barricades in 1848 and the ring of Archbishop Sibour who had been murdered in 1857. The high proportion of clerics arrested and shot by the *communards* is an indication of the bitter hostility towards the Church felt by some of them.

Following the defeat of the Commune, a superficial revival of religious fervour swept through France. National and monarchist pilgrimages were organized to such shrines as Paray-le-Monial and Lourdes. The basilica of the Sacred Heart was built on Montmartre in partial atonement for the sins of the nation. The Organic Articles were abolished and the Church regained control of education and the right to establish universities. The Government treated the Holy See with respect and even with subservience. Jules Simon, the new Minister of Religion, was a deist but he always consulted the nuncio about episcopal appointments and manifested an ingratiating concern about a candidate's 'orthodoxy'; Dupanloup maliciously remarked, 'M. Simon will be a cardinal before I am'.

Cardinal Mathieu later expressed the opinion that the subsequent violence against the Church was entirely due to the tactless way in which Catholics behaved at this time. As usually happens during times of official conformism, spies and informers flourished; civil servants, officers and mayors suspected of being irreligious were dismissed; priests rebuked school teachers for singing the *Marseillaise* and republican tradesmen were denounced from the pulpit and boycotted; troops once again marched to church in columns of four. Only a few Catholics such as Bishop Guilbert of Gap realized that 'To wish to link or identify religion with any form of government whatever is surely to compromise the Church and the clergy, as well as to commit a glaring mistake'. In July 1876 Guilbert publicly declared that the Church could live under all forms of Government; the early Christians had accepted the rule of Nero; contemporary Catholics in France should not associate the fate of the Church with that of the monarchy. Unfortunately, few French Catholics were prepared to follow Guilbert's advice.

Although the Government was Catholic and monarchist, it proved impossible to restore the monarchy, partly at least because of the existence of rival candidates and the fact that Catholics were so divided themselves. Veuillot supported the Comte de Chambord. 'Henri de Bourbon's programme', he wrote in 1871, 'leaves a deep impression. One is astonished at this simplicity, this serenity, this grandeur . . . No man has spoken thus'. Veuillot's astonishment was not reduced by the fact that he himself had composed the programme. However, 'King Henry V' insisted on his full legitimist claims and he even refused to abandon the white flag of Henry IV. This gave rise to the jibe that Henry IV considered Paris to be worth a Mass, whereas Henry V did not consider France to be worth a serviette or a handkerchief. Liberal Catholics usually supported the Orleanist candidate, the Comte de Paris, and there was also a Bonapartist claimant, the Prince Imperial. By the very fact that the Assembly was unable to restore the monarchy, it slowly and inevitably established and consolidated the Third Republic.

The Assembly was the most sincerely Catholic parliament in France since 1789, but Catholics in the Assembly included men of different political views who had little in common except their loyalty to a Church of which they often had a very different understanding. Most Catholic deputies were not tempted to adopt extreme policies; they were prepared to face political realities and were well aware of the need for compromise. Catholicism was strongest among the supporters of the Bourbons, but many legitimists were open to contemporary influences and they included such leading Liberal Catholics as Dupanloup and Falloux. However, if Liberal Catholicism was strong in the French Parliament, it was weak in the French Church at large, where conservative and Ultramontane forces had been immeasurably strengthened by their victory at the recent Vatican Council. In 1871 Pius IX himself expressed his love for France, the eldest daughter of the Church, and warned against the evil of Liberal Catholicism; it was to be feared even more than the revolutionary Commune. Two years later, the Pope again referred to those who would spread revolution under the pretence of reconciling liberty and Catholicism. Ultramontane Catholics as well as opponents of the Church were quick to point out that Liberal Catholics had been rejected by the Roman authorities in theory as well as in practice.

Consequently, attempts by Liberal Catholics to govern pragmatically according to the art of the possible were jeopardized by the efforts of French Ultramontanes to achieve their unrealistic aims. Led by Veuillot, the Ultramontanes hoped that the French Government might help to restore the temporal power of the Pope and they collected petitions in support of this end. However, following their defeat in the Franco-Prussian War, most Frenchmen regarded the prospect of another war with horror. Supported by Dupanloup, Thiers deplored the fact that the issue of the temporal power had been raised again and even the Pope rebuked the Ultramontanes on the grounds that their reaction was incompatible with Christian charity. Nevertheless, anti-clericals and republicans were able to indulge in anti-Catholic propaganda and to condemn all Catholics as political reactionaries and war mongers.

On the whole, the religious policies adopted by the National Assembly were neither immoderate nor extreme. but public opinion could not ignore the spectacular pilgrimages and exaggerated sermons which seemed to reflect the true spirit of Catholicism, clerical and reactionary, exclusive and dominating. Frenchmen felt humiliated when they were told to repent for the sins of the nation and called upon to return to the past as their only hope of salvation. The country as a whole was no longer monarchist nor Catholic but indifferent or hostile. Most

Frenchmen were republicans, radicals or socialists, and were certainly opposed to the policies of a monarchist and Ultramontane minority. Many committed Catholics and perhaps even the majority of French Catholics were also alienated by the clerical and monarchical claims made by some of their co-religionists.

After 1848, the extension of the vote had ensured the political domination of the Catholic Church for more than twenty-five years through the local influence of squires and parish priests. However, after 1876, universal suffrage became a weapon in the hands of the enemies of the Church as republicans came to dominate the electorates and the parliaments of the Third Republic. The election of 1876 which gave the republicans a clear majority in the Chamber of Deputies was more typical of French opinion and more decisive than the election of 1871. Conservative ranks were weakened by internal dissensions. It seemed more reasonable and would better secure internal stability to put republicans in charge of a republic. Finally, in order to secure peace abroad, it was necessary to put an end to Catholic demands in favour of the restoration of the temporal power of the Pope.

In 1877 the Pope asked the clergy and faithful throughout the world to obtain from their Governments effective resolutions which would ensure his independence as Head of the Church. Catholic Committees in France proposed to send an address to the Pope and to petition the French Government, but these committees were dissolved at the instigation of left-wing politicians who accused Catholics of wanting to provoke another war. Some of the bishops issued imprudent pastorals and one of them sent an open letter to the President as well as copies to the mayors and magistrates in his diocese. The forces of the left eagerly seized this opportunity to attack the Church in Parliament. Léon Gambetta associated the clerical party with political reaction; he quoted Archbishop Darboy, who had argued that the policies of Pio Nono would result in a break between the Church and modern states, and bring to an end the Concordat with France. Gambetta concluded with his famous call to arms:

> There is one thing which, like the *Ancien Régime*, is hateful to the country; it is the domination of clericalism. I only translate the sentiments of the French people in saying . . . 'Clericalism, there is the enemy!'

The deputies then invited the Government to suppress the 'unpatriotic' agitation in support of Ultramontane views.

The Government was in an impossible position. Republicans were firmly in control of the Chamber of Deputies, while a Catholic President was supported by a Catholic Senate. However, republicans also won control of the Senate in 1879 and the President resigned. The republicans who now controlled the Presidency, the Senate and the Chamber of Deputies could take revenge for the past and establish themselves more securely for the future. French Catholics had generally identified themselves with the forces of political reaction and would now be made to pay the price. One of the few French priests who still argued that the Church could live under all forms of Government, the *Abbé* Georges Frémont, noted that it was too late to avoid disaster:

> Because it has bound up its cause with that of Royalism, the clergy of France has finally convinced everyone who believes in things popular and democratic that between the Church on the one hand and progress, the Republic and the future on the other, there is no relationship possible but the most deadly hatred.

Although the republicans intended to destroy the political influence of the French Clergy, they did not for the moment wish to destroy the existing relations between Church and State; the Concordat effectively limited the authority and the influence of the Church. In any case, many republicans recognized that most Frenchmen still respected the Church even if they were not prepared to vote in its interests. The republicans therefore first turned their attention to the work of the Church in education. Ferry's education law of 1879 cancelled privileges granted to the Church by excluding churchmen from the councils supervising schools or restricting the right to confer degrees to public institutions. Ferry also tried to restrict the right to teach by denying it to non-authorized religious congregations and in particular to the Jesuits. When the Senate refused to accept this particular article, the Cabinet retaliated by calling on religious congregations to apply for official recognition within three months, except for the Jesuits who were to be dissolved.

Jesuits and other unauthorized religious remained in their houses waiting to be evicted by the secular authorities. Bishops, aristocratic ladies and distinguished laymen kept vigil in monastic chapels and processed out with the religious when the gendarmes arrived. Monks who had fought during the war wore their military decorations. Egged on by a cheering crowd, 400 soldiers laid siege to a monastery at Nîmes which had been empty for the last four years. Altogether, between nine and ten thousand monks were evicted from some 260 houses. However, many of the evicted religious quickly and quietly gathered together again, the schools of authorized religious remained as yet undisturbed, and it proved impossible to staff the State schools without employing nuns.

Nevertheless, Ferry began the creation of a State system of education which was eventually capable of taking over every area of education. He had started to construct a strictly secular educational system based on free and compulsory education in 'neutral' public or Government schools which gave no religious instruction whatever. In 1880 fees for primary education in public schools were abolished and provision was made to establish public schools for girls. In 1882 religious instruction in public schools was abolished. In 1886 legislation prohibited religious from teaching in public schools and it was declared that these should be staffed as soon as possible by an exclusively lay personnel. The Government not only passed a series of laws controlling Catholic education and depriving religious of the right to teach, but also moved towards the establishment of a secular state and restricted the rights and privileges of priests and religious, particularly those engaged in charitable and social work. In 1884 divorce was legally sanctioned and authorized congregations were ordered to pay a special tax on the deaths of their members, though not all the congregations complied. More and more the civil authorities took over charities which had once been the responsibility of the Church.

The policies of Leo XIII were based on the necessity of recognizing the republican form of Government which had been freely chosen by the French people and on his efforts to unite divided French Catholics in support of the Church and of France. The Pope rejected Catholic conspiracies against the republican régime while continuing to support the interests of the French Church. Leo recognized that much of the anti-Catholicism and anti-clericalism in France was partly a reaction against Catholic supporters of the monarchy and clerical opponents of the Republic. By refusing to accept the Republic which was clearly supported by most Frenchmen, Catholics were playing into the hands of the enemies of the Church. Leo XIII, therefore, attempted to persuade French Catholics to accept the Republic and to reject their royalist sympathies. At first, he gently advised French Catholics, but then he firmly began to demand that they should give their support to the existing Government.

French Ultramontanes in particular were alarmed at the prospect of reconciliation. In October 1880 the Pope pointed out to the Archbishop of Paris that some French Catholics supported by their bishops were demonstrating in favour of the monarchy, whereas the Church was only concerned with religion and did not reject any particular form of Government. The death of 'Henry V' in 1883 further divided the monarchists and Leo wrote to the French bishops suggesting that French Catholics should forget their differences in the interests of Catholicism. However, some French Catholics formed a Counter-Revolutionary League devoted to the destruction of the Republic. They claimed the support of the Pope in spite of *Immortale Dei* which made it clear that he did not disapprove of democracy and *Libertas praestantissimum* in which he had deplored the use of force as a means of securing political ends. Thus, French monarchists not only threatened to split the Church in France and endanger the position of the Church within the Republic, but they also jeopardized the Pope's social and political policies in the Church throughout the world. Leo XIII, therefore, arranged that the Primate of Africa, Cardinal Lavigerie, should act on his behalf.

Cardinal Lavigerie, the Archbishop of Algiers, was not an enthusiastic republican. He had been an imperialist during the Second Empire, a legitimist after 1870 and had even urged the Comte de Chambord to attempt a *coup d'état*. However, the Cardinal was a devout Catholic and a French patriot who became angry with the royalists when he saw that they simply wanted to use the Church for their own political ends. He also feared the socialists and the radicals. But he was prepared to accept the Republic in order that the Church might be left in peace to reform itself and to educate its clergy, and perhaps most of all, to secure the money, protection and prestige of France for his missionary work and his efforts to suppress slavery in north Africa.

The time seemed ripe for compromise. Moderate republicans began to recognize that the Pope and at least some of the French bishops would welcome a reconciliation. Moderate Catholics began to see that some of the moderate republicans wanted to end the persecution. The danger was from the two extremes, from right wing Catholics who used the Church in the interests of their politics and left wing radicals who would have happily tried to destroy the Church. When Leo XIII appointed a realistic and diplomatic nuncio to France, the civil and ecclesiastical authorities had been able to come to a reasonable understanding over the appointment of bishops. In 1883 even Jules Ferry defended clerical salaries and diplomatic relations with the Holy See to the fury of the left who accused him of turning republicans into Ultramontanes.

Much of the anti-clerical legislation at the time hadmore than a touch of studied defiance, a hint of Voltairian glee and the pigheadedness of personal prejudice. Moderate men had been willing to go to extremes against the Church in order to show their contempt for the right and to secure the support of the left. However, by 1887, moderate republicans felt that they had gone far enough. They had laicized education, restored divorce to the civil code, removed religion from ceremonies of the State, smoothed the way for secular funerals, restricted religious processions, allowed work on Sundays, abolished hospital and military chaplains, extended conscription to seminarians and reduced clerical stipends.

Furthermore, France at the time was politically and internationally isolated. The Tsar of Russia was unwilling to associate with reckless radicals, while Leo XIII was restoring the diplomatic prestige of the Vatican and cultivating good relations with Germany. Meanwhile, Catholic missionaries were playing an important part in the spread of the French colonial empire: Gambetta himself said that anti-clericalism was not for export. Finally, persecution and extreme radicalism were not necessarily politically popular or socially acceptable at home and the support of Catholics seemed more than marginally important when the Republic was threatened with a *coup d'état* by General Boulanger in 1889.

Lavigerie first ensured that the Government did not intend to indulge in any anti-Catholic measures which might further alienate Catholics at a time when he was trying to win them over. On 12 November 1890 the Cardinal gave a formal lunch to important civil and military officials in Algiers. In his speech, he called on French Catholics to 'rally' to the Republic and so avoid the dangers which were threatening both the Church and the Nation. He concluded by drinking a toast to the French navy, while a band of White Fathers played the *Marseillaise*. Lavigerie's speech provoked a storm of protest from Catholic royalists who did not find it easy to change the political allegiance of a life-time and who claimed that the Cardinal was not acting on behalf of the Pope. The Pope himself did not immediately support the Cardinal and for more than a year royalists were able to condemn the *Ralliement* as the personal policy of Lavigerie and to adopt even more extreme and intransigent positions.

Most of the French bishops maintained an attitude of cautious reserve; 'Rabbits in mitres', Lavigerie called them. However, it is only fair to point out that they could hardly be indifferent to their existing pastoral responsibilities and they were largely dependent on the good will and the financial support of royalist families. Furthermore, the anger of the royalists was not simply an irrational protest of outraged loyalty or the selfish outburst of thwarted politicians. The monarchists were being asked to sacrifice a hopeless case which they loved for a hopeless cause which they detested. They had enough evidence that some republicans were simply hoping to divide Catholics even more, while the Panama scandal of 1892 did not show the republican deputies and senators who had taken bribes in a particularly attractive light. In any case, was the Pope entitled to give orders in matters of political allegiance? *Le Temps* justly pointed out that Ultramontanism in favour of the Republic was no less dangerous than Ultramontanism directed against it, while the prudent Monsignor d'Hulst asked what would happen if Catholics were ordered to support the restoration of the monarchy?

Consequently, even a year later, French Catholics had not united in rallying to the Republic in spite of constant pressure from Rome on the French bishops and clergy. In January 1892 five of the six French cardinals issued a declaration which was immediately accepted by seventy-five other bishops; they denounced the sins of the Republic against the Church and exhorted Catholics to continue to resist secular encroachments on the spiritual realm; however, the cardinals also exhorted Catholics to give a 'frank and loyal acceptance of political institutions'. Leo XIII does not seem to have been satisfied with this declaration because in the following month he issued the encyclical *Inter innumeras sollicitudines* where he tactfully but firmly declared that it was the obligation of Catholics to play their part in the Republic and to work from within to correct any wrongs done to the Church, 'for the civil power is of God and always of God'.

A spokesman for the Government welcomed the 'new spirit, the spirit which tends to reconcile all Frenchmen round the ideas of good sense, justice, and charity'. The encyclical was also welcomed by some republican and left-wing magazines, and received a great deal of support from most of the bishops, clergy and laity including many of those who had previously been hostile. However, many other French Catholics remained intransigent and Catholics were now divided between the *Ralliés* and those who simply rejected the Pope's policies. The editor of the *Univers,* Eugène Veuillot brother of Louis immediately supported

Leo XIII, but his sister Élise, 'the Iron Virgin', did not and she established a rival newspaper.

As a political manoeuvre the *Ralliement* failed. It was quite impossible to convert Catholic monarchists into loyal republicans overnight and by 1898 the *Ralliement* as a short-term expedient was clearly unsuccessful. There is some evidence that Leo XIII hoped that the return of Catholics into the French political arena might eventually result in the restoration of the monarchy and this was the declared aim of some French extremists, but such a restoration was by now practically impossible. If the Pope hoped to see the emergence of a French Catholic party like the Centre Party in Germany which could unite French Catholics, defend the interests of the French Church and pursue a moderate political line, he was also disappointed. Such a hope ignored the historical background and intransigence of many French Catholics as well as the strength of anti-clericalism. The immediate effect of the *Ralliement* was simply to divide French Catholics further and so encourage them to adopt even more extreme positions. The old monarchist party which had suffered a series of defeats since 1870 would in time be transformed into *Action Francaise*, a logical but unhappy result of political Catholicism. *Action Francaise* under the leadership of Charles Maurras, the atheist who was described by Pius X as a great defender of the faith, would eventually become the 'Catholic Party', the champion of the Church against the Third Republic.

On the other hand, the *Ralliement* was not a complete failure. The Pope's desire that French Catholics should accept the Republic, coupled with his encouragement of Social Catholicism and support for an intellectual revival, strengthened liberal elements within French Catholicism and helped to foster a new spirit. French Catholics no longer had simply to choose between a form of conservative or liberal Catholicism, but between accepting a situation or rejecting it and ultimately they had to decide between a form of political Catholicism or religious Catholicism. Leo XIII might also have been thinking in terms of the future and Catholic participation in French politics during the next two or three generations. French Catholics needed time to accept in practice as well as in theory the legitimacy of all forms of government which allowed the Church reasonable liberty to fulfil its mission and which preserved order and respected morals. In this sense, the success of the *Ralliement* came with the heroism of the French clergy during the first World War when Catholics fought and died for the Republic and with the contribution which Catholics made to the political life of France before and after the second World War. Finally, it is quite possible that Leo XIII was not only thinking of the future of the Church in France, but of the Church throughout the world and more especially of the future of Social Catholicism. When Lamennais prophesied the advent of a Pope who would lead the Christian nations into a new age, the young Joachim Pecci had been preparing his doctoral thesis in Rome; half a century later, as Pope Leo XIII, he was beginning to steer the Church in the direction which Lamennais had indicated.

'The Affair'

One crucial reason for the immediate failure of the *Ralliement* was the history of the *Dreyfus Affair*. Alfred Dreyfus was a well-to-do republican officer; he was Jewish, but the family religion was a matter of heritage rather than conviction. In 1894 he was falsely accused and convicted of selling secret military information to the Germans. He was cashiered, sentenced to deportation for life and during the next four years suffered the severest possible solitary confinement on Devil's Island. Dreyfus had been convicted on a mass of evidence which was circumstantial, malicious or false and as a result of undisclosed secret 'evidence' submitted to the court.

The actual conduct of the case was almost bizaare. The public was excluded whenever military secrets were mentioned and these included the only real piece of evidence produced. The prosecution witnesses and even the so-called experts were inconsistent and occasionally flatly contradicted themselves, while one of the General Staff's special investigators actually confused two Dreyfuses in his reports. The central document in the case was a handwritten list of classified material given to the Germans by a French officer. There was a remote similarity between Dreyfus' handwriting and that of the list, but there were also striking differences. Furthermore, as an artillery officer, Dreyfus would not have made the mistakes which were to be found on the list, while a reference to 'manoeuvres' could not possibly apply to Dreyfus and this was a matter of military record.

Nevertheless most French commentators at the time were convinced that Dreyfus was guilty. Jean Jaurès, the socialist leader, demanded the death penalty and Georges Clemenceau, one of the leaders of the Radical Party, who opposed capital punishment felt that it should still be used in the case of Dreyfus, the 'traitor'. Even the leaders of the French Jewish community accepted the verdict without question and subsequently seemed less concerned about his guilt or innocence than the dangers of arousing anti-Semitic feeling in the event of a public controversy. These fears were not unjustified. When an early pamphlet defended Dreyfus in 1896, the Socialist press dismissed it as a Jewish trick to create doubts about the guilt of a traitor.

Anti-Semitism in France was as old as the Middle Ages and as recent as the writings of Comte Arthur de Gobineau in the middle of the nineteenth century. Voltaire was one of the great prophets of modern anti-Semitism as well as of anti-clericalism. He described the Jews as 'an ignorant and barbarous people, who have combined the most sordid greed with the most detestable superstition'. A century later, Charles Fourier proclaimed that the most shameful of all France's evils had been the admission of Jews to citizenship. The socialist Proudhon demanded the abolition of the Jewish religion itself: 'Not for nothing have the Christians called them deicides. The Jew is the enemy of mankind. That race must be sent back to Asia or exterminated'.

Anti-Semitism in France was reinforced by the immigration of thousands of Jews from Galicia and the Ukraine after 1870. Between 1870 and 1894 almost a third of the anti-Semitic books published in France were written by Catholic priests. A few were the works of perverted fanatics like *Père* Henri Desportes who repeated mediaeval tales of ritual murder and as a result was removed from his position in a seminary by the Archbishop of Rouen. A few more writers revived the old accusation that the Jews had been responsible for the betrayal and crucifixion of Christ. Most of them, however, based their hostility to Jewish financiers on a mistaken sense of social and economic justice, and suspicions of the 'Syndicate' especially after the collapse of the *Union Générale* in 1881.

The *Union Générale* raised a capital of some 25 million francs in the spring of 1878. Its prospectus claimed 'the special autograph blessing of our most Holy Father, Pope Leo XIII', and Catholics of the old nobility, small landowners and several religious orders invested in the company whose 500 franc shares were worth 3,000 francs by November 1881. Jewish and Protestant banks were outmanoeuvered by the *Union Générale* which won mining and railroad concessions throughout the Balkans. Suddenly, large blocks of its stock were sold for a fraction of their current value by unknown speculators, the *Union* was destroyed and many Catholic stockholders were ruined. There seemed to be only one possible, logical and obvious explanation: the Syndicate, the legendary Internationale of Jewish finance, had brought about the destruction of the *Union*. Suspicions and fears of the Syndicate were further reinforced six years later when several Jews were compromised in the financial corruptions associated with the collapse of the Panama Canal Company in 1887.

In 1892 *La Libre Parole* was founded by Édouard Drumont who had formerly advanced the interests of a leading Jewish financier, but who had recently returned to Catholicism and written a massive work in two volumes which was partly cause and part effect of the new wave of anti-semitism. *La France Juive*, published in 1886, combined history, sociology and political economy in an attempt to illustrate that as the Jews rose to power, the French nation declined. Within two years no less than 127 editions were printed and the book was also published in Germany, Spain and Poland. Drumont simply dared to say what so many other Frenchmen were thinking and some of his remarks contained enough truth to be memorable; 'The Rothschilds believe they belong to the aristocracy', he wrote on one occasion, 'Hirsch [another rich Jewish banker], on the other hand, believes that the aristocracy belongs to him'.

Drumont's racist prose appealed to the prejudices of the time:

> The Semite is business-like, greedy, intriguing, subtle, and crafty; the Aryan is enthusiastic, heroic, chivalric, disinterested, and open, trusting to the point of naiveté. The Semite is a son of the earth hardly ever grasping anything beyond the present moment; the Aryan is a son of the heavens ceaselessly preoccupied by higher aspirations; one lives in the real world, the other in the ideal.

Drumont published a series of articles on Jewish infiltration into the army and several other nationalist newspapers took up the theme. These articles occasioned several duels between Jewish and anti-Semitic army officers. Dreyfus himself was almost deprived of his position on the General Staff as a result of anti-Semitism and it is more than probable that anti-Semitism was a factor in his eventual degradation.

In June 1895 Major Georges Picquart, who incidentally was a Catholic, was appointed Chief of Counterintelligence. Picquart had been one of the few instructors at the War College who had not been impressed by Dreyfus. He was not anti-Semitic on political or religious grounds, but tended to despise Jews socially; seeing Dreyfus glance at the stripes torn from his uniform during his degradation, Picquart had observed: 'He looks like a Jewish tailor estimating the value of the cloth'. Picquart found his new section in a state of some confusion and set about the necessary reorganization. A few months later French counterintelligence recovered the draft of a letter addressed to a Major Esterhazy from the wastepaper basket of the German military attaché. Picquart therefore began to investigate Esterhazy and discovered that his handwriting seemed identical with the list which Dreyfus had been accused of writing. As Picquart turned his attention to the file on Dreyfus, he discovered how flimsy was the evidence on which the Jewish officer had been convicted.

Count Marie Charles Ferdinand Walsin-Esterhazy was a rogue and a fraud whose standard of living always exceeded his income. He also had ambitions to be recognized as an outstanding soldier. On one occasion, while he was in charge of the records of his unit, he took the opportunity to write a glowing account of the part he had played in a battle in which he had not even fought. In order to obtain a rank which he considered appropriate to his talents, he joined the Papal Legion in May 1869 as a second lieutenant before enlisting in the French Foreign Legion. He later obtained a permanent commission in the French regular army.

It would seem that in July 1894 Esterhazy called on the military attaché of the German Embassy and offered to provide secret military information in return for a suitable reward. French counterintelligence actually intercepted the coded message sent to Berlin, but never bothered to alert the French agents watching the Embassy and Esterhazy, sometimes in uniform, continued to visit the German attaché. Characteristically, Esterhazy exaggerated the significance of the information which he had in a list prepared for the attaché before 'leaving for manoeuvres'. The actual documents were sent to Berlin, but the covering note or list was torn into pieces and thrown into the wastepaper basket. The cleaning woman, acting on behalf of French counterintelligence, recovered the pieces and gave them to her contact, a Major Hubert Joseph Henry.

Picquart's investigations coincided with increasing speculation about the guilt or innocence of Dreyfus as well as the justice of the legal processes which had led to his conviction. Not unnaturally, though erroneously, the Chief of Staff and Minister of War suspected Picquart of leaking information to Dreyfus' supporters and he was ordered to leave Paris and to inspect the situation along France's eastern borders. During Picquart's absence, Major Henry became acting Chief of counterintelligence. He deliberately altered and falsified documents in order to provide further evidence against Dreyfus and even employed the services of a professional forger.

Just before Picquart was due to return to Paris, he was ordered to Marseilles and then to Algeria and Tunisia. He was later posted to the Libyan border, presumably because the risks of mortality there were noticeably higher. Picquart, therefore, wrote an account of what he knew which he entrusted to his lawyer with instructions that it should only be divulged on his express orders or if he died mysteriously. Picquart also told his story to a superior officer in Libya who ordered him to return to Paris in an effort to secure justice. The investigating officer in Paris, however, dismissed and even tried to discredit Picquart's story.

By October 1897 the danger of public revelations had increased to such an extent that the General Staff resorted to treachery. In return for immunity from prosecution, Esterhazy placed himself at the service of counterintelligence. However, *Le Figaro* published a letter from Mathieu Dreyfus accusing Esterhazy of writing the list and so forced the Government and the Army to conduct an inquiry. The Prime Minister became convinced that he must either defend the army, the hope and the glory of France, or risk losing office, while other members of the Government were afraid of strengthening the forces of the opposition by revealing the vile conduct of which certain army officers had been guilty. Consequently, the Prime Minister ridiculed the claims of the Dreyfusards, referred to secret documents justifying the conviction and explained that there was not a shred of evidence against Esterhazy. He then made his famous declaration, '*there is no Dreyfus affair*', to a tremendous ovation from the deputies. The Government investigation simply whitewashed Esterhazy after another pretence of examining the evidence. Esterhazy himself was acquitted at a court martial on the basis of evidence which was never produced and never existed, while Picquart's testimony was heard in secret and the impression was deliberately created that his case had been destroyed on the basis of further secret evidence.

Not everyone, however, was convinced and in November 1897 *Le Figaro* published the first article on the Dreyfus case by Émile Zola, though the owner cancelled the series because of declining circulation. Zola was bitterly attacked by the opponents of Dreyfus as a writer who had sold his services to the Jews. Zola replied with his famous article, *J'Accuse*! which appeared in *L'Aurore* on 13 January 1898. Clemenceau's newspaper which had a normal circulation of about 30,000 copies sold nearly ten times that number. Addressing the President of the Republic, Zola claimed that a court martial had recently dared to acquit Esterhazy and in so doing had delivered a supreme blow at the administration of truth and justice. He then went on to accuse and to list by name those who were responsible for committing injustice and concealing the truth.

Zola's protest was hailed throughout the world, though there were some significant exceptions. *Civiltà Catholica* declared:

> The Jews have invented the allegation of a judicial error. The plot was worked out at the Zionist Congress in Basle, invoked ostensibly to discuss the deliverance of Jerusalem. The Protestants made common cause with the Jews for the creation of a syndicate . . . The Jews allege a judicial error. The real error was that of the Constituent Assembly which granted them French nationality. That law must be repealed.

It was at this time that thousands of Catholic children learned to call their chamber pot a 'Zola' and Georges Bernanos, François Mauriac and Charles de Gaulle learned of the terrible lies being told by the Jews and their supporters. Jewish stores were sacked and synagogues desecreated. In such a civilized country as France duels were inevitable and Picquart had the satisfaction of wounding Henry in the arm.

Zola was brought to trial on the charge that he had accused the judges of acquitting Esterhazy on the orders of the Government. The jury was prejudiced, the public audience was hostile and the trial would inevitably be a mockery. However, Picquart was called to give evidence. Sooner or later the march of events was going to force the army to disclose its precious, secret and forged evidence. Picquart himself, dismissed from the army, brought formal charges against Esterhazy and others of having forged incriminating evidence. Representatives of the German and Italian Governments, including the military attaché involved, earnestly declared that they had never had any dealings with Dreyfus. Public confidence was being eroded and, in an effort to satisfy the rising criticism, the Minister of War revealed the 'evidence' against Dreyfus. The Dreyfusards were now able to concentrate on proving that this evidence was irrelevant or forged and that the court martial had been illegal.

Picquart, who was able to show that at least one of the letters was an invention, found himself accused of espionage, arrested and imprisoned, though the investigating magistrate ordered Esterhazy's arrest at the same time. The Government was forced to employ another expert to examine the dossier on Dreyfus and on this occasion the fact of forgery was revealed. Henry was arrested and later committed suicide in prison. The Dreyfus case, however, was still far from over. After all, there was still *some* evidence against Dreyfus and members of the Government as well as the public at large remained hostile to a judicial review; the security of the nation must not be sacrified to the enemies of the army.

By autumn 1898 Charles Marie Photius Maurras had become a fanatical racist and militarist; he was convinced that the decline of France had been caused by the contamination of the race by Jews, Protestants and other inferior foreigners who must be expelled. Maurras now rallied the opponents of Dreyfus. What Henry had done was unimportant, only his motive mattered. To forge evidence proving the guilt of a traitorous Jewish officer was the act of a patriot not a criminal. Henry was a victim of the 'Syndicate of Treason', Jews, Protestants and Freemasons; he was the first martyr in a holy cause; he must now be avenged and his memory sanctified!

> In the state of confusion in which the national parties find themselves, we have not been able to give you the great funeral which your martyrdom deserves. We should have flourished the bloodstained tunic on our boulevards as well as the bloodstained blade, we should have borne the coffin in a procession and worshipped the shroud as if it were a black flag. It will be to our shame that we did not attempt this. But patriotic feeling, although diffused and multiplied against itself and still is capable of action, has nevertheless been resuscitated.

La Libre Parole organized a fund for Henry's widow and children which was supported by 15,000 subscribers who contributed 130,000 francs. The names and remarks of the donors to the fund were recorded in a volume of seven hundred pages and they included the following examples from the clergy:

> A country priest who is making the most ardent vows for the extermination of the two enemies of France – the Jew and the Freemasons. Five francs . . .
>
> An unimportant priest of the Potevin who will chant the Requiem for the last of the Yids with pleasure. One franc.
>
> *Abbé* Cros, ex-lieutenant, for a floor mat of Yidskin in order to trample them under foot morning and evening. Five francs.

Such remarks illustrate how some Catholics were identifying the Church with anti-Semitism and how the fate of Dreyfus was becoming associated with the future of the nation and the survival of the Third Republic.

The President of the Republic, Félix Faure, was opposed to granting Dreyfus a retrial and he therefore won the support of right-wing forces including right-wing Catholics. However in February 1899 he died in the arms of another man's wife. Clemenceau wrote that there was 'not one less man in France', but a more sympathetic editor stupidly recorded the traditional lament, *Ainsi est mort un grand président dans la pleine exercise des ses fonctions*. A Catholic correspondent simply reported that Faure was 'said to have died suddenly after a cup of tea at a soirée given by a rich Jewess'. The election of the new president, Émile Loubet, was regarded by opponents of Dreyfus and supporters of the right as nothing less than calamitous and on the day of Faure's funeral, the leader of the League of Patriots, Paul Déroulède, made his pathetic and unsuccessful attempt at a *coup d'état*. However, when Déroulède was put on trial, he was acquitted.

Vincent de Paul Bailly, the editor of the bitter and extreme Catholic periodical *La Croix*, eventually resisted the temptation of becoming involved in the *coup*, but Déroulède was supported by other intransigent Catholics and the Government, not unnaturally, began to become concerned about their activities as well as the influence of *La Croix* with its readership of over half a million. The threat to the Republic was lifted on 4 June when some anti-Dreyfusards abused the President at a race meeting and one of them bashed his top hat with a walking stick. Their stupid and offensive behaviour proved to be a turning point as the forces of the Left supported by thousands of ordinary citizens rallied against the threat to the Republic from the aristocracy, the army and the Church.

In an effort to distract public attention from the corruptions of the republican régime, supporters of the Left continued to proclaim that Dreyfus was innocent and René Waldeck-Rousseau was chosen as Prime Minister to form a cabinet to defend the Republic. Waldeck-Rousseau had a justified reputation for honesty, but he was not above manufacturing a false dossier of incriminating evidence against supporters of the right nor above tolerating that system of spying on the opinions and private lives of Catholic officers with a view to preventing their promotion which discredited Combes' ministry in 1904.

On 9 February 1899 the criminal chamber of the Court of Cassation declared that the conviction of Dreyfus in 1894 was void. On the following day the Government ordered that the Dreyfus case should be tried again before the entire Court of Cassation. On 29 May the Court annulled the verdict of 1894 and referred the case once again to the military authorities at Rennes. Dreyfus was then brought home to face another court martial after being on Devil's Island for just over four years. In June Picquart was also released and acquitted of the charges brought against him after spending three hundred days in prison. However, the judicial procedure during Dreyfus' court martial was again most unsatisfactory; more 'evidence' was manufactured against him and one of his lawyers was wounded in an assassination attempt. On the other hand, the German authorities categorically denied having had any dealings with Dreyfus, the evidence against him was shown to be worthless and the French Government put pressure on the generals for an acquittal. However, by a vote of five to two, Dreyfus was again found guilty of treason, but with extenuating circumstances; he was sentenced to ten years, five of which had already been served.

The London *Times* declared that 'A thrill of horror and shame ran through the whole civilized world'. People throughout the world, except in Russia and French Canada, expressed their disgust at the verdict. Queen Victoria was horified, the Attorney General of Montana suggested sending missionaries to France as well as to Africa, the people of Chicago boycotted French goods and William James expressed his satisfaction at belonging to a Republic, forgetting for the moment that France was one. Clemenceau declared:

> France is now a country with no security either for the liberty, the life or the honour of her citizens. A horde ganged up on us, a praetorian guard, a host of monks who have savagely burnt all that forty centuries of human effort have accomplished.

La Croix, on the other hand, proclaimed that 'Justice has been done. Dreyfus has been condemned. As Frenchmen we rejoice over it. As Catholics we praise God for it'.

The Government then decided to end the Affair once and for all in time for the Paris Exposition in 1900. In September 1899 Dreyfus was pardoned and on 1 January 1900 the Prime Minister introduced a general amnesty preventing any further litigation on the Affair. This measure deprived Picquart and Zola as well as Dreyfus himself of the opportunity of proving their innocence by legal means and the Dreyfusards, particularly Picquart who had most to lose, were angry with Drefus who was willing to accept the situation. Picquart, who had been disgraced by accusations of forgery and disloyalty, broke with Dreyfus and deliberately turned down all later attempts at reconciliation. Apart from obvious qualities of courage and endurance, Dreyfus seems to have been an unlikely hero. He has been described as at best a neutral hero and at worst an ungrateful egocentric.

Charles Péguy once remarked: 'We might have died for Dreyfus, but Dreyfus would not have died for Dreyfus'. Theodore Herzl claimed: 'One can't even guarantee that he would have been on the side of the victim if someone else had suffered the same fate in his place'. On 12 July 1906 the Court of Cassation annulled the Rennes verdict and unanimously declared that Dreyfus was innocent of all charges. The Government then restored Dreyfus and Picquart to the army and promoted them in spite of the inevitable protests. However the passions aroused by the case were not speedily cooled and in 1908 when Zola's ashes were transferred to the Pantheon, Dreyfus would be shot in the army by a fanatic who was apprehended at the scene, duly tried and unanimously acquitted by a Parisian jury.

For a generation the Affair dominated the political life of France. Republicans seized the chance of political revenge for the embarrassments suffered during the Panama scandal and used the Dreyfus case as a means of political self-preservation and the basis of a renewed and reunited anti-clericalism. Dreyfus, it was argued, was the victim of those who would defend the army, right or wrong. It was even claimed that Dreyfus had been destroyed by a Jesuit conspiracy. But at the very least Catholics had joined the military, nationalists and royalists in resisting the demands of Jews and Protestants, anti-clericals and Freemasons for a revision of Dreyfus' sentence. The anti-clericals enjoyed the support of a massive press campaign in presenting themselves as a dedicated brotherhood in pursuit of justice. Since an innocent man had been rescued from Devil's Island by anti-clericals, not by churchmen, it was implied that Catholics put the demands of order and expediency over those of truth and justice.

Of course, the line between Dreyfusards and anti-Dreyfusards did not neatly coincide with such divisions. There were anti-Semitic and nationalist radicals and Socialists as well as Catholic Dreyfusards. The largest Socialist party, the French Labour Party, reflected the anti-Semitism of many workers and was bitterly opposed to Dreyfus. In spite of the association of anti-Semitism with the opponents of Dreyfus, most of the French Jews did not in fact support him. Picquart, on the other hand, risked everything including his life in the effort to clear Dreyfus. Maître Edgar Demange, Dreyfus' lawyer, was a devout Catholic

Emile Zola

and the son of an officer. One of the two judges who had the courage to dissent from the absurd verdict that Dreyfus was guilty with extenuating circumstances was also a pious Catholic. In time most of the outstanding writers and artists came out in support of Dreyfus and these included Charles Péguy and Jacques Maritain. In an interview with a correspondent of *Le Figaro*, Leo XIII declared: 'Happy the victim whom God considers so just as to liken his cause to that of His own sacrificed Son'. The Pope's remark alarmed Catholic extremists and pious French ladies made novenas for the reformation of the 'heretical' Pope.

However, although a couple of hundred Catholics were members of the Committee for the Defence of Right, thousands of them joined Déroulède's League of Patriots. Furthermore, Catholic periodicals as well as those which supported Dreyfus had a vested interest in concealing the existence of Catholic Dreyfusards. The anti-clerical press mercilessly exposed every example of Catholic prejudice such as the fact that three hundred priests (out of 55,000) had subscribed to a memorial for Henry or that *Civiltà Cattolica* had declared that 'The Jew was created by God to act the traitor everywhere'. Too many Catholics were blind to the possibility that an injustice had been committed and remained silent or hostile during a moral campaign to establish the truth.

Many opponents of Dreyfus believed that even if the evidence had been forged, the army officers of France should not be disowned for the sake of a single Jewish captain. But other opponents who were not influence by anti-semitism or jingoism found it impossible to believe that dozens of officers, ministers or politicians had behaved criminally or that all of them had been wrong about Dreyfus. The opponents of Dreyfus included such men of integrity as Albert de Mun who referred to

> Frenchmen anxious to keep intact that which is most precious to them, that which remains in the midst of our struggles and party discords the common ground of our invincible hope – the honour of the Army.

It was easier to recognize the innocence of Dreyfus after the event, though for years later, honest and intelligent men could still maintain that he had been guilty.

Many Catholics were influenced by *La Croix*, which not only became increasingly shrill in its defence of the army but identified Catholicism with the anti-Semitism sweeping through France which even threatened at one stage to overthrow the Government. *La Croix* advocated intransigent, fundamentalist and even credulous religious and political attitudes: the de-Christianization of France was the result of the activities of Jews, Protestants and Freemasons; natural disasters were retributions for sin, while the 'flu epidemic of 1889 was attributed to the decline in religious observance. Vincent de Paul Bailly seriously maintained that only those places had been occupied during the Franco-Prussian War where public prayers had not been offered. On another occasion *La Croix* declared that until the infideltiy of France had been expiated,

> Christ must inflict on the Eldest Daughter of the Church a punishment reminiscent of his own passion. That is why he has allowed her to be betrayed, sold, jeered at, beaten, covered with spittle, and crucified by the Jews.

During the Affair, *La Croix* maintained that it was not a question of whether Dreyfus was guilty or innocent, but whether the enemies of the Army would be allowed to triumph over its friends; free inquiries were not to be permitted on such issues, while the terms Christian and anti-Jewish were inseparable. In 1899 Leo XIII informed the directors of *La Croix* that he deplored 'the spirit and tone of their newspaper' and in the following year, he ordered the Assumptionists to discontinue their association with the journal.

Catholics retaliated to the bitter republican attacks on the Church by creating that tightly-knit community of individuals who not only felt persecuted, but who too easily imagined that their opponents were united in a conscious and sinister design to destroy them. Furthermore, the Army provided the one career in which monarchists and Catholics were still able to serve the nation and was the only institution which had not fallen into the hands of their enemies, the conspiracy of Jews, Protestants and Freemasons. Many Catholics in France and elsewhere adopted the theory of a conspiracy against the Church pursued especially by Freemasons. It is true that during the Third Republic, Freemasons and republicans became convinced that they would have to destroy the Church before they could achieve their aim of creating a secular society in France. Masonic lodges became centres of anti-clericalism and republicans found it convenient to discuss their plans at masonic meetings. But any conspiracy against the Church was a perfectly open one and the allegations against freemasonry do not account for or explain but only describe one example of anti-Catholic propaganda and political action.

On the whole, masonic membership was regarded as a means to an end, providing protection and opportunities to men who shared similar secular and republican assumptions. There is little doubt that the support or the opposition of Freemasons could make or break a man, particularly at the local or the provincial level. However, the Grand Orient tended to be rather circumspect in dealing with real politics at the national level and even more so at the international level. Similarly, republican deputies and senators rewarded and strengthened their republican supporters by recommending them for public concessions, state tobacco kiosks or sub-post offices and it was not unknown for them to recommend the children of 'good republicans' to the attention of examiners. A deputy might warn a board of examiners that the daughter of a good party supporter was 'shy' during oral examinations and the board might respond by asking the deputy the sort of questions on which she was least likely to be shy.

However, French Catholics were convinced that the full force of a terrible conspiracy was being waged against them and their sense of real as well as imagined persecution created subconscious fears and hatreds which resulted in some incredible and almost pathological manifestations. Between 1895 and 1897 Catholics were publicly fooled by the memoirs of a 'Diana Vaughan' who described from her American convent how she had been corrupted by a group of satanists who were behind the masonic movement, how she had slept at the foot of a statue of Lucifer and see the devil on a throne of diamonds; 'always listen to the voice of reason', he had said. Miss Vaughan was due to appear at a mass meeting in Paris during 1897, but in her place appeared her inventor, Léo Taxil, who formerly made his money from anti-clerical pornography.

On 4 May 1897 there was a funeral in Notre Dame for 118 victims of a fire at a charity bazaar. For the first time in twenty-five years the President of the Republic and leading ministers were present at a religious ceremony. The preacher took the opportunity to castigate the crimes which France had committed against Religion. Men had relied on science and defied God, but God had used science against them; the marquee had been set on fire by an electrical short-circuit! The Church had been betrayed and so God had sent an Angel of Death to avenge it; so much life and beauty had been trampled into the bloodstained mud and destroyed in the heat of the fire; 'By the dead bodies strewn along the way, ye shall know that I am the Lord'.

The Dreyfus Affair added nothing to French politics, but revealed with startling clarity the divisions between supporters and opponents of the Revolution who might otherwise have been able to establish a *modus vivendi* before the outbreak of the first World War. By reviving the old issues of religion and the regime, the Affair for a time destroyed the possibility of uniting Catholics, monarchists and conservative republicans against more radical political forces. The Affair also stimulated the movement towards the separation of Church and State. Francis de Pressensé, for example, had written a book on Cardinal Manning and was himself drawn towards the Church. However, he was alienated during the Dreyfus Affair and later became one of the most influential supporters of the campaign to separate Church and State.

Separation of Church and State

The first anti-Catholic legislation passed by the Government was directed against religious orders and against the Assumptionists in particular. The Law of Associations required religious order to apply for authorization from the Government. If orders refused, their members were to be dispersed and their property auctioned, though former religious would receive pensions from the proceeds of the sales. This legislation effectively ended the reconstruction of Catholic education which had quietly resumed after Ferry's attacks. Some 138 unauthorized congregations out of a total of 753 decided that it was pointless to apply for recognition. Assumptionists, Jesuits and Carmelites dispersed or went into exile and handed over their schools to the secular clergy.

Many priests and religious communities went to Spain or Italy, Belgium or Britain, though many others stayed behind and replaced their cassocks and habits with secular suits. The young Teilhard de Chardin accompanied the rest of his community to the island of Jersey. He recorded how the fathers disguised themselves in lay dress provided by local sympathizers and, as a result of their ignorance of contemporary fashions, how some of them wore top hats with sporting flannels and motoring caps with morning coats. The Carmelite Prioress of Laval went even further and appeared in a scarlet mantle and mauve dress studied with stars.

The tension increased when Émile Combes replaced Waldeck-Rousseau. Combes was a former lecturer in a junior seminary who became a narrow, anti-clerical, provincial, radical Freemason. Combes punished the innocent with the guilty, though the former clearly outnumbered the latter. He was determined to tear French youth from clerical clutches and in spite of the assurances and protests of

Waldeck-Rousseau, he enforced the strictest interpretations and even indulged in chicanery in applying the law. There were a few exceptions. The political importance and significance of Trappists or Cistercians were obviously limited. France could not afford to lose the medical services of the Hospitaliers of St John of God, while the missionary work of the White Fathers or the Society for African Missions was regarded as more valuable than a fleet of gunboats or a division of *Légionnaires.* However, most other orders including fifty-four congregations of men and eight-one congregations of women were dissolved.

In spite of riots in Brittany and the protests of moderate Frenchmen, Combes closed schools which had been established by authorized congregations since their date of authorization. By October 1903 he had closed over 10,000 primary schools, though almost 6,000 had reopened, two-thirds of which were staffed by 'secularized' brothers and nuns. Originally, there were about 20,000 Catholic schools in France and by September 1904 Combes was able to boast that he had closed almost 14,000. It was impossible at the time to adopt a system of education which was exclusively secular because of the costs involved and the implied threat to religious and political liberty. Nevertheless, a law was passed in 1904 which ordered authorized congregations to close their schools and to abandon all teaching within the next ten years. Combes succeeded in closing a third of the schools run by religious congregations and deprived some 150,000 children of their schools. Less than half of these were absorbed into the public schools; most of the rest joined other Catholic schools with a bitter and justified sense of grievance against the Government.

Combes was deliberately provactive and cruel. Former monks were forbidden to preach in spite of the fact that, as *La République Francaise* put it, 'Everyone cannot be like M. Combes and, after leaving the cassock, make a living out of politics'. Combes and most of the deputies would have willingly deprived members of dispersed congregations of their elementary right to earn a living. If former monks and nuns had not been able to continue teaching in schools as 'lay' staff, there would have been even more cases of poverty-stricken former religious than there were. Three bishops who petitioned on behalf of the religious were deprived of their salaries, soldiers were forbidden to spend their leisure time in Catholic circles, churchmen were excluded from certain State examinations, crucifixes were once again removed from the law courts. The navy was traditionally religious and so nuns were removed from naval hospitals, a battleship was named after Ernest Renan, the

Good Friday fast on shipboard was abolished and so was the Mass of the Holy Spirit at the beginning of term in the naval academy.

As early as December 1902 Combes deliberately invited a direct clash with the Holy See on the most crucial issue in relations between Church and State, the right of the French Government to nominate bishops. In order to avoid choosing unsuitable candidates, French politicians had unofficially consulted the nuncio before sending names to Rome. Combes simply ignored this practice and the Pope refused to accept his candidates. Combes for his part laid the matter before the Chamber of Deputies and raised the possibility of cancelling the Concordat and separating Church and State. Initially, Combes might have been simply trying to intimidate the Roman authorities into accepting his interpretation of the rights of the French Government under the Concordat. He himself apparently shared the common view that a disestablished Church would be more dangerous than a salaried clergy. On the whole, the Government supported the Concordat and only a minority of the deputies were opposed to it. Yet within three years most of the deputies were in favour of separation and a reluctant Government was forced to follow their lead.

Shortly after the quarrel over episcopal nominations began, Leo XIII died and was replaced by Pius X. The chance of pursuing Leo's policies was lost when the Austrian Emperor vetoed Cardinal Rampolla who was within thirteen votes of the number required and eight votes ahead of Cardinal Sarto. The cardinals indignantly rejected the Emperor's veto and gave Rampolla an extra vote to prove it. However they appreciated that it would be difficult for a Pope to rule the Universal Church effectively without the respect of the major powers and that to elect a Francophile against the expressed wishes of Austria and the Triple Alliance might result in subsequent difficulties.

Pius X was a devout pastoral priest with a heavy sense of responsibility. He was much less familiar than his predecessor with the ways of the world and unlike his predecessor he did not 'enjoy' the papacy. The new Pope had little conception of the importance of diplomatic expertize to spiritual men with spiritual objectives living in an uncomprehending materialistic society. Pius was undoubtedly courageous and honest, but he lacked any sense of timing or even any capacity for manoeuvre in the battle against anti-clericalism and scepticism. The new Secretary of State, Merry del Val, shared many of his master's qualities and attitudes; he was also young, brash and incisive at a time when experience, caution and even 'studied evasiveness' were the qualities needed.

Pius X manifested his willingness to compromise by accepting one and rejecting the other of the two episcopal nominations. The French Government, however, noted only the refusal and declared that no other vacancies would be filled until their earlier nominations had been accepted. The Pope was clearly distressed at the prospect of leaving sees vacant, but he refused to give way and Combes once again retaliated by raising the issue of disestablishment. Combes did not realize that there had been a change in Vatican policies and only recognized the change when it was too late. Unlike Leo XIII, the new Pope was not a Francophile, nor did he indulge in vain hopes that the French Government might some day help to solve the Roman Question. On the contrary, the improvement in relations between the Italian Government and the Holy See enabled Pius X to take a stronger line with France.

Pius X and Merry del Val did not renounce Leo's policy of *Ralliement*, but they progressively undermined its spirit and its strategy. Merry del Val thought that Leo's policies of 'appeasement' and encouraging an alliance between Catholics and conservative republicans had proved disastrous. Merry del Val believed that Catholics should unite with anyone, including monarchists, in support of Catholic and papal interests – an attitude which threatened to create the sort of ghetto mentality which Leo XIII had anxiously tried to avoid – and the French Assumptionists were restored to the favour and confidence of the Pope. In short, although Pius X would not welcome the separation of Church and State in France, he was, if necessary, prepared to end the Concordat and he openly discussed the advantages that might follow disestablishment.

Combes' ministry lasted less than three years, but during that time all the issues affecting relations between Church and State which had troubled France for over a century had been raised again: the freedom of Catholic education, the expulsion of religious orders, the secularization of civil ceremonies, deadlock over episcopal nominations, papal control of French bishops, and finally the Roman Question itself. The Roman Question had virtually disappeared from the realm of international politics. Although Pius X was still the 'Prisoner of the Vatican', a *modus vivendi* had been established and the papacy maintained a theoretical rather than a practical position. In April 1904, however, President Loubet of France defied Catholic protocol by paying a State Visit to King Victor Emmanuel in Rome.

Originally, Rampolla and Merry del Val reacted to the proposed State Visit with a combination of conciliation and firmness. Loubet himself hoped to be received by the Pope if only unofficially. However, the Roman authorities feared that such a visit might seem to be a feeble acceptance of the French action as well as an example of the declining significance of the papacy which might in turn encourage other countries in their dealings with the Holy See and the Catholic Church. In an effort to avoid friction, Merry del Val agreed to meet the French Foreign Minister and the editor of *Le Figaro* determined to revenge himself on the Minister who had recently given evidence in a lawsuit against the newspaper.

Le Figaro informed its readers that the Foreign Minister, *'putting the interests of the country above ministerial solidarity'*, was rightly trying to secure an audience with the Pope and that the Prime Minister would probably first hear the news from *Le Figaro*. Combes was furious, the Foreign Minister had to deny the story and this public denial seemed a further humiliating insult to the Holy See which had already made a considerable concession in allowing the Secretary of State to meet the French Foreign Minister in the first place. Consequently, when the President returned to France, Merry del Val decided to issue a protest which was sent to Catholic Governments throughout the world. Inevitably, there was a leak and the protest appeared in the French press.

It would have been difficult for an anti-clerical forger to have composed a document which would have proved more provocative to public opinion in France. The French Government and people were told that they ought to be grateful for the privilege of protecting Catholic interests in the east and for the large number of French cardinals. The French nation should apparently be willing to sacrifice its security in support of the papacy's quarrel with Italy; a quarrel which was hardly regarded as a real issue even by Roman authorities. Finally, copies of the protest, unlike the original, included a sentence to the effect that the nuncio was only staying on in France beceause the fall of Combes' government was confidently expected. Few Frenchmen were aware of the background to the protest and Catholics as well as republicans were outraged. They all regarded the temporal power of the Pope as a dead issue, whereas they had supported the State Visit in the hopes of detaching Italy from the Triple Alliance. The French ambassador was recalled from the Vatican and, with the widespread support of public opinion, Combes put further pressure on the Holy See and renewed his threats of disestablishment.

The formal break took place as a result of differences over papal control of French bishops. Two French bishops, detested by conservative forces in their dioceses, were the subjects of scandalous gossip. One was accused of spending nights in orgies with actresses and the other of competing with his secretary for the affections of an eccentric Carmelite prioress. The second bishop was also accused of paying a gang of youths to beat up his secretary as the latter was leaving the convent late one night. Other accusations included wearing a masonic apron in a masonic procession, misappropriating funds, promising to give a titular canonry and ordaining a natural son. In July 1904 Merry del Val summoned the two bishops to Rome to answer the accusations made against them. It is significant that the crucial charge levelled against the bishops at Rome was that of informing the civil authorities about ecclesiastical secrets and they were ordered to resign. Combes had some legal justification for refusing to accept their resignations, though with his typical meanness, he also stopped their salaries on the grounds that they had left France without permission. Merry del Val refused to give way and the formal diplomatic break occurred on 30 July 1904.

The diplomatic break with the Holy See and the threat to separate Church and State in France were part of Combes' effort to put pressure on the Pope. But by his actions, he was supporting forces in favour of separation and creating a situation which he could no longer control. In fact, he more or less committed the Government to the policy of separation. However, before separation actually took place, Combes had been forced to resign. Under Combes' ministry, the high principles of the Dreyfusards had been replaced by a crude ideological support for a corrupt republican 'establishment'. Combes' persecution of religious congregations seemed as cynical as the methods employed against Dreyfus. The Government never made any secret of the fact that official posts were reserved for its own supporters, but in October 1904 the deputies learned that the promotion of army officers was based on secret reports prepared by Freemasons. One officer, for example, was reported to be very cold, very reserved and had been present at his son's first communion. A nationalist deputy was found dead, murdered, it was said, by the masons or the police. Further evidence of espionage conducted by the Government included the confidential investigation of the deputies themselves and Combes was forced to resign.

Some of the supporters of separation regarded it as a means to an end: 'complete secularization of the State, and an end to the influence of the Church'. Ferdinand Buisson maintained that 'Democracy, impelled by a wonderful instinct of its needs and of its immediate duty, is preparing to detach the nation, families and individuals from the Church'. However, the very different political interests of the various forces in the Chamber of Deputies ensured that the Bill on the separation of Church and State would be moderate and non-punitive; it was more liberal and conciliatory than had been expected and was drawn up in such a way as to avoid offending the religious sentiments of Catholics.

The French State recognized absolute freedom of conscience, but France would be a neutral country tolerating all forms of religion and giving public support to none. Most ecclesiastical property including churches and cathedrals would be handed over to local bodies subject to the control of the State. However, these *associations cultuelles* could federate together, establish reserve funds and recognize the rights of the ecclesiastical hierarchy. The Government would no longer pay clerical stipends, though there was to be a transitional period and existing pension rights would be safeguarded. Other privileges were maintained. Military and hospital chaplains could still be paid from public funds, while seminarians who proceeded to ordination and the parochial ministry were free from military service. New ecclesiastical rights were recognized; bishops could freely correspond with the Roman authorities and could adjust diocesan or parochial boundaries.

On the whole, the Roman authorities regarded separation as an evil to be avoided if this could be done without loss of prestige. The Pope himself was not unaware that separation of Church and State might have a beneficial effect on priests thrown onto their own resources and that it would strengthen his authority over French bishops who in future would be appointed only hy himself. However, as a pastoral bishop, Pius X was also aware of the hardships which the French clergy might suffer and, as Head of the Church, he was very conscious of the insult offered to the Holy See by the unilateral actions of the French Government.

Most French Catholics tended to share the Roman point of view. There were a few Catholics in the tradition of Lacordaire or Montalembert who supported the principle of separation, but most Catholic separatists at the time were influenced by their hostility to the Republic and became loyal supporters of the Concordat when the Government officially adopted the policy of separation in 1904. Consequently, moderate Catholics and republicans who supported a sensible compromise were threatened by radical politicians seeking to dominate the Church or by intransigent Catholics influenced by their hatred of republicanism. In the event, most of the Catholic press, many French priests and bishops eventually came out against the law largely because opponents of the law were a more homogeneous and vociferous group than its supporters.

The arguments on both sides were finely balanced. Some Catholics argued that separation would produce a more enthusiastic clergy, whereas others maintained that the effects might prove demoralizing. Cardinal Gibbons himself pointed out that French Catholics might not accept their obligation to support the Church financially, while financial dependence on wealthy French Catholics might entail an unfortunate political as well as social dependence. In fact, if Catholic benefactors had not proved as devoted and loyal as they did, many priests might have suffered at the hands of wealthy but capricious patrons. Furthermore, the need to collect money would obviously distract priests from other more pastoral or intellectual pursuits. A Church supported by the State could also afford the luxury of bishops who were remarkable for their intellectual and pastoral abilities rather than for their financial skills.

In the past, there were sufficient examples of unhappy episcopal appointments to justify Monsignor d'Hulst's complaint that the Government was 'poisoning' the episcopate. On the other hand, the Government had also appointed many worthy men including some more 'liberal' bishops than the Roman authorities themselves might have liked. Subsequent episcopal appointments caused many French Catholics to regret the separation of Church and State. Future French bishops would be chosen in the interests of papal politics and some of the bishops appointed over the next few years later proved hostile to the policies of Pius XI; a sizeable number supported *Action Francaise* which inevitably caused difficulties when that movement was condemned. Furthermore, the Roman authorities did not allow French bishops to meet in assembly until 1951 and one perceptive commentator remarked, 'There used to be bishops, but no episcopate. Now there are not even bishops'.

However, if the Holy See and the French Church were united in their opposition to separation of Church and State, they were divided over their attitudes towards the *associations cultuelles*. These associations were the only embodiment of the French Church which the Government was prepared to recognize, groups of French citizens engaged in the activity of worship. The associations were regarded in legal terms as similar to any other clubs or organizations formed for particular purposes. The law, therefore, did not define the nature of the association, did not mention Pope or bishops, nor even stipulate that an orthodox Catholic priest should be a member of each association. This legal 'neutrality' seemed incomprehensible to Catholics who could not conceive of the Church without Pope or bishops and who expressed their fears that the associations might be infiltrated or even dominated by schismatics, heretics or infidels. Their fears proved to be unrealistic, but they were reinforced by the explicit threats of some anti-clericals, while the danger of schism undoubtedly influenced the Roman authorities. Nevertheless, when it became obvious that the law separating Church and State would pass without any further concessions being made, many Catholics including most of the influential French clergy argued in favour of accepting the associations. The law would allow the ecclesiastical authorities to impose their own rules on the associations which would necessarily involve the laity in parochial affairs and to some extent spare the clergy the inevitable embarrassments associated with exclusive financial responsibility. The Roman authorities, however, were influenced by other considerations.

Several reasons have been offered to explain the publication of *Vehementer*, which has been seen as a reaffirmation of papal authority over a more accommodating French hierarchy or as a demonstration of the purity of a supernatural Church. However, it would seem that the Roman authorities were bitterly opposed to the fact that the French Government was imposing a new legal constitution on the French Church without making the least effort to secure the consent of the Holy See. Diplomatic relations had been broken in 1904. During the following year France had unilaterally abolished the Concordat and then independently proposed to separate Church and State as if the Vatican did not exist. These seemed crushing blows to the international prestige of the Holy See. Other nations, particularly Switzerland, Spain and Portugal, might be tempted to follow the example of France unless the papacy manifested its determination to defend the interests of the Church. Merry del Val explained:

> It is not only the French Church and its well-being that is at stake; it is the good of the whole Church. If the system of *cultuelles* is allowed to take root in France – a system which implies pillage on the one hand, laicization on the other, and ultimately state control –we will be responsible for the spread of this disastrous system to

> all the other Catholic countries. Imitation will be inevitable, and Freemasonry is everywhere preparing to insist that governments follow similar policies. It is a disguised form of secularization, where the hierarchy is subjected to the opinions of the laity, be it private individuals, the courts, or the state. The western churches will undergo the fate of the eastern churches, tightly reined-in by *laïques* who interfere in church administration. It will be a clear belittling of the Holy See, whose authority and control are rejected both in theory and practice.

The encyclical *Vehementer* published in February 1906 condemned the unilateral abolition of the Concordat, the Law of Separation and the principle of separating Church and State. The imposition of *associations cultuelles* was described as an attempt to force a constitution on the Church without consultation and against its wishes. Furthermore, the constitution was opposed to the hierarchical constitution of the Church established by Christ. The Law of Separation subjected the Church to the secular power, encouraged schism and placed authority in the hands of the laity, whereas ecclesiastical authority was vested in the clergy and the hierarchy. The institution of the Catholic Church was incompatible with a law which did not recognize the hierarchy and the duty of French Catholics now was to follow the lead given to them by the Pope.

From the Roman point of view, the material interests of French Catholicism could not be compared to the spiritual interests and international prestige of the papacy. When the Pope was told how many millions of francs were involved, he replied that it was the good, rather than the goods of the Church that he was defending and that he could always appoint a Franciscan as Archbishop of Paris, if an Archbishop could not fulfill his duties without a palace or a budget. The French bishops, on the other hand, were less concerned about the details of Vatican diplomacy, which were themselves relics of a former and worldly greatness, than with the effective exercise of the Church's ministry which to some extent at least depended on money and property. The French bishops were more afraid of the consequences of administrative chaos or financial disaster on the future of the French Church than with the unlikely threat of schism or the vague dangers of Erastianism.

Meanwhile, twenty-three leading Catholic intellectuals signed an open letter in which they declared that the proposed organizations of the *Associations cultuelles* incorporated all the safeguards which the Church needed. The alternative was to surrender the traditional religious heritage of France, to turn medieval churches and cathedrals into barns or dance halls, and to transform Catholicism into a private religion which had little influence on society and was controlled by those who provided the largest financial support. However, the French Church would not be allowed to decide the issue independently of the Roman authorities, whose handling of the situation certainly left something to be desired.

The international prestige of the Holy See could be preserved either by securing an agreement with the French Government or by refusing to accept the Law of Separation. To reject the Law might well salvage papal prestige because of the considerable financial sacrifices involved which could win the respect and admiration of 'neutral' observers and might even provoke a reaction against the 'persecuting' French Government. However, the Holy See could not give the impression of making sacrifices on behalf of others. It was necessary for the French bishops themselves to reject the associations. The Roman authorities could then prohibit the associations without any embarrassment.

Merry del Val decided to use a plenary assembly of the French bishops to achieve the aims of the Roman authorities. The Secretary of State has been described as having 'a notion of authority such as one might have cherished in Spain three centuries earlier' and hiding 'steel beneath the velvet of great natural benevolence and exquisite politeness'. He adopted 'an extremely hierarchic view of the Church's organization, regarding Catholics as subject in all things to the bishops, and the latter as taking their cue from Rome'. Merry del Val recognized that the French bishops might actually vote in favour of the associations and he therefore imposed secrecy on the bishops under pain of canonical suspension. Then, even if the bishops did oppose the policies of the Holy See, only the bishops themselves would know and the Roman authorities had long experience of dealing with disgruntled bishops. The Secretary of State also ensured that the French hierarchy was clearly aware of the Pope's attitude; only if the bishops were virtually unanimous in accepting the associations would he himself reluctantly accept them.

Merry del Val believed that to accept the associations would prove to be:

> a victory for all these young priests and Catholics who have been

won over to the freedom of the critical school, the advanced democratic school and all those who dream of reforms and novelties where the human and lay elements attempt to hold in check the divine and supernatural, and where the time-honoured structure of the Church would be turned upside down, in favour of the new Church of their dreams adapted to the ideas of modern lay society'.

He further explained:

I am very anxious, because I clearly see that we are at a turning-point in history for the Universal Church. All the forces of evil and international freemasonry are ranged against the Church; and it is France which is in the front line of this struggle at this present moment. What happens in France will serve as an example to everyone else, and that is why the decision is of the greatest importance'.

By the time the French bishops met in assembly in May, 1906, it was widely rumoured that nearly all the archbishops and some two thirds of the bishops were in favour of accepting the associations. After all, if it was feared that ecclesiastical property might fall into the wrong hands, the refusal to accept the associations simply increased this danger. It was impossible to foresee that the French Government would in fact leave churches, though not presbyteries, in the hands of the parish priests, or that attempts by schismatic associations to obtain possession of Catholic properties would be consistently rejected by the French courts. Furthermore, since recent elections had clearly shown that the electorate was largely indifferent to the fate of the Church, the case in favour of rejecting the associations seemed less convincing than ever.

The French bishops voted in secret on three specific points. In the first place, they demonstrated their solidarity with the Pope by almost unanimously condemning the Law of Separation. On the crucial issue of establishing associations – '*à la fois canoniques et légales*' – forty-eight bishops voted in favour and only twenty-six against. The bishops then went on to approve by fifty-nine votes to seventeen statutes prepared by Archbishop Fulbert-Petit of Besançon allowing the French Church to establish committees that would have fulfilled the purposes of the associations. At the same time, a sub-committee of curial cardinals meeting in Rome was evenly balanced on the question of accepting the *associations cultuelles*.

Merry del Val, however, refused to give way and in August 1906 the

Pope issued his encyclical *Gravissimo officii* forbidding Catholics to form *associations cultuelles.* The establishment of associations according to French Law could not be done without violating sacred rights which were indispensable for the very existence of the Church. Other forms of association were also ruled out unless legal safeguards were given that the divine constitution of the Church, the immutable rights of the hierarchy and the papacy, would be securely and irrevocably guaranteed. Since the decisions of the episcopal assembly had been kept secret, the encyclical exploited the distinction between the three questions; the willingness of the French bishops to accept the associations was not even mentioned and the Pope gave the impression that he was simply confirming their unanimous condemnation of the Law of Separation. Angered by this cynical dishonesty, Bishop Lacroix revealed the truth in the pages of *Le Temps*. Merry del Val, however, continued to maintain that the Holy See and the French hierarchy were united in their approach and even his closest friends were induced to believe him. Yet the diplomatic mendacity of the Secretary of State is probably easier to understand and to forgive than the sacrifices and burdens which he imposed on the French Church.

The period of time allowed for the formation of associations expired in December when the Government was legally entitled to confiscate all ecclesiastical property including churches and cathedrals. The Government tried to compromise by extending the period of grace and then attempted to force the issue by expelling the papal *chargé d'affaires.* The Government did not behave as responsibly in seizing his records including some of his confidential reports on French priests which were leaked to the press. The publication of these reports helped to discredit the ecclesiastical system which had been responsible for them, though the French Republic was also dishonoured by the way in which it had used them. The Government attempted to safeguard clerical pension funds and the property of ancient religious establishments, but these attempts were also rejected by the Roman authorities. A series of decrees and circular allowed the Church to continue without setting up the associations; buildings intended for worship could be placed at the disposal of priests by their legal owners, the various communes. At the same time, episcopal palaces and seminaries, presbyteries, schools and halls as well as pension funds and funds for Masses were seized by the Government.

The Pope stood firm and the Church of France stood with him, though many French churchmen did not approve of his actions. One prelate who did not sympathize with Ultramontanism rather thought that his colleagues had received what they deserved: 'They wanted an infallible Pope', he said, 'they have got one'. The French Church was finally separated from the French State, but perhaps even more important, the Holy See had finally dominated the Gallican Church; all its episcopal appointments were now firmly in the hands of the Vatican authorities. Meanwhile, in many French parishes only the church remained as the material sign of that great institution which had once been the wealthiest in France and most of these churches were not owned by 'occupied'. Only new churches and a few chapels belonging to nineteenth-century benefactors were independent of the civil authorities. The parochial clergy were deprived of any official standing within their communities, they celebrated at altars where they were only allowed on sufferance, many of them were miserably poor and totally dependent on the charity of their flocks. The number of ordinations fell and the decline in attendance at Church continued.

In financial terms, the sacrifices imposed on the French Church by the Roman authorities were considerable. The ban on associations also deprived French Catholics of the means of re-building their material resources on a legally secure basis. When the ban was lifted in 1924, fifty years of effort were needed to replace the resources lost in 1906. In 1924 Pius XI would justify the change in papal policy by emphasizing the different character of the associations and the changed political situation, though the French Government had been willing to make concessions in 1907 which were far more valuable than those granted in the 1920s. It was hoped that the new associations might be able to recover some of the church property which was still unallocated. But as a result of episcopal intransigence and the opposition of radical politicians, this was only finally restored by Marshal Pétain in 1941, when it was worthy barely one per cent of what the Church had lost in 1906.

The anti-Modernist reaction in France as elsewhere suppressed new intellectual, social and political movements in the Church. French scholars such as Duchesne or Blondel had to endure the embarrassment of a French hierarchy joining Merry del Val in supporting the legend that Lazarus, Mary and Martha had evangelized Gaul; and this in spite of the fact that Canon Vacandard had already demonstrated that the legend went no further back than the eleventh century. But at the very time of defeat, a new spirit seemed to be stirring in the French Church. A new sense of social awareness had been aroused among Catholics in the upper and middle classes. A new sense of man's need for God would soon be found among intellectual and literary figures. The spirit of lay initiative began to spread and a more apostolic clergy seemed to emerge and find their voice. Internal conflicts which had so weakened French Catholicism declined as did the forces of anti-clericalism since the Church was no longer so politically involved. At the beginning of the twentieth century the French Church had lost its status as a national institution, was losing its numerical claim to respect and had suffered continuous and finally decisive political defeats. Furthermore, like other Catholic Churches throughout the world, it was dominated by the See of Rome. Nevertheless, following the separation of Church and State, a new vitality seemed to surge through French Catholicism and from the struggles of the nineteenth century, a new period of ecclesiastical history had undoubtedly begun.

George Tyrrell

VIII: Pius X and the Condemnation of Modernism

Leo XIII helped to create the modern papacy by restoring its international prestige. Pius X became one of the founders of the modern papacy through his encouragement of a greater sense of pastoral concern and through his internal reforms of the Church. However, Pius X's reforms were restricted to the institution of the Church itself. He did not share Leo's concern with social issues nor his interest in the intellectual revival of Catholicism. Pius X prepared for the liturgical revival by promoting more frequent communion, reforming the breviary and restoring Gregorian chant. He paid particular attention to the formation of the clergy and was responsibile for the reorganization and improvement of diocesan seminaries. He laid down uniform rules governing the discipline and studies in seminaries. He urged bishops to be careful in selecting candidates, to be demanding in the examinations preceding ordination and to be diligent in supervizing newly-ordained priests. He urged priests to be assiduous in prayer and meditation, devoted to the reading of good books especially the Bible and to examine their consciences frequently. Daniel-Rops has pointed out that Pius X also tried to enhance the authority of the Holy See and to tighten ecclesiastical discipline by reforming the curia and controlling bishops throughout the world. The new code of Canon Law emphasized the role of the Roman authorities in the choice of bishops. Furthermore Pius X checked the least move towards disobedience or doctrinal error. He therefore condemned the 'Modernists' at at least tolerated the activities of conservative and integrist Catholics.

It has been argued that after the triumph of Ultramontanism and the failure of Liberal Catholicism, the development of 'Modernism' would have been impossible if Pio Nono had been succeeded by an equally intransigent Pope. Leo XIII's more open attitude, however, encouraged a new generation of Catholic scholars who tried to reconcile contemporary scientific and historical discoveries with the faith, the theology and the apologetic of the Catholic Church. Louis Duchesne, for example, was himself a pupil of the Liberal Catholic archaeologist Cavalliere de Rossi. Duchesne applied critical methods to the study of ecclesiastical history, though, unlike his own pupil, Alfred Loisy, he quickly learned to avoid commenting on more dangerous theological or biblical questions. Duchesne conceded that the development of the early Church and its teaching were influenced by the same historical factors which governed other contemporary secular developments. However, the ecclesiastical authorities felt that this concession did not sufficiently recognize the role of the Holy Spirit and the intervention of divine providence. Duchesne's *Early History of the Church* was put on the Index in spite of the fact that it had received an *imprimatur* from the Master of the Sacred Palace.

According to Buonaiuti, the movement known as 'Modernism' had its origin in the conflict between two generations of scholars. The older generation suspected or condemned more modern ideas and ignored or rejected the conclusions of historical and biblical criticism. Buonaiuti described their intellectual approach in the following way:

> In the ecclesiastical schools two fundamental assumptions dominate the method of teaching. One is that Christian revelation is primarily of a doctrinal character; in other words, it is a revelation of dogmas which the Church professes to have received from Christ and the Apostles, from the very beginning of Christianity; the other is that Christianity is identical with the dogmatic definitions of the councils, particularly of the Council of Trent and of the Vatican Council. The task of the professor of Dogmatic Theology is simply to supply the evidence that the dogmatic formulations of the councils are supported by scriptural texts. The professor of Church history has no task other than to demonstrate that the dogmas, the laws, the organization and the discipline of the Church were in existence in the Church from the beginning and that they have remained unimpaired throughout the centuries of Christian history. No great effort is needed to discover that the professors of Dogmatic Theology twist fragments of scriptural texts from their context to make them fit the definition of the councils, and that the professors of Church history twist the facts of history to make them fit into the dogmatic theological pattern designed by those councils.

Catholic scholars like Pierre Batiffol or Marie-Joseph Lagrange accepted the principles of scientific and historical criticism without necessarily indulging in radical theological conclusions or theological reductionism. However, conservative Catholics who had already diverge considerably from more liberal scholars refused to make any distinctions and simply identified ecclesiastical reformers with radical theologians, political liberals with dangerous philosophers. One conservative scholar made a significant appeal for a 'return to an *integral* and intransigent Catholicism, in the true supernatural sense of that word' and more enlightened theologians were accused of attempting to destroy the faith. At the beginning of the twentieth century, Maurice Blondel commented,

> With every day that passes, the conflict between tendencies which set Catholic against Catholic in every order – social, political, philosophical – is revealed as sharper and more general. One could almost say that there are now two quite incompatible 'Catholic mentalities', particularly in France.

Consequently, when Loisy was condemned, other scholars like Lagrange fell under suspicion, while advocates of ecclesiastical reform or social and political action were also associated with the 'heresy' of Modernism.

There were, however, several very different and distinct forms of 'Modernism' and it was possible to accept one and to reject another. The only common attitudes adopted by all the Modernists seem to have been an undue confidence in contemporary developments and a rejection of that unconditional obedience which the Roman authorities had come to expect. In 1912 Pius X actually told a group of priests that the love of the Pope was an important means of sanctification. That love should be manifested in deeds as well as words; the Pope and the Vatican bureaucracy which acted in his name should be obeyed without limit. The opposition of the Modernists to papal and Roman autocracy remained a common factor among many of those who were able to remain in the Church as well as among those who left it or were expelled.

'Historical' or 'biblical' Modernists included scholars who accepted the implications of biblical or historical criticism as well as those like Loisy who eventually rejected the sacred character of the scriptures or the unique and eternal truthfulness of biblical revelation. As a result of his biblical studies, Loisy not only concluded that the scriptures were historically unreliable but he surrendered his belief in the Virgin birth and the fact of Christ's resurrection. Loisy argued that belief in Christ as the Son of God was a creation of Christian faith meditating on and transforming the Jesus of Nazareth. According to Loisy, the object of historical criticism was to rediscover the historical figure of

Jesus and remove the 'veils' of faith. He therefore offered a purely natural account of Christ and the origins of Christianity which undermined the basic claims of the Church. Loisy also concluded that ecclesiastical statements, papal or conciliar decrees, were subject to the same relativity as biblical claims and were not infallible. He began to deny the supernatural character of religion, though he still wished to serve the Church, 'an essential institution and the most divine upon earth', the educator of the human race, the guarantee of the peace of society and the happiness of the family.

Loisy's lectures and writings especially on the nature of prophecy, the historicity of Genesis and the authorship of the Pentateuch provoked a great deal of criticism from other Catholics. Students were forbidden to attend his lectures, he was restricted to teaching ancient languages and finally lost his chair at the Institute Catholique in Paris. Following the publication of *Providentissimum Deus* in 1893 he made a rather equivocal submission and one of his articles was officially condemned by the Archbishop of Paris. In 1902 Loisy created a sensation when he published *The Gospel and the Church* in answer to the work of the Liberal Protestant, Adolph von Harnack. Loisy argued that a radical historical criticism of the origins of Christianity justified the full, rich, corporate life of the Catholic Church rather than the reduced and diluted faith of Protestantism. The Church with its hierarchy, dogma and liturgy was the necessary form in which the Gospel was preserved, expressed and developed. Christianity had grown from an original seed, changing as it developed, but was still essentially the same and had flowered into the Catholic Church. True Christianity was to be found not in its origins but in the life of the Church. *The Gospel and the Church* was condemned by the French bishops and then put on the Index by the Holy Office.

Loisy's qualified submissions and ambiguous attitudes manifested a genuine hesitancy which has given rise to more serious charges. It has been said that he continued to live as a priest and even tried to promote his own candidature for the episcopate after losing his faith. For a long time, his personal beliefs could not be reconciled with his public statements or his apologetic. In the second edition of *The Gospel and the Church*, he added a discussion distinguishing the actual or immediate witness to the life and teaching of Christ from the understanding of Christians after his death. Had this discussion appeared in the first edition, it would have modified the enthusiastic welcome given to the book by Blondel or von Hügel as well as the cautious interest shown by later opponents like Pius X and Batiffol.

However, during the first decade of the twentieth century, Loisy suffered a series of blows which no doubt helped to destroy his faith. In 1903 several of his books were put on the Index. Loisy submitted to the condemnation of his books, offered to surrender his lectureship and to suspend any work on which he was engaged. The Pope then cruelly questioned his sincerity, demanded an unqualified submission and urged him, like Clovis, to burn what he had adored and adore what he had burned. However, it is only fair to add that on another occasion, Pius X told Loisy's bishop to 'Treat him kindly, and if he takes one step towards you, take two towards him'. Loisy could not have remained unaffected by the political conflicts between Church and State in France, the condemnation of Modernism and the integrist campaign. On the feast of St Thomas Aquinas 1908 he was formally excommunicated when he refused to submit to the measures taken against Modernism. Any hopes of a reconciliation were destroyed by the condemnation of the *Sillon* in 1910: 'The Roman Church', wrote Loisy, 'has no heart'.

'Dogmatic' or 'theological' Modernists included opponents of scholasticism as well as writters like Buonaiuti or Tyrrell. Buonaiuti interpreted the tradition of the Church as the collective spiritual experience of Christianity rather than cold dogmatic formulas or legal definitions. Tradition was dynamic, not static, and could not simply be identified with the earlier decisions of the official organs of ecclesiastical Government. Tyrrell became convinced that in order to avoid the unnecessary and damaging conflicts between science and religion, Christianity must adapt itself to contemporary realities. An evolving Catholicism could survive, but the conflict between modern thought and traditional Catholic theology was such that neither could accept the other without being destroyed.

Tyrrell removed the dichotomy between dogma and scientific or historical knowledge by arguing that theology was the inadequate expression of the living experience of the Church. Revelation consisted in that living experience and not in its intellectual formulation which varied according to the intellectual capacities and needs of men living at particular times. The Catholic Church mediated the fullest experience of God, Christ and the spiritual life, but the theological system of the Catholic Church was neither an adequate nor an immutable statement of absolute truth. Faith was not an assent to a series of formulations and Catholicism was not merely a system of practical observances regulated by theology. Catholicism was primarily a life and 'the Church a spiritual organism in whose life we participate'; theology was 'an attempt of that life to formulate and understand itself'.

The 'political' Modernists rejected political and social conservatism and tried to reconcile Catholicism with democracy and socialism. Antonio Fogazzaro was a novelist and a poet. In his novel, *The Saint*, he argued that ecclesiastical teaching should be modified in the light of evolutionary theories and that the dogmas of the Church should be adapted to contemporary needs. Fogazzaro urged the Pope to reform the Church and to end the evils of falsehood, clerical domination, avarice and obscurantism which were to be found in the Church. At one time, Fogazzaro was on the editorial board of *Rassegna Nazionale* which maintained that Italian Catholics should accept the *Risorgimento*. The hero of his novel *Daniele Cortis* advocated the freedom of the Church within the state and the formation of a non-confessional party independent of ecclesiastical control.

Romolo Murri was one of the founders of Christian Democracy. He supported political and social, but not theological reform. He himself was scholastically orthodox; he had welcomed the election of Pius X and approved of the condemnation of Loisy. In Murri's opinion, the definition of papal infallibility had freed Catholics from the need to engage in theological disputes and they could now concentrate their attention on social issues. Nevertheless, in 1906 his review, *Cultura sociale*, was officially banned partly at least because of a letter which he had published from Tommaso Gallarati Scotti;

> Since the death of Pope Leo the Roman Curia has assumed towards the world of thought a reactionary attitude reminiscent of the days of Pius IX, when the Church was at war with everything and everybody . . . There are very many of us in Italy today who, having an ardent faith, feel unable to adapt ourselves to a clerical policy which seriously threatens that Catholic intellectual progress for which we desire to work energetically so long as God grants us life . . . We cannot in all sincerity uphold official Catholic policy.

At the same time, Scotti was very careful to explain his position in some detail;

> I know that people from all walks of life will seek to brand us as rebels; I know that they will refuse to take account of our open profession of the Catholic faith, of the integrity of our lives, of the

> honesty of our words and deeds . . . Rebels? Perhaps: words mean so little. But we are rebelling not against the Church's dogma, not against the hierarchical authority in its divine mission on Earth, not against the prescribed forms of worship – we declare outselves to be united in a single faith with the most ignorant old woman in Christendom – but against a false concept of authority which corrupts men's souls and seeks to penetrate even into the life of the nation, against a religious ignorance that invests profane, transient and conjectural things with the character of eternal truths, and would compel a people to observe outmoded and threadbare forms without permitting it that spontaneous development which alone can create new institutions and new forms of Christian civilization.

In due course Murri himself was excommunicated by Pius X, though the Pope also gave him a monthly allowance when he fell on hard times. Murri later renounced the priesthood, married and became a radical deputy. However, he was eventually reconciled just before his death in 1943 by Pius XII.

The term 'institutional' Modernists might be used to describe those who advocated the internal reform of the Church, the election of bishops, the abolition of compulsory celibacy, and the reform of education, especially seminary education. As early as 1898 Hermann Schell's books had been put on the Index. Schell advocated the need for improvements in Catholic education and argued that the Catholic spirit should be Christian rather than medieval or Latin. He condemned Roman authoritarianism as harmful to the authorities themselves as well as to their subjects; authoritarianism resulted in immaturity and an unhealthy dependence. Schell also became involved in that movement towards a more personalized religion which existed at the turn of the century.

Schell discussed the relationship between the subjective dispositions of the inquirer and the rather 'rationalistic' approach to apologetics which had become almost traditional in the Church. The obvious danger in a personalist approach is that the subjective element might be substituted for objective content and simply result in a sentimental theology of 'religious feeling'. Schell attracted the attention of the Roman authorities when he challenged the objective validity of the systematic scholastic approach to theology, though his ideas on sin, redemption and the general judgment had also given rise to suspicions. However, Schell was making a genuine attempt to reconcile the Catholic faith with contemporary thought and it was not unjust to condemn him for his 'agnosticism' or 'theological sentimentalism'.

In general, 'Modernists' tended to argue that man had a need for the divine which, rising into consciousness, took the form of a religious sense or religious feeling which was equivalent to faith. Revelation was man's interpretation of his religious experience and although this interpretation was necessarily expressed in conceptual or intellectual forms, these forms might become antiquated so that new forms of expression had to be found. The notion that God revealed absolute truths which were in turn promulgated by the Church in the form of immutable statements of unchangeable truths was regarded as incompatible with an evolutionary understanding of human development and the cultural and religious life of man.

It is, however, important to remember that some of the more extreme statements of the Modernists were made after their expulsion from the Church and it is by no means certain that they would have gone to such extremes if they had not been excommunicated. Furthermore, and in spite of the opinion of Pius X, Modernism was not an organized movement plotting the destruction of Christian orthodoxy, nor even a distinct party advocating a doctrinal system contradicting that of scholasticism. The Modernists did not begin with philosophical presuppositions or *a priori* principles when they criticized Catholic teachings or accepted biblical criticism. They questioned the presuppositions of scholasticism and tried to reinterpret traditional teaching as a result of their academic research and their willingness to accept the findings of modern scholarship.

However, the ecclesiastical authorities became so concerned about some of the conclusions reached by the Modernists that they failed to recognize the reality of the genuine problems with which the Modernists were attempting to deal. The Roman authorities, in particular, were often at least incompetent in dealing with the personalities and issues involved; the authorities were the products of an ecclesiastical tradition that had left them incapable of dealing with Modernism. For their part, not all the Modernists showed the restraint and devotion manifested by Schell in Germany, Laberthonnière in France or Semeria in Italy. These scholars were characteristic of the best of Modernism and they were eventually able to exercise an enduring and beneficial influence on the Church in the twentieth century. Most of the Modernists fell between the two extremes, but the 'movement' as such was largely influenced by some of the worst representatives of Modernism. Finally, the Roman authorities and the Modernists themselves by believing or attributing such extremes to each other helped to create that crisis and climate in the Church which had such disastrous effects.

Some of the Modernists were unduly influenced by current evolutionary, immanentist or pragmatic fashions of thought and adopted ideas which it would be difficult if not impossible to reconcile with historic Christianity. Some Modernists were undoubtedly guilty of philosophical pragmatism or even completely agnostic in their theological approach. Some were guilty of historical scepticism or at least adopted a biblical or historical positivism and a scientific or historical approach which excluded the supernatural. Some of them seemed in danger of adopting historical or theological relativism, over-emphasizing critical rationalism or accepting a philosophical immanentism which rejected the metaphysical and the transcendent, and in its extreme form reduced religion to ethical considerations.

Pius X clearly opposed 'modern' ideas and their advocates within the Church. Biblical criticism was rejected with the condemnation of Loisy. The condemnation of Laberthonnière illustrated that the Roman authorities were still unwilling to tolerate theological or philosophical developments which were not inspired by scholasticism. The condemnation of Fogazzaro revealed their unwillingness to adopt ecclesiastical reforms. Contemporary political principles were condemned with the suspension of Murri and the Pope's criticisms of Bishop Geremia Bonomelli of Cremona who advocated a more liberal line on relations between the Holy See and the Italian State.

In 1903 the Pope approved of the decree of the Holy Office which put five of Loisy's works on the Index. In 1905, he insisted that Catholic Action should always be controlled by ecclesiastical officials. In 1906 Pius X warned the Italian clergy of the dangers of insubordination and suspended those who joined the National Democratic League. In the same year two works by Laberthonnière and Fogazzaro were put on the Index, though the Pope assured the latter of his paternal affection. Murri was suspended in April 1907 and in the following June the Pope issued a letter on the errors of Hermann Schell. In July the Holy Office issued *Lamentabili* and put works by Le Roy, Houtin and Dimet as well as the international review *Coenobium* on the Index. During the following month, the Holy Office instructed religious superiors how to protect their subjects from dangerous errors.

The Pope published his encyclical *Pascendi* in September 1907. The anonymous authors of *The Programme of Modernism* were excommunicated in the following month. During November the Pope issued a *motu proprio* which decreed that all Catholics were bound in conscience to accept past and future decrees of the Biblical Commission in the same way that they accepted the doctrinal decrees issued by the Sacred Congregations and approved by the Pope. During 1907 and 1908 Minocchi was suspended, while Tyrrell, Schnitzer and Loisy were excommunicated along with the publishers, editors, authors and collaborators of *Il Rinnovamento*. The Pope's campaign finally came to an end with the imposition of the anti-Modernist oath on 1 September 1910.

Monsignor Umberto Benigni seems to have invented the expression 'Modernism', which he described as *omnium haeresium complexus*. With the Cardinals Tuto and Billot, Benigni has also been suggested as the author of *Pascendi*. Incidentally. Tuto later went mad, while Billot was forced to resign after the condemnation of *Action Francaise* in 1926. However, the principal author of the doctrinal part of Pascendi was apparently Father Joseph Lemius. Several theologians had submitted different versions which failed to satisfy the Pope. Merry del Val then asked Lemius to produce a draft which delighted Pius X. *Pascendi* and *Lamentabili* can both be seen in the tradition of such papal encyclicals as *Mirari vos* and *Quanta cura*; in fact, *Lamentabili* was clearly modelled on the *Syllabus of Errors*, though restricted to two issues, the understanding of dogma and the interpretation of the Bible. The encyclical listed the errors of Modernism in 65 theses mostly taken from Loisy. Many of these, however, were torn from their contexts and sometimes sentences were added to reinforce the original sense or to take it to its logical conclusion or sometimes even to extremes. Some of the propositions condemned seemed to imply that Catholics could not even make use of a moderately conservative biblical criticism.

Pascendi tried to draw a picture of the typical Modernist as apologist and reformer, theologian and philosopher, historian and scripture scholar. The encyclical tried to draw a composite picture of the principal ideas of a Loisy or a Tyrrell in apologetics and reform, theology and philosophy, history and biblical criticism. The 'doctrines' and 'heresies' of the Modernists were synthesized and their historiography, philosophy and theology were found to be contrary to every ecclesiastical doctrine and to lead to agnosticism and phenomenalism, immanentism and symbolism and so to pantheism or atheism. In this sense, *Pascendi* gave form to a heresy which as outlined did not exist and collected as a whole what no single individual had ever held. In spite of this, several

Catholic commentators have argued that the Pope was trying to deal with the logical conclusions of ideas being advocated at the time and that, although the official ecclesiastical reaction to Modernism might have been regrettable, the original condemnation was nevertheless justified.

Several recommendations were made to combat the dangers of Modernism. Scholasticism was to form the basis of theological education and those Catholic professors who favoured Modernism were to be removed. Bishops were ordered to establish councils to fight against Modernism particularly social Modernism, to censor books by their *nihil obstat*, to confiscate any Modernist writings, and to report every three years to the Roman authorities on the success of these measures and the beliefs of their clergy. Clerical conferences were to be allowed to meet only occasionally and special reliable Catholic institutes of study were to be established. This last provision, the only positive recommendation made, was never fully implemented.

Pius X proceeded to pack the Biblical Commission with conservative scholars so that distinguished writers like Batiffol or Lagrange had to suffer the embarrassment of listening to pronouncements which obliged Catholics not to question the Mosaic authorship of the Pentateuch, the unity of Isaiah, the priority of Matthew or the Pauline authorship of Hebrews. Other measures included the imposition of the anti-Modernist oath on all candidates for ordination, on priests receiving faculties for hearing confessions or preaching and on professors in seminaries and universities. Seminarians were forbidden to read secular newspapers or magazines, while their lecturers had to submit their textbooks and lecture notes to the bishops for approval. The bishops for their part, were required to supervize the teaching given in seminaries and universities, and to establish vigilance committees to seek out Modernists and to counteract their teaching.

A few days after the publication of *Pascendi*, Buonaiuti anonymously published *The Programme of Modernism* in which he maintained that the Modernism described and condemned in the encyclical was merely a creation of those theologians who had composed the encyclical. The Frankenstein monster had never existed except in the distorted picture drawn quite deliberately by reactionary theologians in the curia. Buonaiuti unsuccessfully appealed to the Pope not to reject those of his children who were only seeking after the truth. He later wrote,

Pope Pius X

> Therefore, with all that I can summon in the way of authoritative weight by my word and my testimony, as the result of these thirty years of suffering that the condemnation of Modernism by *Pascendi* has procured for me, I must here solemnly avow that never, in the history of Christian tradition and spirituality, has a greater outrage been perpetrated upon that regard for truth which is the elementary obligation of every human being. Modernism was not in any respect what *Pascendi* claimed that it was.

Other bishops and theologians denied that the condemnations could be applied to the Modernists. Joseph Schnitzer wrote,

> Although the image of modernism as drawn by the encyclical *Pascendi* was described as accurate by those who were opposed to or unfamiliar with its ideas, those most intimately concerned, whose views were at stake, all agree that it was a caricature in which they could not recognize themselves.

George Schwagiers wrote, 'The modernist views as portrayed by the encyclical *Pascendi* were not advocated in this way by any of the real or alleged modernists'. Bishop Dandolle of Dijon believed that no Modernist in practice, ever had a wing span equal to the enormous spread outlined by Pius X'.

Archbishop Eudoxe-Irenée Mignot who was familiar with the results of biblical criticism was also friendly with Loisy. He defended *The Gospel and the Church* against some of its critics, though he himself was not uncritical of some of its limitations. The Archbishop continued to correspond with Loisy even after the latter's excommunication. Mignot also criticized the policies adopted by Pius X and justified taking the anti-Modernist oath as an act of respect which did not necessarily imply assent to all its propositions. Bishop Lucien Lacroix of Tarentaise was a liberal republican whose hopes of preferment disappeared with the ending of the concordat. When Loisy was excommunicated, the bishop wrote to him,

> I read this morning, in *La Croix*, that one is forbidden to correspond with you. That inspires me with an irresistible desire to write to you, to tell you again of my lively and profound sympathy. It is beyond my comprehension that, in the twentieth century . . . such antiquated proceedings should be brought into play: it is childish, grotesque and odious.

Lacroix later resigned his bishopric because of his opposition to the political and academic policies adopted by Pius X.

The curia seems to have believed that there was a widespread Modernist conspiracy, originating in Germany and France, which was attempting to destroy the faith of the Church. In fact, some of the popular sympathy for the social programme of the Centre Party in Germany was lost as a result of the anti-Modernist campaign. Several devout and loyal Catholics in Germany suffered like Catholics in other countries from the witch hunt which was at least tolerated by the Roman authorities. Albert Ehrhard commented, 'The current Roman condemnations constitute a mortal threat to conscience and religious learning in the Catholic world. They are a sin against the Holy Spirit'. Resistance to the anti-Modernist oath was particularly strong in Germany where professors who did not exercise a parochial ministry were later dispensed from taking the oath by the Roman authorities.

The superior of the seminary at Perugia was dismissed for having allowed his students to read Loisy and Fogazzaro. Canon Ulysse Chevalier came under attack simply because he did not believe in the authenticity of the Holy Shroud or in the transportation by angels of the Holy House at Loreto. Historians like Batiffol and biblical scholars like Lagrange were subjected to unjust criticism and even disciplinary action; Lagrange was later removed from his position at the Biblical School in Jerusalem. Several periodicals ceased publication including *Annales de philosophie chrétienne* and *Revue d'histoire et de littérature religieuse* which declared that it could no longer survive in the context of the 'inquisitorial system set up in the Church'.

Francis P. Duffy was a philosophy professor in the seminary of the archdiocese of New York and the editor of the *New York Review* from 1905 until 1908. This review tried to keep its readers abreast of contemporary scholarly developments, but was eventually forced to close down as a result of pressure from the Apostolic Delegate. In the face of this situation, Duffy decided that he too would close his books and he went to work in a parish. His statue, in battledress as chaplain of the 69th Regiment, New York National Guard, stands today just above Times Square. The *New York Review* is forgotten, but Duffy, as played by Pat O'Brien in 'The Fighting 69th', is part of American Catholic folklore.

Several other Modernists and their sympathizers managed to stay in the Church without changing their opinions, quietly deploring the policies adopted by the ecclesiastical authorities. Lucien Laberthonnière was not a biblical or a theological Modernist, but he was critical of scholasticism and Roman authoritarianism. He was able to accept the findings of biblical criticism without indulging in theological reductionism or rejecting dogmatic beliefs which he maintained could be justified by religious experience. Edouard Le Roy was a close friend of Teilhard de Chardin and both men greatly influenced each other. Following the condemnation of Modernism and his own book, *Dogme et critique*, Le Roy quietly continued his work without altering his views. In 1931 he adopted the same course of action when four more of his books were put on the Index.

The number of biblical or theological Modernists has often been exaggerated. To the claim that 15,000 French priests were Modernists, Loisy replied that there were not even 1,500 while a later suggestion would reduce the number to 150. However, there might well have been many more Modernists, if political and social Modernists were to be included and especially if the number included critics of the institutional Church. In any case, the failure to track down more than a few Modernists seems to have been an important reason for the imposition of the anti-Modernist oath and might well have been a factor in the subsequent influence of the integrists who attempted to detect secret Modernists and to extend ecclesiastical authority to cover practically every aspect of life.

The integrists equated Catholic belief with an extremely conservative uniformity in all spheres of human activity, secular as well as religious, which was to be accepted or rejected as a whole. A rather literally translated version of part of Benigni's 'Policy of the *Sodalitium Pianum*' would read as follows:

> We are integrist Roman Catholics. Just as the word indicates, the integrist Roman Catholic accepts integrally the doctrine, discipline and directions of the Holy See, and all their legitimate consequences for the individual and for society. He is "papalist", "clericalist", anti-modernist, anti-liberal, and anti-sectarian. And so, he is integrally counter-revolutionary, because he is the adversary not only of the Jacobin Revolution and of sectarian radicalism, but equally so of social and religious liberalism . . .
>
> We consider the spirit and existence of so-called Catholic liberalism and democracy, intellectual and practical modernism, whether radical or moderate, and all the consequences of these, as sores in

the human Body of the Church . . .
We are entirely:

- against any attempt to lessen, put in second place, or conceal systematically, the papal claims for the Roman Question, to set aside the social influence of the Papacy, or to make laicism predominate.
- for the unwearying claiming of the Roman Question according to the rights and instructions of the Holy See . . .
- against democracy, even when it is called Christian, but always more or less poisoned with demoagoic ideas and facts, against liberalism, even when it purports to be economically and socially orientated, which by its individualism leads to the break-up of society . . .
- against anti-militarism and utopian pacifism, exploited by the Sect in the aim of weakening society and putting it to sleep under the nightmare of Jewish Freemasonry . . .
- against the doctrine and the deeply anti-Christian fact of the separation of the Church from the State . . .
- against "modernized" philosophical, dogmatic and biblical education which, even when not completely modernist, becomes similar at least to an archaeological or anatomical education . . .
- for ecclesiastical education which is inspired and guided by the glorious traditions of Scholasticism . . .
- against the exploitation of the clergy and "Catholic Action" by any political or social party in general, and in particular against the infatuation for "social involvement" that some desire to impart to the clergy and to "Catholic Action", ostensibly to "get them out of the sacristy", only for them to return there too infrequently, or on the quiet, or at the very least with a mind possessed by the outside world . . .
- against the mania, or the weakness, of so many Catholics who want to appear "fully up to date", "truly people of their time" . . . completely ready to display their tolerance, to blush at, if not to speak ill of, the disciplinary measures taken by or for the Church . . .
- against everything which is opposed to the doctrine, tradition, discipline and spirit of integrally Roman Catholicism;
- for everything which is in accordance with this last.

The integrists considered the Modernists to be particularly dangerous, not only because they seemed to threaten the whole dogmatic system, but because they operated from within the Church, disguised their 'heresy' and wrote anonymously or under pseudonyms. Tyrrell, for example, published his attack on 'Romanism', *The Church and the Future*, for private circulation, in a limited edition, under a pseudonym, with a French subtitle to imply that it was translated. Consequently, it is hardly surprising that the self-styled defenders of the faith should have retaliated in kind. Benigni established a secret society, the *Sodalitium Pianum*, to organize the fight against Modernism; members of the society passed information and co-ordinated contacts, established international as well as local agencies and publications.

The integrists included *Père* Le Floch, a Holy Ghost Father and superior of the French Seminary in Rome, the *Abbé* Emmanuel Barbier who could not even tolerate any mention of Liberalism or Modernism, Social Catholicism or democracy, and the *Abbé* Boulin, alias Roger Duget, who believed that the Freemasons were behind everything and who was later suspended by his own bishop. Benigni himself had offices in Milan, Fribourg, Vienna, Berlin, Cologne, Brussels, Ghent and Paris, while integrist magazines could be found in France, Switzerland, Italy, the Netherlands, Germany and Austria. These included *La Vigie, La critique du Libéralisme, La foi catholique, La Revue internationale des Sociétés Secrètes, Riscossa, Difesa, Liguria del Popolo* and *Unità cattolica*. Code names and aliases were adopted and Benigni himself had no less than twelve. Modernism was 'the disease'. The Pope became 'Lady Micheline' or 'Michel' and Merry del Val was 'Miss Romey' or 'George'. *Osservatore Romano* was known as 'Oswald', Benigni's confidential circular was 'Nelly' and *Sapinière* was 'Quentin'. The Benedictines were 'carpenters', the Capuchins were 'tailors' and the Jesuits were 'Nasly'.

The integrists poured out a stream of personal attacks and calumnies which not only divided Catholics throughout the world, but provided enemies of Catholicism with plenty of ammunition against the Church itself. Reputable journals of theology were forced to cease publication and even ungrounded accusations of Modernism left innocent men under suspicion, debarring them from higher ecclesiastical office or restricting their teaching careers. Those who tried to defend themselves were usually ignored by the Roman authorities, though when the integrists themselves finally came under attack, they then accused the Church of weakening under the attacks of its enemies. The integrists denounced practically all the leading Catholic scholars at the time and almost all the prominent workers in social or political fields; these included Cardinal Amette of Paris and Cardinal Piffl of Vienna, Cardinal Mercier and Cardinal Van Rossum, Paulin Ladeuze, Rector of Louvain, Pierre Batiffol and Henri-Marie Baudrillart, Rectors of the Catholic Institutes at Toulouse and Paris, Marie-Joseph Lagrange and Antonin Sertillanges, Jules Lebreton and Ferdinand Prat. The integrists also delated Angelo Giuseppe Roncalli, the future Pope John XXIII, for an article which he wrote in 1911.

When it became known that Antonino De Stefano, the historian who later left the Church, was about to launch the *Revue Moderniste Internationale,* a priest friend came to stay with him. The guest was left alone for a few hours and proceeded to photograph all the correspondence connected with the review which he then sent to the Holy Office. As a young priest, Giorgio La Piana, later professor at Harvard, met an unknown priest on a train going to Rome. This unknown companion confidentially revealed his sympathies with Modernism and Piana revealed that he too shared similar views. A few days after arriving in Rome, Piana was summoned to explain himself and immediately sent back to his diocese; the unknown traveller had been a curial official. Cardinal Archbishop Pietro Maffi of Pisa, himself a victim of the integrists' campaign, maintained that their attacks had resulted in a general feeling of mistrust, paralysis and inability to act. A single newspaper, he complained, could decide the fate of a whole diocese. 'Of course, anyone who acts may make a mistake', he declared, 'but since mistakes are pounced upon while good deeds go unnoticed, most people decide to play safe and do nothing'.

Pius X was apparently prepared to tolerate the use of any methods or any allies in his fight against Modernism.

> In a duel, you don't count or measure the blows, you strike as you can. War is not made with charity: it is a struggle, a duel. If Our Lord were not terrible, He would not have given an example in this too. See how he treated the Philistines, the sowers of error, the wolves in sheep's clothing, the traders: He scourged them with whips!

Cardinal Gasparri reported later,

> Pope Pius X approved, blessed, and encouraged a secret espionage association outside and above the hierarchy, which spied on the members of the hierarchy itself, even on their Eminences the

Cardinals; in short, he approved, blessed, and encouraged a sort of Freemasonry in the Church, something unheard of in ecclesiastical history . . . And not only did Pius X approve, bless and encourage the *Sodalitium Pianum*, but the denunciations emanating from it also afford the explanation for some serious attitudes adopted by Pius X in the government of the Church, although in this the Holy Father was, I do not doubt, in perfect good faith.

The integrist campaign was particularly vicious in France. 'If you ever treat of the Modernist crisis', a professor at the Catholic Institute told Jean Leflon, 'do not forget to tell how much we suffered'. Pius X used to call Modernism the '*mal francese*' of the Church; this was the Italian description of venereal disease. Certainly, France was one of the centres of Modernism. Most of its scholars, supporters and publishers were French. Duchesne was one of its precursors, Loisy one of its leaders. Archbishop Mignot has been described as its moderator and Bishop Lacroix as its bishop. The Pope's determination to destroy all appearances of social and political as well as doctrinal Modernism received the enthusiastic support of those French Ultramontane descendants of Louis Veuillot whose religion was practically identified with French monarchism and political reaction.

Even if it is possible to forgive some of the Pope's excesses in his campaign against Modernism, it is difficult to understand his speed in beginning the campaign, especially since most of the clergy condemned or humiliated simply and sincerely wanted to work for the reform of the Church. The campaign began within a few months of his election and without an adequate or even a prudent investigation. The delay in issuing the condemnation resulted from difficulties in satisfying the Pope's desire for one which would be effective and all-embracing. The impulsive attitude of Pius X seems to have been the result, at least in part, of pressure from the Archbishop of Paris as well as other French and curial prelates opposed to the 'democratic *abbés*' and who regarded the defeat of the 'intellectual *abbés*' as the first necessary step in their campaign. Leo XIII had refused to give way to their pressure, but the election of the new Pope provided them with another opportunity of pursuing their aims.

Several Christian Democratic priests who had flourished during the later part of Leo XIII's pontificate were silenced by Pius X. Paul Naudet established worker's clubs, addressed meetings and conferences, and established *La Justice sociale*, a publication which supported

Christian Democracy. Naudet accepted the results of biblical criticism and did not take the condemnation of Loisy too seriously. He also defended the separation of Church and State in France. After the condemnation of Modernism, *La Justice sociale* was also suppressed and Naudet was forbidden to write. The integrists found another victim in the left-wing republican Jules Lemire who was condemned and forbidden to say Mass, though Benedict XV later lifted the suspension and Lemire was never again subjected to ecclesiastical censure or disciplinary action. But the greatest tragedy was the condemnation of the *Sillon*, described by one historian as 'the finest religious movement among youth that France has ever known'.

Marc Sangnier, a devout Catholic, devoted his life and considerable personal fortune to the cause of *Ralliement*. In 1894 he established the *Sillon*, a religious movement of missionary and social concern which succeeded in avoiding the paternalism associated with so many Catholic social movements. Sangnier hoped to enable young people to live a full Catholic life as individuals and members of society, and to overcome social and religious barriers. The Sillonists provided instruction, recreation and Christian fellowship for organized groups of workers. Sangnier received many marks of favour from Leo XIII who decorated him with the Order of St Gregory the Great as well as from Pope Pius X himself. On the election of Pius X, Leon Harmel arranged a pilgrimage for Sangnier and some twenty Sillonists who were received in audience by the Pope, while in the following year, a group of Sillonists took over the duties of the Swiss Guard.

Sangnier was a democrat and he used democratic means to fight anti-Catholic legislation. Originally, the Sillonists won the support of right-wing Catholics in France by their defence of the Church and their patriotic loyalty. But when the *Sillon* engaged in political activity as a democratic and republic party of social concern, most French bishops and the Ultramontane press became increasingly hostile especially after the condemnation of 'Americanism'. In 1903 members of the *Action Française* began a relentless attack on the *Sillon* whose members defended themselves by asserting their rights to engage in social and political activities independent of the ecclesiastical authorities and so by implication acknowledging their affinities with Liberal Catholicism and even with the policies of *L'Avenir.*

Sangnier and the Sillonists prided themselves on their doctrinal orthodoxy, their fidelity to the Vicar of Christ in matters of faith and morals, and they explicitly dissociated themselves from doctrinal or biblical Modernists. Nevertheless, their orthodoxy was questioned and they were calumniated following the condemnation of Modernism. In 1910 an integral attack appeared in *Osservatore Romano* and in August of the same year a papal letter which undoubtedly used hostile right-wing sources condemned the *Sillon*. This condemnation not only reflected the opinions of integrist Catholics and extreme Ultramontanes, but even the theories of Joseph de Maistre himself. Sangnier at once submitted;

> I know that my attitude will disappoint certain anti-Clericals, and especially, perhaps, certain reactionary Roman Catholics who counted upon my not submitting. But I do not regret having to suffer for my faith, and I hope that God will accept the offering of my grief, since I shall be happy if by this sacrifice I may still serve the cause to which I have devoted my life, and help to give to the Republic a moral inspiration and to the democracy a Christian spirit. Since I am, and intend to remain, above all a Roman Catholic, the question does not even arise whether I shall or shall not submit to the discipline of the Church.

It is said that Benedict XV later acquitted Sangnier of the errors which Pius X had condemned. Certainly, Sangnier's sacrifice did serve his cause. In 1912 many young priests and former Sillonists joined his *League of the Young Republic* which he established to defend Christianity, to support democracy and the Republic, and to work for social and economic reform. In later years many former Sillonists would be found working in those social and pastoral movements in France which would prove to be so important in the history of the Church during the twentieth century. Sangnier himself was eventually elected as the first president of the *Mouvement Républicain Populaire*, a party which helped to free the French Church from its former reactionary associations.

Meanwhile, however, as Archbishop Mignon recognized, the condemnation of the *Sillon* was an obvious victory for that right-wing, monarchist, anti-semitic and anti-democratic *Action Francaise* which enjoyed the support of Pius X but would be condemned by Pius XI. When some of the works of Charles Maurras were put on the Index in 1914, the Pope did not promulgate the condemnation because of his contributions to the fight against Modernism and the *Sillon*. Maurras himself never changed his agnostic if not pagan attitudes, though as leader of *Action Francaise*, he was careful to avoid repeating his attacks on 'the

Jew' who had cast darkness from the cross over all humanity and on the Church which for eighteen hundred years had monstrously soiled the world.

In 1913 a group of enterprising Belgian and German Catholics succeeded in investigating the *Sodalitium Pianum* and they reported their discoveries to the Holy See. Floris Prims was a priest and a lawyer, and the secretary of the superior of the Belgian Dominicans, Jan Routen, one of Benigni's victims. In order to learn the truth, Prims joined the *Sodalitium Pianum* and became an intimate confidant of Arnold Jonckx, Benigni's chief agent in Belgium. Cardinal Mercier and Cardinal Maffi unsuccessfully tried to get a private audience for Prims, but the priest had to be content with informing Merry del Val, who refused to take any action until Prims could substantiate his charges with documentary evidence.

At the same time, Merry del Val was clearly worried that the activities of the *Sodalitium* might be publicly revealed and he tried to curb Benigni. However, the Pope and the Secretary of State apparently gave way when Benigni threatened to cease publication rather than moderate his denunciations. Benigni told Jonckx:

> You received my letter in which I announced to you the future departure of Nelly [*Corrispondenza*], and later you received a telegram saying that Nelly was not going to leave. Here is the explanation: Nelly's papa [Benigni], informed Michel [Pius X] and George [Merry del Val] that Nelly preferred to leave, once she discovered that she was not allowed to do anything. You should know the prudence of George is immense, or to put it squarely: he is a coward. His prudence is a heavy burden for Nelly; he is always afraid that Nelly is going to make trouble . . . If that is the way things are handled, the child is going to become anaemic. That is why papa had taken the decision to let her leave. But then Michel and George came to tell me that they would never allow her to leave, because they loved the nice girl very much.

Nine months later, however, Merry del Val ordered Benigni to cease publication.

> Nelly is going to close shop. Miss Romey [Merry del Val] commands it. She is scared to death of Nelly as well as of her Daddy. Miss Romey has killed Nelly's business, because now she is only allowed to sell things that people can get much better elsewhere. But my

> business ethics and my own profit tell me that I should not reconcile myself to this policy. Yesterday I saw Miss Romey. She is in terrible shape and feels deserted by everybody. It is her own fault. Simply a result of her own defects. It is pitiful . . . But when I left we were on good terms. She asked me always to inform her and Lady Micheline [Pius X]. That is what I will do, of course, for the profit of our business.

Cardinal Rampolla, Leo's Secretary of State, felt obliged to protest against the activities of the extremists, but the most famous protest came from Archbishop Mignot to Benedict XV's future Secretary of State. Mignot pointed out that the Church had lost the services of many of its best scholars and pastoral priests as a result of spyings and denunciations. Ecclesiastical studies had dramatically declined and an undue concentration on 'test book theology' seemed the best guarantee of furthering ecclesiastical ambition.

> The perpetuation of this state of things will mean an inferior clergy, more concerned with the externals of worship than with the spiritual realities of interior religion – a clergy which will understand nothing of the intellectual and moral difficulties of the time, or of the movement of ideas, and the Church will be the loser. Such a clergy will stand motionless amidst a world on the march, a world whose light they ought to be. Neither their minds nor their hearts will be opened to those who are besieged by doubt, and so much in need of them.

On the 3rd of September 1914 Cardinal Archbishop Giacomo della Chiesa of Bologna was elected Pope. On the very first day that the new Pope went into his office, he found in his desk an unopened letter addressed to his predecessor, Pius X. Bishop Giovanni Pellizari of Piacenza, a well known extremist, had written a confidential letter denouncing the Archbishop of Bologna as a dangerous Modernist. The new Pope immediately informed Benigni that his services were no longer required and mistakenly imagined that he had thereby brought the activities of the *Sodalitium* to an end. Merry del Val was replaced by Cardinal Domenico Ferrata who had himself been denounced by the *Sodalitium* for supporting the victims of integrist attacks when he was apostolic nuncio in Paris. On a later occasion when Benedict received another prelate who had been accused of Modernism, he remarked, 'I hope you are now sure of Our orthodoxy: We are infallible'. The duties of the Congregation of the Index were transferred to the Holy Office, while a new congregation of seminaries and universities under Cardinal Mercier became more positive in its approach to education and matters intellectual.

Benedict's first encyclical, *Ad Beatissimi*, was written within a few months of the opening of the World War. Although the new Pope repeated the condemnations of his predecessor, he also condemned the activities of the integrists.

> Let no private person, by the publication of books or newspapers or in public speeches, comport himself as a teacher in the Church . . . With regard to those things about which – where the Holy See has not pronounced its own judgment – it is possible in due faith and discipline to discuss the pros and cons, it is certainly permitted to everyone to give and maintain his own opinion. But in such discussions let everyone refrain from excess in speech, which may cause grave offence against charity; let everyone freely defend his own opinion, but with courtesy, and let him not accuse others of suspect faith or lack of discipline for the simple reason that they hold different views from his own. We also wish our sons to refrain from those appellations which have recently begun to be used to distinguish Catholics from Catholics . . . faith is either professed wholly or not at all. There is therefore no need to add epithets to the profession of Catholicism; it is enough for each one to say 'Christian is my name and Catholic my family name'; but let all who call themselves so, be so in very truth.

The Pope again officially censured the *Sodalitium Pianum* in 1921. During the Great War the German High Command was informed that there was important information about the French Catholic conspiracy against Germany among Jonckx's papers. However, the papers only provided evidence of the sordid activities of the integrist Catholics and after the War, they were returned to the Belgium Government for use in a case against Jonckx who was eventually sentenced to death for collaborating with the enemy. Photocopies were deposited in the seminary at Roermond in Holland and in 1921 a dossier of the most important information was sent to the Holy See. Shortly afterwards the Cardinal Prefect of the Congregation of the Council finally ended the activities of the *Sodalitium Pianum*. At least one of Benigni's agents left the Church and the priesthood, while Benigni himself joined *Action Francaise* before becoming an informer for Mussolini, supervising the Vatican mail on behalf of the Italian secret service.

If the pontificate of Pius X seemed to show that the Catholic Church had finally come out against the theological and biblical scholarship, the social, economic and political developments, the institutional and ecclesiastical reforms advocated during the nineteenth century, the pontificate of Benedict XV dramatically illustrated that Catholicism was not permanently committed to such a reaction and the new Pope himself would show that the Church was not totally unprepared to meet the problems and the challenges of the new age.

Conclusion

The shooting at Sarajevo brought the complacent optimism of the nineteenth century to an end. When Pius X was asked to bless the Austro-Hungarian armies, the Pope sternly replied, 'I bless peace, not war'. In some ways, the career of Pius X epitomized the history of the papacy during the nineteenth century. In spite of obvious limitations, all the Popes during the nineteenth century were hard-working men of high principles; none of them was morally corrupt, none of them was weak, none of them was even guilty of the nepotism which marred the histories of their predecessors during the seventeenth and eighteenth centuries. However, the Popes of the last century usually reacted unfavourably to many of the social, economic and political movements which were increasingly influencing and on the whole benefitting countries in the western world. The Popes also rejected the attempts of some Catholics to re-present the theological and biblical teaching of the Church in the light of scientific and historical developments and new patterns of thought.

At the same time, although millions of indifferent or nominal Catholics refused to follow the lead of the Papacy and so provided evidence of that process of dechristianization which seemed such a feature of the age, the Popes could not have carried the Church with them, if they had not spoken for the convictions of most of the clergy and the laity. Minorities and individuals might have opposed papal decisions or questioned their timeliness, but with few exceptions they usually concurred once the Popes had spoken. On the whole, Catholics in the nineteenth century enthusiastically welcomed the increased and more effective authority of the papacy. The danger that the Catholic Church might disintegrate into national bodies controlled by local rulers or bishops disappeared as Catholics closed their ranks against – and in an effort to win – a world whose indifference and hostility had been augmented by the forces of revolution. Certainly, Ultramontanism so united the Church throughout the world that it was able to maintain that unity even during two world wars.

Although the papacy and Catholicism became increasingly hostile and even obscurantist in their opposition to the world of the nineteenth century, Catholics were not content to remain on the defensive, but tried to convert those who did not share or were even opposed to their views. Assisted by hierarchies directed more and more by the Holy See, priests, religious and laity endeavoured to fulfil the Church's mission to preach the Gospel to every creature. The greatest numerical gains were made in the missionary fields of Asia, Africa and the Pacific. Further conversions resulted from the development of Uniate Churches in the east, while a significant, though relatively small, number of notable converts joined the Catholic Church from the Anglican and Protestant Churches.

At first, it might seem that in spite of the expansion and revival of Catholicism, the 'Catholic' areas of Europe were precisely those that were being dechristianized. In 1789 the Catholic Church was closely identified with political, economic and social structures which were first challenged and then were shattered. Meanwhile, intellectual developments appeared to undermine the very foundations on which Catholicism was based. Consequently, the Catholic Church seemed less prominent in the political, economic, intellectual and cultural life of Europe at the end of the nineteenth century than it had been during the early part of the eighteenth century. However, one of the limits of the church historian is that he is unfamiliar with the ways in which God works in history. A century is but a short time in the history of a Church which has been forced to endure much darker periods in its past and it is questionable to what extent Europe has ever been 'christianized' let alone 'dechristianized'. Even during the so-called 'ages of faith' the moral and intellectual claims of the Church were openly despised, while the history of inquisitions, wars and crusades hardly provide much evidence of the adoption of 'Christian' attitudes.

In spite of dechristianization, secularization and anti-clericalism, perhaps the most significant feature of the development of Catholicism during the nineteenth century was the revival of old orders, the restoration of the Society of Jesus, the advent of new congregations and societies, and the creation of innumerable associations which involved the laity in service and worship. During the nineteenth century, it would seem that more organizations, both lay and religious, emerged in the Catholic Church than during any previous century of its history or indeed in the history of any other Christian Church. The majority of the new organizations were devoted to service and education, to the poor and under-privileged, the sick and the aged. They endeavoured to evangelize present and future generations in the western world as well as to extend Catholicism in missionary territories. Furthermore, the foundation and restoration of these organizations were encouraged and closely controlled by the Holy See.

An important aspect of this development was the active part played by the laity, both men and women, though these were often subject to clerical control. The emergence of a dedicated laity had important implications for the future and might be symptomatic of a growing distinction between nominal and practising Catholics, between the faithful and those who were put partially converted or in the process of being 'dechristianized'. Somewhat ironically, more of the new congregations and movements originated in France than in any other country. France provided more missionaries than any other nation; the Society for the Propagation of the Faith which collected more money for the missions than any other Catholic agency was founded in France; so was the Society of St Vincent de Paul which enlisted more laymen in the service of the Church throughout the world than any other movement before or since.

The church historian can but inadequately record what the faith really meant to those millions of people who are the Church. During the nineteenth century the beginnings of the Liturgical Movement strengthened public worship, there was an increased emphasis on the sacraments, especially the Eucharist, on devotions to the Sacred Heart and the Blessed Virgin, while the circulation of spiritual reading, old and new, would suggest that the practice of private prayer and meditation was widespread. Thousands of Catholics were faithful in frequenting the sacraments and the observance of their religious duties. These 'committed' Catholics were probably more numerous than in the eighteenth century and it is even possible that the proportion of genuinely committed Christians in the 'ages of faith' was no greater than it was in the nineteenth century.

It is probable that the average level of intelligent faith and morality among the clergy of the nineteenth century was higher than it had been even during the thirteenth century; it was certainly higher than it had been at the time of the Reformation. Although the attitudes of the ecclesiastical authorities to clerical training did not always help the clergy to meet the problems presented by the intellectual, economic and political developments of the age, there does seem to have been a general improvement in their moral qualities, their sense of discipline, their spiritual earnestness and their faithfulness to their pastoral responsibilities.

Perhaps the most significant event in the history of the papacy during the nineteenth century was the loss of the temporal power which provided the Holy See with the opportunity of enhancing its spiritual and moral authority. Reluctantly and not by choice, the papacy was emancipated from its dependence on a form of power which was contrary to the precepts of the Gospel, but which the collapse of the Roman Empire and the conditions of medieval Europe had seemed to impose. The Holy See could now become a more religious and a less political institution. Catholics in general could only come to terms with the modern world after ceasing to deplore the evils of the age and critically examining the weaknesses and the faults of the Church itself. French Catholics in particular believed that the de-Christianization of France was the result of the forces of the Revolution or the machinations of republicans, Freemasons and Jews. Catholics throughout the world were influenced to a greater or lesser extent, by the French experience and their involvement in supporting the temporal power of the Pope which appeared to be a somewhat similar situation. The need for a critical self-analysis could not be restricted to the political point of view in the hopes of achieving immediate political gains, but it had to be undertaken for religious reasons by Catholics who understood that the Church could no longer live and function within the old framework of Church and State.

Since the seventeenth century the Church especially but not exclusively in France had relied on its political power and influence, silencing opposition whenever this was possible. These policies finally succeeded in isolating the Church from the French and the Italian nations. The Church had abandoned the total cultural sphere for the political field in which it was at least possible to imagine that 'Christendom' still survived. The Church throughout Europe ceased to be a missionary Church and the papacy simply tried to preserve its 'power', its static position, by making concordats, for example, the basis of its policy. Political Catholicism, however, ultimately resulted in the formation of a ghetto mentality among Catholics and by the end of the nineteenth century, the Church had to rediscover 'religious' Catholicism and try to extricate itself from the impasse into which it had been led by 'political' Catholicism. The condemnation of *Action Francaise*, the signing of the Lateran Treaty, the decrees of the second Vatican Council, the publication of *Populorum Progressio* – subjects to be discussed in greater detail in a sequel to the present work – have all been stages in that process. Yet it still remains to be seen whether the Catholic Church and the Holy See have finally and completely abandoned the realm of power politics in favour of strictly religious policies . . . 'It was not with a cheque drawn on Caesar's bank that Jesus sent His Apostles out into the world' . . .

'In the world you will have tribulation;
but have courage:
I have overcome the world'.

A select bibliography

Acton, J.E.E.D. *Ignaz v. Dollinger Briefwechsel mit Lord Action.* Edited by V. Conzemius. 3 vols. Munich, 1963-70.

Letters from Rome [by 'Quirinus'] London, 1870.

Lord Acton and the first Vatican Council: A Journal. Edited with an introduction by Edmund Campion, Sydney, 1975.

Lord Acton. The Decisive Decade 1864-1874 Essays and Documents Edited and written by Dammian McElrath, James C. Holland et al., Louvain, 1970.

Adolfs, R. *The Church is Different.* London, 1966.

Anon. *The Little Treasury of Leaflets.* 4 vols. Dublin, n.d.

Aretin, K.O. von. *The Papacy and the Modern World.* London, 1970.

Aubert, R. *Le Pontificat de Pie IX.* Paris, 1952.

Barmann, L.F. *Baron Friedrich von Hügel and the Modernist Crisis in England.* Cambridge, 1972.

Barruel, A. de *The History of the Church during the French Revolution.* London, 1794

Memoirs illustrating the history of Jacobinism. London, 1797.

Barry, C.J. (Ed.) *Readings in Church History The Modern Era 1789 to the Present.* Westminster, 1965.

Bazin, R. *Pius X.* London, 1928.

Bedeschi, L. *La Curia Romana durante la crisi modernista Episodi e metodi di governo.* Parma, 1968.

Bettenson, H. (Ed.) *Documents of the Christian Church.* London, 1944.

Biddiss, M.D. (Ed.) *Gobineau: Selected Political Writings.* London, 1970.

Blakiston, N. (Ed.) *The Roman Question: Extracts from the dispatches of Odo Russell from Rome 1858-1870.* London, 1962.

Bodley, J.E.C. *The Church in France.* London, 1906.

Bottalla, P. *The Pope and the Church considered in their Mutual Relations Part II The Infallibility of the Pope.* London, 1870.

Briggs, C.A. and von Hügel, F. *The Papal Commission and the Pentateuch.* London, 1906.

Brodhead, J.N. *The Religious Persecution in France 1900-1906.* London, 1907.

Brogan, D.W. *The Development of Modern France* (1870-1939). London, 1940.

Buehrle, M.C. *Rafael Cardinal Merry del Val.* London, 1958.

Buonaiuti, E. *Pilgrim of Rome. Edited by C. Nelson and N. Pittinger.* Aberdeen, 1969.

Burtchaell, J.T. *Catholic Theories of Biblical Inspiration since 1810.* Cambridge, 1969.

Bury, J. B. *A History of the Papacy in the Nineteenth Century (1864-1878).* London, 1930.

Butler, C. *The Vatican Council.* 2 vols. London, 1936.

Cappellari, M. *Triomphe du St-Siège et de l'Eglise,* Lyon, 1833

Cesare, R. de. *The Last Days of Papal Rome 1850-1870.* London, 1909.

Chadwick, W.O. *Catholicism and History. The Opening of the Vatican Archives* Cambridge, 1978.

Chateaubriand, R.F.A. Vicomte de. *Genius of Christianity or The Spirit and Beauties of the Christian Religion.* Paris, 1854.

Memoirs. 6 vols. London, 1902.

Cobban, A. *A History of Modern France.* 2 vols. London, 1961.

Copleston, F. *History of Philosophy.* Vol. IX. London, 1975.

Cragg, G.R. *The Church and the Age of Reason 1648-1789.* London, 1960.

Dal-Gal, H. *Saint Pius X.* Dublin, 1954.

Daniel-Rops, H. *A Fight for God.* London, 1966.

Our Brothers in Christ. London, 1967.

The Church in an Age of Revolution. London, 1965.

Dansette, A. *Religious History of Modern France.* 2 vols. Edinburgh-London, 1961.

Delumeau, J. *Catholicism between Luther and Voltaire.* London, 1977.

Devas, R. *Ex Umbris Letters and Papers hitherto unpublished of the fathers Lacordaire, Jandel, Danzas.* Rugeley, n.d.

Döllinger, J.J.I. von. *Declarations and Letters on the Vatican Decrees 1867-1887.* Edinburgh, 1891.

The Church and the Churches. London, 1862.

The Pope and the Council [by 'Janus'] . London, 1869.

Dru, A. *Péguy.* London, 1956.

The Church in the Nineteenth Century: Germany 1800-1918. London, 1963.

Dupanloup, F.A.P. *The Ministry of Preaching An Essay on Pastoral and Popular Oratory*. London, 1890.

The Papal Sovereignty: viewed in its relations to the Catholic Religion and to the Law of Europe. London, 1860.

Ehler, S.Z. and Morrall, J.B. (Eds.). *Church and State Through the Centuries. A Collection of historic documents with commentaries.* London, 1954.

Ellis, J. Tracy. *American Catholicism.* Chicago, 1955.

Catholics in Colonial America. Baltimore, 1965.

The Catholic Priest in the United States: Historical Investigations. Collegeville, 1971.

The Life of James Cardinal Gibbons. 2 vols. Milwaukee, 1952.

Falconi, C. *The Popes in the Twentieth Century*. London, 1967.

Ferrero, G. *The Two French Revolutions 1789-1796.* New York, 1968.

Fogarty, G.P. *The Vatican and the Americanist Crisis: Denis J. O'Connell American Agent in Rome, 1885-1903.* Rome, 1974.

Fogazzaro, A. *The Patriot.* London, 1906

The Saint, London, 1906.

Forbes, F.A. *Life of Pius X.* London, 1919.

Fryer, W.R. *Republic or Restoration in France? 1794-7.* Manchester, 1965.

George, H. *Progress and Poverty: an inquiry into the cause of industrial depressions, and of increase of want with increase of wealth. The Remedy*. London, 1883.

Greaves, R.W. "Religion", *New Cambridge Modern History*. Vol. VII. Cambridge, 1957.

Guillou, M.J. Le. "The Mennaisain Crisis", *Concilium.* Vol. VII. 1967.

Hales, E.E.Y. *The Catholic Church in the Modern World*. London, 1958.

Pio Nono A study in European politics and religion in the nineteenth century. London, 1956.

Revolution and Papacy 1769-1846. London, 1960.

Heimert, A. and Miller, P. (Eds.) *The Great Awakening Documents Illustrating the Crisis and Its Consequences.* Indianapolis and New York, 1967.

Heyer, F. *The Catholic Church from 1648 to 1870.* London, 1969.

Hoare, F.R. *The Papacy and the Modern State.* London, 1940.

Hogarth, H. *Henri Bremond.* London, 1950.

Holmes, J.D. *More Roman than Rome*

English Catholicism in the Nineteenth Century. London, 1978.

Hughes, H.L. *The Catholic Revival in Italy 1815-1915.* London, 1935.
Jalland, T.G. *The Church and the Papacy An Historical Study.* London, 1949.
Jedin, H. *Ecumenical Councils of the Catholic Church An Historical Outline.* Edinburgh, London, 1960.
Jemolo, A.C. *Church and State in Italy 1850-1950.* Oxford, 1960.
Joyce, L.D. *Church and Clergy in the American Revolution.* New York, 1966.
Lacordaire, J.B.H. *Jesus Christ God God and Man Conferences delivered at Notre Dame in Paris.* London, 1887.
Life: Conferences delivered at Toulouse. London, 1875.
Thoughts and Teachings. London, 1902.
Lamennais, F.R. de. *Affairs de Rome.* Paris, 1836-7.
Essay on Indifference in matters of Religion. London, 1895.
Observations on the promise of teaching the Four Articles of the Declaration of 1682. London, 1822.
Larkin, M. *Church and State after the Dreyfus Affair.* London, 1974.
Latourette, K.S. *A History of the Expansion of Christianity.* Vols. IV-VI. Grand Rapids, 1971.
Christianity in a Revolutionary Age. Vols. I-III. Grand Rapids, 1970.
Lebrun, R.A. *Throne and Altar The Political and Religious Thought of Joseph de Maistre.* Ottawa, 1965.
Lefebvre, G. *The French Revolution from its origins to 1793.* London, 1962.
Leflon. J. *La Crise Révolutionnaire 1789-1846.* Paris, 1949.
Lewis, D.L. *Prisoners of Honor The Dreyfus Affair.* New York, 1973.
Lilley, A.L. *Modernism A Record and Review.* London, 1908.
Lively, J. (Ed.) *The Works of Joseph de Maistre.* London, 1965.
Loisy, A. *The Gospel and the Church.* London, 1903.
Loome, T.M. "The Enigma of Baron Friedrich von Hügel – as Modernist", *Downside Review.* Vol. XCI. 1973.
Maguire, J.F. *Pontificate of Pius the Ninth.* London, 1870.
Maistre, J.M. Comte de. *Letters on the Spanish Inquisition.* London, 1838.
Oeuvres. Montrouge, 1841.
The Pope considered in his relations with the Church, Temporal Sovereignties, Separated Churches, and the Cause of Civilization. London, 1850.
Manning, H.E. *Petri Privilegium Three Pastoral Letters.* London, 1871.
Religio Viatoris. London, 1888.

The Independence of the Holy See. London, 1877.
The Temporal Power of the Vicar of Jesus Christ. London, 1880.
The True Story of the Vatican Council. London, 1877.

McClelland, J.S. (Ed.) *The French Right de Maistre to Maurras.* London 1970.

McManners, J. *Church and State in France 1870-1914.* London, 1972.
The French Revolution and the Church. London, 1969.

Mills, A. *The Life of Pope Pius IX.* London, 1877.

Mohler, J.A. *L'Unité de l'Église.* Brussels, 1839.
Symbolism or exposition of the Doctrinal Differences between Catholics and Protestants as evidenced by their symbolical writings. London, 1894.

Montalembert. C.F.R. de. *Catholic Interests in the Nineteenth Century.* London, 1852.
L'Eglise Libre dans L'État Libre. Paris, 1863.
Pius IX and Lord Palmerston. London, 1856.

Moody, J.N. (Ed.) *Church and Society Catholic Social and Political Thought and Movements 1789-1950.* New York, 1953.

Moore, T.E. *Peter's City An Account of the Origin, Development and Solution of the Roman Question.* London, 1929.

Moss, C.B. *The Old Catholic Movement, Its Origins and History.* London, 1948.

Murray, J.C. *We Hold These Truths Catholic Reflections on the American Proposition.* London, 1961.

O'Clery, The. *The Making of Italy.* London, 1892.

Odegard, P.H. (Ed.). *Religion and Politics.* Rutgers, 1960.

Ozanam, F. *Letters with a connecting sketch of his life* [by A. Coates]. London, 1886.

Pagani, G.B. *The Life of Antonio Rosmini-Serbati.* London, 1907.

Poulat, E. *Integrisme et Catholicisme Intégral. Un reseau secret international antimoderniste: La Sapinière (1909-1921).* Paris, 1969.
Histoire, dogme et critique dans la Crise Moderniste. Paris, 1962.

Pratt, J.W. *Religion, Politics, and Diversity The Church-State theme in New York History.* New York, 1967.

Purcell, E.S. *Life of Cardinal Manning Archbishop of Westminster.* 2 vols. London, 1896.

Ranchetti, M. *The Catholic Modernists.* London, 1969.

Ratté, J. *Three Modernists: Alfred Loisy, George Tyrrell, William L. Sullivan.* London, 1968.

Reardon, B.M.G. *Liberalism and Tradition Aspects of Catholic Thought*

in Nineteenth-Century France. Cambridge, 1975.
Roman Catholic Modernism. London, 1970.
Renan, E. *The History of the Origins of Christianity Book I Life of Jesus.* London, n.d.
Roe, W.G. *Lamennais and England The Reception of Lamennais's Religious Ideas in England in the Nineteenth Century.* Oxford, 1966.
Rosmini-Serbati, A. *Of the Five Wounds of the Church.* London, 1883.
Sheppard, L.C. *Lacordaire A Biographical Essay.* London, 1964.
Simon, W. (Ed.) *French Liberalism 1789-1848.* New York, 1972.
Soderini, E. *Leo XIII, Italy and France.* London, 1935.
The Pontificate of Leo XIII. London, 1934.
Spencer, P. *Politics of Belief in Nineteenth-Century France.* London, 1954.
Sweet, W.W. *The American Church An Intepretation.* London, 1947.
Trevor, M. *Prophets and Guardians Renewal and Tradition in the Church.* London, 1969.
Tyrrell, G. *Autobiography and Life.* Arranged, with supplements, by M.D. Petre. 2 vols. London, 1912.
A Much-Abused Letter. London, 1906.
Christianity at the Cross-Roads. London, 1910.
Through Scylla and Charybdis or The Old Theology and the New. London, 1907.
Vidler, A.R. *A Century of Social Catholicism 1820-1920.* London, 1964.
A Variety of Catholic Modernists. Cambridge, 1970.
Prophecy and Papacy A Study of Lamennais, the Church and the Revolution. London, 1954.
The Church in an Age of Revolution 1789 to the present day. London, 1961.
The Modernist Movement in the Roman Church. Cambridge, 1934.
Wallace, L.P. *Leo XIII and the Rise of Socialism.* Duke, 1966.
Wangermann, E. *From Joseph II to the Jacobin Trials.* Oxford, 1959.
Woodruff, D. *Church and State in History.* London, 1962.
Wrangler, T. 'Emergence of John J. Keane as Liberal Catholic and Americanist', *American Ecclesiastical Review.* Vol. 166. 1972.

Index

E

F

G

K

L

M

N

S

T

V

W

Z